Case Studies on Women in Business

Case Studies on Women in Business

Third Edition

Konnie Kustron

Eastern Michigan University

with

Kimberly Kustron

SAN DIEGO

Bassim Hamadeh, CEO and Publisher
Jennifer Codner, Senior Field Acquisitions Editor
Anne Jones, Project Editor
Celeste Paed, Associate Production Editor
Trey Soto, Licensing Specialist
Natalie Piccotti, Director of Marketing
Kassie Graves, Senior Vice President of Editorial
Jamie Giganti, Director of Academic Publishing

Kendall-Hunt Publishing Company previously published this book.

Cover image copyright © 2011 iStockphoto LP/aijohn784.
⠀⠀⠀⠀⠀⠀⠀⠀© 2020 iStockphoto LP/AaronAmat.
⠀⠀⠀⠀⠀⠀⠀⠀© 2019 iStockphoto LP/Portra.
⠀⠀⠀⠀⠀⠀⠀⠀© 2020 iStockphoto LP/dragana991.
⠀⠀⠀⠀⠀⠀⠀⠀© 2019 iStockphoto LP/MangoStar_Studio.
⠀⠀⠀⠀⠀⠀⠀⠀© 2018 iStockphoto LP/FilippoBacci.

Printed in the United States of America.

cognella® | ACADEMIC PUBLISHING
3970 Sorrento Valley Blvd., Ste. 500, San Diego, CA 92121

We dedicate our book to all women who have struggled and excelled in business. May we continue to step, occasionally stumble and leap forward to make our dreams come true.

Contents

Acknowledgments

WE WANT TO acknowledge our deep appreciation to our coauthors, family, work colleagues, friends, and acquaintances, who have provided content in authoring this book. Several took the time to share their employment and career experiences with trepidation, courage, joy, and trust.

We thank our grandmothers, who are both immigrants, and our mother for the women we have become. We looked at our family history during our research and realized that our journey of awareness and empowerment began years and years ago and is connected through the generations.

Our grandmothers' and perhaps great-grandmothers' paths and determination are reflected in us and by us in the 21st century. Our father, too, should be given credit for supporting his daughters. He always said, "Plant the seedling now. Don't wait. Otherwise, there will never be a tree to give you shade when you or others need it or an apple or pear when you are hungry." His words encouraged and empowered us since we were young.

And, to our three sisters, Karol, Kathy, and Kristine, we thank you for your editing and candid feedback. We are wiser and more AWARE of the bond of family by working on this successful project.

About Your Authors

Authors

Kimberly Kustron is sales leader, executive health care consultant, and pharmacist. She received her bachelor of science in pharmacy from Ferris State University and began her career as a retail pharmacist and sales representative for Eli Lilly and Company. After holding several sales positions, Ms. Kustron selected Bayer/Talecris Corporation to expand her pharmaceutical sales and marketing career in management. As their senior national sales director, she led the Specialty Sales organization promoting life-saving plasma-derived medications to both physicians and hospitals with revenue in excess of $1 billion. Following that role, she formed her own healthcare consulting company, and provided expertise to venture capitalists in the United States and abroad regarding specialty pharmacy and manufacturer investments. Having held senior management positions in sales, sales operations, corporate accounts, training, and marketing, her 25 years' experience is vast and diverse. She is is currently in management for a global biopharmaceutical corporation specializing in rare medical disorders. Ms. Kustron is a member of the Arizona Pharmacists Association, Michigan Pharmacists Association, Pharmacy Consultants, National Osteoporosis Foundation, National Association of Mentally Ill, Immune Deficiency Association, and the Arizona Professional Women's Association.

Konnie Kustron is a professor in the School of Technology Studies and Professional Services Management at Eastern Michigan University (EMU) in Ypsilanti, Michigan. She is also a member of the Women and Gender Studies Department. Professor Kustron teaches a variety of technology, business education, and law classes at EMU at both the undergraduate and graduate levels. Ms. Kustron also has 2 years of academic, administrative experience as associate dean for EMU's College of Technology and 17 additional years of business and corporate management experience.

Professor Kustron received her BS with honors in prelaw from Michigan State University and her JD from the Michigan State College of Law. She is a licensed attorney and an active member of the Michigan Bar Association. She is a Quality Matters reviewer for online classes, and she has a Michigan Department of Education Standard Teaching Certificate with an endorsement in CTE—Business Administrative Management and Operations (52.0299). Ms. Kustron is also a consulting editor for the *Journal of Education for Business.*

Professor Kustron is a recipient of an Eastern Michigan University Alumni Teaching Award and a Dean's Outstanding Faculty Award. She is a chapter author in the *Internet Guide for Michigan Lawyers*, a winner of the "Award of Excellence in the Best Publication" category given by the Association for Continuing Legal Education. Professor Kustron is the author of three law books with the international publisher, Bookboon.

Contributing Authors

Katrina Bezak has a passion and love for oncology and hematology. She is currently the regional director for Oncology Services for Karmanos Cancer Network, where she provides focused leadership for all aspects of oncology. She has responsibility for overall strategic direction, business development, performance improvement, physician collaboration, market influence, market share growth, patient satisfaction, and operations. Dr. Bezak has a special expertise in cancer network integration, best practice adoption, and completion of goals and initiatives of the cancer service line. Previously, she was the cellular therapy program manager at Yale New Haven Health Cancer Hospital in New Haven, Connecticut, and an inpatient hematology nurse practitioner at Mayo Clinic in Rochester, Minnesota. Dr. Bezak has a doctor of nursing practice and master of business administration from

Johns Hopkins University, a master of nursing from Georgetown University, and a bachelor of nursing from Wayne State University.

Dr. Bezak is the author of "Jingle Bells" and "More Than a Nanny."

Mary E. Blair is currently the executive vice president at Cornerstone Consulting Organization, LLC. She has global accountability for all supply chain and training activity, including materials, planning, and logistics. Previously, Dr. Blair was the senior vice president and chief supply chain officer for Accuride Corporation, leading global supply chain initiatives and strategies. Prior to Accuride, Dr. Blair was the vice president of global procurement at United Components, Inc. (UCI). Dr. Blair also has extensive global supply chain experience from working at Navistar and General Motors. Dr. Blair is also an adjunct professor at Oakland City University. Dr. Blair was recognized in 2017 as a STEP (Science, Technology, Engineering and Production) Ahead top 100 women awardee. Dr. Blair has also served on the board of Junior Achievement and the University of Evansville.

Dr. Blair received her undergraduate degree from Ferris State University and earned an MBA from Central Michigan University. She is also a graduate of Capella University, where she earned her PhD in business leadership. Dr. Blair serves as an adjunct professor at Oakland City University, located in Oakland City, Indiana.

Dr. Blair is the author of "International Negotiations."

Melinda Carlson received her BS and MS degrees in business education with a concentration in leadership from Eastern Michigan University (EMU) in Ypsilanti, Michigan. She was a high school teacher for 12 years and has been an adjunct lecturer at Washtenaw Community College and EMU for over 10 years. Ms. Carlson is also a trainer for the KN Corporate Services Word, Excel, and PowerPoint based classes in Ann Arbor, Michigan. Prior to teaching, she worked for the Environmental Protection Agency for 5 years where she met her husband. They have four children. Ms. Carlson also served as the Parent-Teacher-Student Organization copresident/treasurer for their children's elementary and high schools. Interests include research in the area of curriculum development and effective teaching strategies for today's classrooms. Other areas of interest include improving community volunteerism. She resides in Ann Arbor, Michigan.

Ms. Carlson is the author of "Intent vs. Perception."

Deborah deLaski-Smith has been a faculty member of interior design and an administrator at Eastern Michigan University for 39 years. She earned her bachelor's degree from Adrian College and completed her master and doctoral programs at Michigan State University. The Interior Design Program is CIDA accredited, and Dr. deLaski-Smith has served as program coordinator. Teaching specialties include environmental/universal design for aging and special-needs populations. Design solutions go beyond the Americans With Disabilities Act to promote successful functionality at home or in the workplace. During her time as an administrator, she served as the associate dean of the Graduate School, interim dean of the Graduate School, and interim dean of the College of Health and Human Services. School director (interim) positions included the oversight of the School of Visual and Built Environments along with the School of Technology and Professional Services Management. Both schools are in the College of Engineering and Technology.

Dr. deLaski-Smith is the author of "Chinese Spinning Plates."

Tierney McCleary is an associate professor in the School of Technology and Professional Services Management at Eastern Michigan University in Ypsilanti, Michigan. She earned her bachelor's in government from the University of Texas at Austin, The Grande Diplome from Le Cordon Bleu in Paris, her master's in foodservice management, and a PhD in communications from Michigan State University.

Dr. McCleary worked in some of the finest kitchens in Paris before returning to her hometown of New Orleans, where she moved through the ranks in high-end restaurants. She was part of the opening and expansion of a catering company and gourmet-to-go operation. After completion of her degrees, she worked as an in-house consultant in the Corporate Food and Beverage Department of Harrah's (now Caesar's) Entertainment. She also worked locally as a food and beverage director and regional food and beverage director for country clubs in Oakland County, Michigan.

Her research interests include accountability systems and motivation in the workplace, friendships and motivation, and trust-building in service provider relationships.

Dr. McCleary is the author of "Too Big to Succeed."

Dorothy McAllen is the interim associate dean and an associate professor in technology management with the College of Engineering and Technology at Eastern Michigan University. She assists with the overall operation of the college, is the director of the college doctoral program, teaches graduate and undergraduate technology-focused courses, and guest lectures in different programs at the university. Prior to earning her PhD and joining Eastern Michigan University, Ms. McAllen served as an officer with the Michigan State Police for 28 years. She was one of the first female troopers hired by the department and was the first female promoted to the lieutenant's rank. In this position, she was responsible for strategic and tactical operations for the multiagency task forces in Detroit and southeast Michigan. She retired as a division commander in charge of technology and business enterprise solutions. Ms. McAllen works closely with the Center for Regional and National Security and serves on multiple advisory boards supporting new and innovative initiatives.

Dr. McAllen received a BS in criminal justice from Michigan State University and both a master's and PhD in technology studies from Eastern Michigan University. Her doctoral research focused on collaboration and interdisciplinary knowledge in understanding national security policies and technological innovation. This research has allowed her to work with other researchers to present their findings at conferences and publish articles focusing on technology, innovation, and national security.

Dr. McAllen is the author of "The Invisible Manager: Workhorse or Glass Ceiling?"

Christina Wall graduated from Florida Institute of Technology in 1998 with a BS in aeronautical science. She obtained her master's degree in interdisciplinary technology, from Eastern Michigan University in 2007. Ms. Wall has worked in the aviation industry for over 20 years, including work on government contracts for the Federal Aviation Administration as well as jobs in airline operations. Additionally, she started and directed the Aircraft Dispatcher Certification Program at the Michigan Institute of Aviation and Technology in 2003. Ms. Wall has taught at Eastern Michigan University since 2003, both as an assistant professor and part-time lecturer in the aviation flight technology and aviation management. She is a member of the University Aviation Association as well as Women in Aviation, International.

Ms. Wall is the author of "Soaring in the Sky."

Preface

THE AUTHORS AND contributing authors of *Case Studies on Women in Business* are women with different backgrounds. There is no pattern in age, gender, race, religion, financial status, independence, education, or career path. Yet, we have been able to collaborate because of the strength in our differences. It is what makes this book unique for teaching and enlightening to read. The core of every case has a foundation of reality to give the reader an appreciation for experiences in employment.

This book is about AWARENESS and preparing the reader and participant for employment in the 21st century. It's not a "how-to" textbook with all the correct answers or solutions to challenges in your career. It is a book to open your mind, your spirit, and your understanding of the common and uncommon, the believable and unbelievable, and the ordinary and extraordinary occurrences in the workplace. You will quickly realize that business and business success is about people.

As a current or future member of the workforce, you will experience at least one if not many of these situations. Minus the unsettling cases, it makes life fun, challenging, and occasionally stressful. The book will not give you specific direction or answers on how to become a CEO (for example) or how to manage professional relationships or succeed in business. What you will gain is insight.

Since the first edition of *Case Studies on Women in Business*, the authors have added a chapter titled, "Ethics and Personal Values." The workplace is forever changing, and two important social themes have emerged: the #MeToo movement and empowerment, which are included in the cases presented here.

AWARENESS of the knowledge that you have a voice and that you are empowered to use it can be world-changing and cathartic. In fact, many voices have been heard by the U.S. Equal Employment Opportunity Commission (EEOC). Since 1963, several laws supporting workers have been enacted in the United States, such as the Civil Rights Act of 1964, the Pregnancy Discrimination Act of 1978, and the Lilly Ledbetter Fair Pay Act of 2009. These are designed to improve the conditions of employment, and more will be fought to ensure diversity, equity, and inclusion for all employees

AWARENESS will make you consciously competent of what's in front of you. It will prepare you to expect the unexpected. Perhaps, it will instill you with confidence and feeling empowered. After reading this book, you will have earned a degree in AWARENESS, which will pave a smoother path for success in your work life.

Introduction

The role of women in the workplace dramatically changed over 80 years ago, starting in the early 1940s with the onset of World War II. Women who had traditionally been homemakers were needed as workers in the United States to support the war effort. Women stepped up to the challenge and were employed in factories, stores, and government agencies in the spirit of national unity. As a group, these women were often referred to as "Rosie the Riveters" (Vergun, 2019) for their dedicated participation in the manufacturing sector. But after the war ended, men returned from the military to resume their jobs and careers (National History Women's Museum, 2007). Women returned to occupational roles more socially acceptable for them. Hence, the "traditional workforce" before World War II resumed.

However, a positive thing happened during this war effort. Women became AWARE that they had other strengths outside of the home and could contribute in ways they never knew. This AWARE-NESS was the catalyst of new thinking for

INTRO FIGURE 1 "These women were welders at the Ingalls Shipbuilding Corporation of Pascagoula, Mississippi, during World War II. (National Archives, 1943, Identifier 522890)." This material is in the public domain in the United States as it is the work of the United States federal government and available for use under 17 U.S.C. § 105.

women—for example: "What if I could …?" and "What if I was …?" and "How could I do…?" Women slowly felt empowered to take a baby step forward or even run forward fast. They fell, got up, and were occasionally pushed down because of their excitement to learn, grow, and contribute to their family and society in a different way. They recognized the possibility of building a "career" rather than just holding a "job" outside of an established female role, too. AWARENESS equated to possibility!

Two decades later, in the 1960s, that possibility took hold, and the United States experienced several societal changes (Walsh, 2010). Many women began to re-enter the workforce in larger numbers, and that trend continues today. Based on data from the U.S. Department of Labor:

- "In 2020, women's annual earnings were 82.3% of men's, and the gap is even wider for many women of color" (Jones, 2021, para. 4). This can be compared to "1973, (when) women made 57 cents per dollar earned by men" (Jones, para. 4).

- "Women earn less than men in nearly all occupations. There are only a handful of occupations where women earn slightly more than their male counterparts, such as health care social workers" (Jones, 2021, para. 6).

- "Women earn less than their same race and ethnicity counterpart at every level of educational attainments. Compared with white men and the same education, Black and Latina women with only a bachelor's degree have the largest gap at 65%, and Black women with advanced degrees earn 70% of what white men with advanced degrees earn. Educational attainment is not enough to close gender earnings gaps. In fact, most women with advanced degrees earn less than white men, on average, with only a bachelor's degree" (Jones, 2021, para. 7).

- "The COVID pandemic has set women's labor force participation back more than 30 years" (Jones, 2021, para. 8). "Unfortunately, the pandemic stalled gains made toward closing the pay gap, and layoffs, and a lack of child care have forced many women out of the workforce entirely. In February 2021, women's labor force participation rate was 55.8%—the same rate as April 1987. And women of color and those working in low-wage occupations have been the most impacted" (Jones, para. 9).

Number of women in the labor force

78,607,961

8,179,017

1920   1930   1940   1950   1960   1970   1980   1990   2000   2010   2020

INTRO FIGURE 2   Workforce Participation Rates by Women for 100 Years
(U.S. Department of Labor, 2020, para. 2)

So, where are we now? Through AWARENESS and an understanding of workforce dynamics, women will be able to experience a more equal work environment. It's going to take patience, determination, and courage to fail and excel and convince society of the benefits of women in the workforce.

This book takes readers through the paradigm shift across eight chapters and 32 case scenarios. It begins with the changing roles of women in the workforce. It progresses to look at specific aspects of the work experience based on gender, including workplace discrimination, work and family, women and leadership, the female entrepreneur, international dimensions, and ethics and personal values.

Each case includes several questions useful for group discussion and personal reflection to accomplish the goal of the authors, which is simply AWARENESS of the challenges both men and women face as today's workers.

Finally, as we close this edition, it is important to recognize that working women are becoming more and more empowered. Recently, the U.S. Department of Labor celebrated the 100th Anniversary of its Women's Bureau (U.S. Department of Labor, 2021b). In recognition of all working women, we also want take this opportunity to thank those who have found the strength to make a difference in this world. We have gratitude for the positive impact they have achieved in the workplace and those who will continue to make progress with their voices.

References

Bureau of Labor Statistics. (2021, May 7). *Economic news release. Table A-1. Employment status of the civilian population by sex and age.* https://www.bls.gov/news.release/empsit.t01.htm

DeWolf, M. (2017, March 1). *12 stats about working women.* U.S. Department of Labor Blog. https://blog.dol.gov/2017/03/01/12-stats-about-working-women

Golden, C. (1991). The role of WWII in the rise in women's employment. *The American Economic Review, 81*(4): 741–756. https://scholar.harvard.edu/files/goldin/files/the_role_of_world_war_ii_in_the_rise_of_womens_employment.pdf

Jones, J. (2021, March 19). *5 facts about the state of the gender pay gap.* U.S. Department of Labor Blog. https://blog.dol.gov/2021/03/19/5-facts-about-the-state-of-the-gender-pay-gap

National Archives. (1943). *86-WWT-85-35* [Image]. National Archives Identifier 522890. https://catalog.archives.gov/id/522890

National History Women's Museum. (2007). *Changing images of women's roles.* https://www.nwhm.org/online-exhibits/partners/1.htm

U.S. Bureau of Labor Statistics. (2021, May 20). *Labor force statistics from the current population survey.* https://www.bls.gov/cps/earnings.htm

U.S. Census Bureau. (2021). *Survey of business owners and self-employed persons (SBO).* https://www.census.gov/programs-surveys/sbo.html

U.S. Department of Labor. (2020). *100 years of working women.* Women's Bureau. https://www.dol.gov/agencies/wb/data/occupations-decades-100

U.S. Department of Labor. (2021a, March 22). *Equal pay for equal work for all women* [Video]. YouTube. https://www.youtube.com/watch?v=ccZjHWlvJMo

U.S. Department of Labor. (2021b). *Women's bureau centennial | 1920 to today.* https://www.dol.gov/agencies/wb

Vergun, D. (2019, March 21). *Rosie the Riveter inspired women to serve in World War II.* U.S. Department of Defense. https://www.defense.gov/Explore/Features/Story/Article/1791664/rosie-the-riveter-inspired-women-to-serve-in-world-war-ii/

Walsh, K. (2010, March 12). The 1960's: A decade of change for women. *U.S. News & World Report.* https://www.usnews.com/news/articles/2010/03/12/the-1960s-a-decade-of-change-for-women

Figure Credits

Fig. 0.1: Source: https://catalog.archives.gov/id/522890.
Fig. 0.2: Source: https://www.dol.gov/agencies/wb/data/occupations-decades-100.

Changing Roles

Soaring in the Sky

By Christina Wall

Overview

This case is about two women during two different periods in history. It begins in the 1940s during WWII with Charlie Ray, a woman whose aspirations are to be a successful pilot. She is offered and accepts a job flying for the Women Airforce Service Pilots (WASP) (Wings Across America, n.d.). This organization hired female pilots to perform flying tasks for the military. While employed, Charlie becomes "in a family way,"[1] and once she "starts showing," her employment is terminated. Firing pregnant employees was common during this time as the medical community feared working could negatively affect maternal and fetal health. Others claimed being pregnant affected a woman's efficiency on the job. The scenario then fast-forwards to Lisa Shay, a present-day airline pilot expecting a baby.

The case compares both pilots' experiences and explores how their employers responded to their pregnancies. It also discusses how

Objectives

- Describe the societal and attitude changes during the past 80 years toward women, pregnancy, and work.
- Compare the legal protections available to working women during WWII versus today.
- Examine when and if an employer must provide work accommodations to a pregnant employee.
- Describe any space and scheduling accommodations an employer must make for an employee breastfeeding her child.

Key Concepts and Words

benevolent sexism, female intensive occupation, FMLA, male intensive occupation, old-fashioned sexism, sex segregation of occupations, women and family initiatives, workplace accommodation

---

1   In the 1940s and 1950s euphemisms were commonly used for the words "pregnant" or "pregnancy." Instead, the terms "expecting," "with child," and "in the family way" were common.

society's views have advanced over the last several decades. As readers will soon question, in aviation, can she really "soar in the sky?"

Scenario

It was early December 8, 1942, and Charlie remembered the day well. One year ago to the day, Japan had declared war against the United States and had attacked the U.S. Navy's Pearl Harbor military base outside Honolulu, killing 2,355 U.S. service members and 68 civilians (History.com Editors, 2020). Germany and Italy had also declared war on the United States, forcing the United States to fight against Germany, Italy, and Japan (National World War II Museum, 2001). The United States was in a global war, and WWII changed everyone's lives. Rationing for daily goods such as sugar and meat was in place, gasoline was scarce, and it took weeks to receive mail from those in the U.S. military.

Most "able-bodied"[2] men had joined the war effort, leaving thousands of unfilled jobs in the manufacturing sector. These were unique circumstances, and single and married women entered the workforce for the first time to fill these jobs. But, unlike many other women, Charlie Ray was already employed.

Back then, most women who went to college became a teacher or a nurse. But not Charlie Ray. During those years, she was a trailblazer as she graduated in June 1940 from college with a business degree. After graduation, she was fortunate to be hired as a bank teller by America the Brave Bank. However, banking was not her passion. Flying was her first love.

Since she was a little girl, Charlie Ray wanted to be a pilot. She admired the determination and courage of Amelia Earhart, and at 23, she learned how to fly. She completed the necessary training and obtained the required licenses, but she rarely heard of pilot job opportunities welcoming to females.

She continued to work at the bank for several months, and she often visited the airport to socialize while hoping she could pick up a few extra dollars being a copilot on a local weekend flight. One day while visiting, she overheard a man talking about the Women Airforce[3] Service Pilots (WASP) and how they were looking for women to join their flight services. WASPs were civilian female pilots who flew

---

2   Although the term "able-bodied" is often replaced with "non-disabled," that was the prevalent term used during WWII.

3   The term Airforce was used during this time instead of the current Air Force.

ferry flights,[4] transported military personnel, and performed test flights on military aircraft. Charlie was immediately interested and applied for the job.

However, Charlie wasn't sure if her husband Michael would approve, and she was worried that she might need her husband's permission to fly as a WASP pilot. Michael had just volunteered to support the war effort by joining the U.S. Army and was deployed overseas in the Philippines. She wrote him a letter to let him know that she wanted to help the war effort, and she could do it by flying.

Before the WASP opportunity, Charlie had considered enlisting in the military hoping to secure a flying position but discovered women could only be nurses in the military. So, she was elated to pursue the newly formed WASP organization. As a part of the application process, Charlie had to disclose her height, weight, and race. Prospective pilots had to be "at least 5 feet, 4 inches tall, pass Army physicals, (and) have a pilot's license" and "have at least a high school diploma and be age 18 to 35" (Oliver, 2016, para. 6). A few days after submitting her application, she was scheduled for an interview.

During the interview process, Charlie was asked to perform various physical tests she successfully passed. Her flying skills were also tested. She was surprised to learn that primarily Caucasian females (Cook, 2006; McLellan, 2000) were hired to fill the 2,000 pilot slots. She knew it would be different flying a military plane, but she would learn.

That Christmas, her husband Michael surprised her with a short leave from the Army because he had been reassigned to the States for a few weeks of special training. He was supportive of Charlie's military flying as a WASP. Charlie put on her new uniform, and her husband was perplexed. It was so large on her. She explained that the military didn't have uniforms for females, and they just had to alter the sleeve and pant length. However, they were forbidden to tailor it to look like a woman's pantsuit.

Charlie flew in January 1944. After flying for the organization for four months, Charlie discovered that she was pregnant. Once "she showed," she was told to take unpaid leave, and it was up to the military's discretion if she could return. When her son Matthew was 6 months old, Charlie wanted to fly again, but there were no "mothers" who were part of the WASP, and the military made no accommodation for

---

4   Ferry flights return an aircraft to its flight base.

women who couldn't meet the demands of the job. It was wartime, and the nurses in the Army Corps were forced to leave the service if they became pregnant. Why should the WASPs be any different? As the war progressed, Charlie was told there were more male pilots available, so there wasn't a strong need for "the girls to fly" (NPR, 2010, para. 5). She decided it was best to abandon flying again.

Four years later, Matthew started nursery school. Charlie was ready to return to her job as a pilot but still needed flexibility in her career and her weekends free. WASP no longer existed (Stamberg, 2012), but Charlie hoped she could fly as a military pilot in the U.S. Air Force and sent in her application to enlist. Although she was accepted to enroll as an officer, her application for a flight position was unfortunately denied, and she returned to her former job as a bank teller. Charlie wondered, why?

Present-Day

After flying for a regional airline for 6 months, Lisa Shay discovered that she was pregnant. She received medical clearance (American Society, 2001) and worked until the last week of her pregnancy because she was healthy and had no pregnancy complications.

Her boss and colleagues gave her a work "baby shower" and wished her the best until she returned. Initially, she took 12 workweeks of leave under the federal Family and Medical Leave Act of 1993 (29 U.S.C. § 2601). Lisa was also very fortunate as her company paid her full salary during the time off. However, when it was time to return to work, Lisa took a 1-year leave of absence to raise her child. The airline was disappointed she didn't return right away. They needed good pilots, and Lisa had regularly volunteered for last-minute flights when another pilot fell ill. By working for a regional airline, Lisa was based in her home city, giving her an easy commute. She took her leave in "good standing," so returning to work for the airline was promising.

PREGNANCY, MATERNITY & PARENTAL LEAVE

"Under the federal Pregnancy Discrimination Act, an employer that allows temporarily disabled employees to take disability leave or leave without pay must allow an employee who is temporarily disabled due to pregnancy to do the same.

An employer may not single out pregnancy-related conditions for special procedures to determine an employee's ability to work. However, if an employer requires its employees to submit a doctor's statement concerning their ability to work before granting leave or paying sick benefits, the employer may require employees affected by pregnancy-related conditions to submit such statements.

Further, under the Family and Medical Leave Act (FMLA) of 1993, a new parent (including foster and adoptive parents) may be eligible for 12 weeks of leave (unpaid or paid if the employee has earned or accrued it) that may be used for care of the new child. To be eligible, the employee must have worked for the employer for 12 months prior to taking the leave and the employer must have a specified number of employees." (EEOC, 2021, para. 5–7)

After taking off the extra time, Lisa looked forward to resuming her job as a pilot. She assumed she would be flying as a pilot on regional U.S. flights like she had and applied to return to work. Lisa also believed she would have a similar schedule. However, her employer had merged with a national airline while she was on leave. Upon her return, she was scheduled to fly cross-country flights and assigned to fly out of Los Angeles (she resided in the Detroit, Michigan area). This required 4 hours of commuting time to LAX (Los Angeles, California), plus the time zone changes from the west to east coasts. Lisa was caught in a quandary.

She talked to her partner, and they decided they would try to make a go of the new schedule. It would be a challenge, being away from home and her son for long periods, but they both felt they were up to the task. The airline offered excellent benefits, and Lisa's seniority was not lost during her leave. However, Lisa had breastfed her child and wished to continue after her return to work. Therefore, she requested that the company provide her with a 20-minute break to express breast milk once every 3 hours.

Although there were some shorter U.S. flights, Lisa's boss did not think it was fair to assign those to Lisa rather than other pilots because she wanted to breastfeed. He discussed her request with Human

Resources, and they agreed that it wasn't possible. The airline reminded her she was a junior pilot and that senior pilots had priority on schedules and routes.

Lisa took a stand on the breastfeeding issue and explored her options and legal rights as a breastfeeding mother and pilot. She felt the airline was forcing her to choose between her job and being a mother and needed an "accommodation" to pump her milk. But the airline responded that as a pilot, the job's essential functions (i.e., flying) meant that the employee must give 100% to the job. There was no type of reasonable accommodation it could provide to a (breastfeeding) pilot that wouldn't compromise airline safety. They insisted the pilot must remain in the cockpit except for regular bathroom breaks.

In frustration, Lisa located a job as a cargo pilot. Her new employer accommodated her breastfeeding schedule with no issues and provided her with a private area. The position gave her regular, scheduled hours but at reduced pay and benefits. Her priority in life was her partner and Matthew, so the trade-off was acceptable. She was lucky to have other employment options in the airline industry, unlike Charlie Ray!

Discussion Questions

1. Why do you believe the WASP recruiter could ask Charlie specific questions of height, weight, and race on the employment application?

2. Do you think an employer today can require certain physical requirements for a specific job using today's standards? If so, which ones and why?

3. Primarily, Caucasian women were hired for the WASP. What additional factors may have contributed to this lack of diversity in the hiring process? Remember, the timeframe for this case is WWII (1941–1945).

4. In the early 1940s, female employees were asked/told or voluntarily left the workforce once it was apparent the worker was pregnant. Why is this not a realistic work policy in today's world? Explain.

5. Fast-forward to the present day. The U.S. Department of Labor (D.O.L.) has published guidelines on employee scheduled breaks and breastfeeding (see Fact Sheet #73). Based on its content, do you believe Lisa's airline employer must accommodate her request?

U.S. Department of Labor _____

Wage and Hour Division   (April 2018)

Fact Sheet #73: Break Time for Nursing Mothers Under the FLSA

This fact sheet provides general information on the break time requirement for nursing mothers in the Patient Protection and Affordable Care Act ("PPACA"), which took effect when the PPACA was signed into law on March 23, 2010 (P.L. 111–148). This law amended Section 7 of the Fair Labor Standards Act (FLSA).

General Requirements

Employers are required to provide "reasonable break time for an employee to express breast milk for her nursing child for 1 year after the child's birth each time such employee has need to express the milk." Employers are also required to provide "a place, other than a bathroom, that is shielded from view and free from intrusion from coworkers and the public, which may be used by an employee to express breast milk."

The FLSA requirement of break time for nursing mothers to express breast milk does not preempt State laws that provide greater protections to employees (for example, providing compensated break time, providing break time for exempt employees, or providing break time beyond 1 year after the child's birth).

Time and Location of Breaks

Employers are required to provide a reasonable amount of break time to express milk as frequently as needed by the nursing mother. The frequency of breaks needed to express milk as well as the duration of each break will likely vary.

A bathroom, even if private, is not a permissible location under the Act. The location provided must be functional as a space for expressing breast milk. If the space is not dedicated to the nursing mother's use, it must be available when needed in order to meet the statutory requirement. A space temporarily created or converted into a space for expressing milk or made available when needed by the nursing

U.S. Department of Labor, "Fact Sheet #73: Break Time for Nursing Mothers under the FLSA."

mother is sufficient provided that the space is shielded from view, and free from any intrusion from co-workers and the public.

Coverage and Compensation

Only employees who are not exempt from Section 7, which includes the FLSA's overtime pay requirements, are entitled to breaks to express milk. While employers are not required under the FLSA to provide breaks to nursing mothers who are exempt from the requirements of Section 7, they may be obligated to provide such breaks under State laws.

Employers with fewer than 50 employees are not subject to the FLSA break time requirement if compliance with the provision would impose an undue hardship. Whether compliance would be an undue hardship is determined by looking at the difficulty or expense of compliance for a specific employer in comparison to the size, financial resources, nature, and structure of the employer's business. All employees who work for the covered employer, regardless of work site, are counted when determining whether this exemption may apply.

Employers are not required under the FLSA to compensate nursing mothers for breaks taken for the purpose of expressing milk. However, where employers already provide compensated breaks, an employee who uses that break time to express milk must be compensated in the same way that other employees are compensated for break time. In addition, the FLSA's general requirement that the employee must be completely relieved from duty or else the time must be compensated as work time applies. *See* WHD Fact Sheet #22, Hours Worked under the FLSA.

FLSA Prohibitions on Retaliation

Section 15(a)(3) of the FLSA states that it is a violation for any person to "discharge or in any other manner discriminate against any employee because such employee has filed any complaint or instituted or caused to be instituted any proceeding under or related to this Act, or has testified or is about to testify in any such proceeding, or has served or is about to serve on an industry committee."

Employees are protected regardless of whether the complaint is made orally or in writing. Complaints made to the Wage and Hour Division are protected, and most courts have ruled that internal complaints to an employer are also protected.

Any employee who is "discharged or in any other manner discriminated against" because, for instance, he or she has filed a complaint or cooperated in an investigation, may file a retaliation complaint with the Wage and Hour Division or may file a private cause of action seeking appropriate remedies including, but not limited to, employment, reinstatement, lost wages and an additional equal amount as liquidated damages.

Additional Resources

- Request for Information on Break Time for Nursing Mothers, Federal Register 75:
- 80073-80079, (2010, December 21): This notice is a request for information from the public regarding the recent amendment to the FLSA that requires employers to provide reasonable break time and a place for nursing mothers to express breast milk for one year after the child's birth. The Department seeks information and comments for its review as it considers how best to help employers and employees understand the requirements of the law.
- Questions and Answers about the Request for Information
- Presidential Memorandum for the Director of the Office of Personnel Management
- OPM Guidance on Nursing Mothers in the Federal Workforce
- Supporting Nursing Moms at Work: Employer Solutions
- CDC Healthier Worksite Initiative, Workplace Lactation Support Program Toolkit
- EEOC Enforcement Guidance: Unlawful Disparate Treatment of Workers With Caregiving Responsibilities
- National Conference of State Legislatures Compilation of State Breastfeeding Laws
- U.S. Breastfeeding Committee, Workplace Support and Coalitions Directory
- International Lactation Consultants Association, Worksite Lactation Support Directory
- The Surgeon General's Call to Action to Support Breastfeeding

For additional information, visit our Wage and Hour Division Website: http://www.dol.gov/whd and/or call our toll-free information and helpline, available 8 a.m. to 5 p.m. in your time zone, 1-866-4USWAGE (1-866-487-9243).

This publication is for general information and is not to be considered in the same light as official statements of position contained in the regulations.

U.S. Department of Labor   1-866-4-USWAGE

Frances Perkins Building   TTY: 1-866-487-9243

200 Constitution Avenue, NW   **Contact Us**

Washington, DC 20210 _____

Fact Sheet #73 (U.S. Department of Labor, 2018). Under Section 105 of the U.S. Copyright Act (17 U.S.C. § 105), this work is a product of an officer or employee of the federal government and is not entitled to domestic copyright protection under U.S. law and is in the public domain.

6. Lisa's employer did not accommodate her request for shorter flights because he didn't believe it was fair to the other employees. What do you think? Was it fair to Lisa? Why?

7. After reading both employers' reactions to Lisa's work requests, which opinion do you support, Lisa's or the airlines? Why?

Assignments

1. Based on historical context, several issues would have been addressed differently in the 1940s versus the current day. Discuss how these situations would have been addressed in both eras (WWII and present) by utilizing the case scenario, resources, and other websites. Use Table 1.1 as a guideline to evaluate criteria.

TABLE 1.1

Subject	WASP	U.S. Commercial Airline
Question of race on an application		
Question of marital status on an application		
Diverse (race) workforce		
Employed while pregnant		
Different standards based on gender		
Salary benefits for pregnancy		
Employed while breastfeeding		
Breastfeeding accommodation		
Employment with spouse approval		
Employment rejection without explanation		

2. In WWII, the Soviet Union had an elite squad of female fighter pilots called the 588th Night Bomber Regiment. How were these pilots different from the U.S. WASPs? See https://www.theatlantic.com/technology/archive/2013/07/night-witches-the-female-fighter-pilots-of-world-war-ii/277779/.

3. Define maternity leave and paternity leave. Which countries do not mandate paid maternity leave? Which countries do not mandate paid paternity leave? Why do you think there is a difference?

4. What type of job could be ideal for breastfeeding mothers because "accommodations" could be made? Is it reasonable to accept that women will always be limited in their career choices because of sex? Debate.

5. Do you think the "sky is the limit" for women in the workforce today? Write a 1,000- to 2,000-word essay supporting your opinion.

6. Charlie had to take unpaid leave for her pregnancy, yet Lisa had options. What is the current standard practice for maternity leave in the United States—unpaid or paid maternity leave? Is an employer required to provide maternity leave? Is childbirth treated as a medical condition? If so, must it be paid? See the materials published by the U.S. Equal Opportunity Commission that discusses the federal Pregnancy Discrimination Act of 1978 (42 U.S.C. § 2000e), which addresses this question. (Tip: Locate the Patient Protection and Affordable Care Act of 2010 (42 U.S.C. § 18001), which amended the Fair Labor Standards Act).

Additional Learning

- The United States Breastfeeding Committee summarizes the "Break Time for Nursing Mothers" law at http://www.usbreastfeeding.org/workplace-law.

- The United States Department of Labor summarizes the Family and Medical Leave Act (FMLA) and resources for employers and employees at https://www.dol.gov/general/topic/benefits-leave/fmla.

- The EEOC has a detailed summary titled "Questions and Answers About Race and Color Discrimination in Employment" at https://www.eeoc.gov/policy/docs/qanda_race_color.html.

- Written information about Women Airforce Service Pilots (WASP) of WWII is available at http://www.npr.org/2010/03/09/123773525/female-wwii-pilots-the-original-fly-girls.

- Frontier Airlines has been sued for failing to accommodate female pilots who are breastfeeding. What is the status of the case? Review it at https://www.aclu.org/cases/freyer-v-frontier-and-hodgkins-v-frontier?redirect=cases/frontier-airlines-eeoc-complaint.

References

ACLU. (2019, December 10). *Freyer v. Frontier* and *Hodgkins v Frontier*. https://www.aclu.org/cases/freyer-v-frontier-and-hodgkins-v-frontier?redirect=cases/frontier-airlines-eeoc-complaint

American Society of Aerospace Medical Specialists (2001). Clinical practice guideline for pregnancy. http://www.asams.org/guidelines/Completed/NEW%20Pregnancy.htm

Barbara, G., Hartmann, H., Hegewisch. A., Milli, J., & Reichlin, L. (2014). Paid parental leave in the United States: What the data tell us about access, usage, and economic and health benefits. Institute for Women's Policy Research. https://iwpr.org/iwpr-publications/report/paid-parental-leave-in-the-united-states-what-the-data-tell-us-about-access-usage-and-economic-and-health-benefits/

Cochrane, D. (2020, May 20). Flying on the homefront: Women Airforce Service pilots (WASP). Smithsonian National Air and Space Museum. https://airandspace.si.edu/stories/editorial/flying-homefront-women-airforce-service-pilots-wasp

Cook, B. (Ed). (2006). *Women and war, a historical encyclopedia from antiquity to the present: Volume one: A-K.* ABC-CLIO.

Fair Labor Standards Act of 1938, 29 U.S.C. § 207(r)(1)-(4) as amended by the Affordable Care Act.

Family and Medical Leave Act of 1993, 29 U.S.C. § 2601-2654.

Garber, M. (2013, July 15). Night witches: The female fighter pilots of World War II. *The Atlantic*. https://www.theatlantic.com/technology/archive/2013/07/night-witches-the-female-fighter-pilots-of-world-war-ii/277779/

Guerin, P. (n.d.). Essential job functions under the A.D.A. Nolo. http://www.nolo.com/legal-encyclopedia/essential-job-functions-under-the-ada.html

History.com Editors. (2020). *Pearl Harbor bombed*. This day in history: December 7. https://www.history.com/this-day-in-history/pearl-harbor-bombed

Lux, J. (2014, January 8). Interview with Kristine Swan Lent Gros Women Airforce Service pilot (WASP) [Video]. YouTube. https://www.youtube.com/watch?v=rA7-aDBDvxo

McLellan, D. (2000, October 23). Adding a missing piece to mosaic of American history. *Los Angeles Times*. http://articles.latimes.com/2000/oct/23/news/cl-40608

National World War II Museum. (2001). A Pearl Harbor fact sheet. http://www.nationalww2museum.org/assets/pdfs/pearl-harbor-fact-sheet-1.pdf

NPR. (2010, March 9). WASP: Women with wings in WWII. Timeline: Female pilots in WWII. http://www.npr.org/2011/06/01/124367587/wasp-women-with-wings-in-wwii

O'Connell, Martin. (1990). Maternity leave arrangements: 1961–85. In work and family patterns of American Women. Current Population Reports, Special Studies series P-23, no. 165. U.S. Census Bureau. Table D.

Oliver, D. (2016, March 25). Flying as a WASP: Women pilots set the standard in 1943. Defense Media Activity-Navy Production. https://www.dvidshub.net/news/194283/flying-wasp-women-pilots-set-standard-1943

Paquette, D. (2017, April 8). She was pregnant and broke. She signed up for Uber—and fell into debt. *Washington Post*. https://www.washingtonpost.com/business/economy/she-had-a-newborn-and-no-money-signing-up-for-uber-drove-her-into-debt/2017/04/07/b5ee9510-05d1-11e7-b9fa-ed727b644a0b_story.html?hpid=hp_hp-top-table-main_maya-730a%3Ahomepage%2Fstory&utm_term=.49e6e7573cf1

Robaton, A. (2016, May 13). When a nursing mom is a commercial airline pilot. CBS Moneywatch. http://www.cbsnews.com/news/when-a-nursing-mom-is-a-commercial-airline-pilot/

Rubin, R. (2016). U.S. dead last among developed countries when it comes to paid maternity leave. *Forbes*. https://www.forbes.com/sites/ritarubin/2016/04/06/united-states-lags-behind-all-other-developed-countries-when-it-comes-to-paid-maternity-leave/#75e609f68f15

Stamberg, S. (2010, March 9). Female WWII pilots: The original fly girls. NPR. http://www.npr.org/2010/03/09/123773525/female-wwii-pilots-the-original-fly-girls

Tan, M. (2015, August 7). Army reviewing rules for maternity, paternity leave. *Army Times.* https://www.armytimes.com/story/military/careers/army/2015/08/07/army-reviewing-rules-maternity-paternity-leave/31285283/

United States Breastfeeding Committee. (n.d.). What is the "break time for nursing mothers" law? http://www.usbreastfeeding.org/workplace-law

U.S. Census Bureau. (2001, November). Maternity leave and employment patterns 1961–1995. https://www.census.gov/prod/2001pubs/p70-79.pdf

U.S. Department of Labor. (n.d.). Family and Medical Leave Act. https://www.dol.gov/whd/fmla/

U.S. Department of Labor. (n.d.). Job accommodations. https://www.dol.gov/general/topic/disability/jobaccommodations

U.S Department of Labor. (2012) *Fact sheet #28:* The Family Medical and Leave Act. https://www.dol.gov/sites/dolgov/files/WHD/legacy/files/whdfs28.pdf

U.S Department of Labor. (2018) Fact sheet #73: Break time for nursing mothers under the FLSA. https://www.dol.gov/whd/regs/compliance/whdfs73.pdf

U.S. Equal Employment Opportunity Commission. (n.d.). Pregnancy discrimination. https://www.eeoc.gov/laws/types/pregnancy.cfm

U.S. Equal Employment Opportunity Commission. (n.d.). Questions and answers about race and color discrimination in employment. https://www.eeoc.gov/laws/guidance/questions-and-answers-about-race-and-color-discrimination-employment

Wings Across America. (n.d.). WASP on the web. http://www.wingsacrossamerica.us/wasp/

Making Life Work Now

Overview

Jenny Tuttle is a 54-year-old divorcee and is excited about her job opportunity as the new office manager at Grand Teton Veterinary Associates. The position offers a good salary with upward mobility. She does not have experience in the veterinary business, but she has been involved in the service industry for many years and is passionate about pets and people.

This past month her youngest daughter Trisha moved back home after her employer laid off a substantial portion of their workforce. Jenny's mother, Agnes, is also living with them. Her mother, age 72, requires additional care because she is in the early stages of Alzheimer's.

Jenny had originally reentered the workforce about 14 years ago to keep herself busy. However, one year ago, she was "officially divorced," and her life situation changed. Now, she must support herself, her daughter, and her mother.

Objectives

- Describe the personal attributes that drive a person's job selection.
- Explain the value of creating a career plan for unexpected life changes caused by external events.
- Examine internally driven needs that can affect job choices and performance.
- Describe the significance of having work-life balance.
- Summarize the importance of effective communication based on generational differences.
- Define ageism and explain its applicability to the case scenario.

Key Concepts and Words

ageism, career goals, career plan, effective communication, embracing change, employee motivation, generational gap, job attribute preferences, job description, job evaluation, personal attributes, transitional life stages

Scenario

Like many divorces, Jenny's was mentally and financially draining. After 26 years of marriage, she and her husband Amell had separated for 5 years. During that time, Amell supported her with a generous income (that he called her "allowance"). As Jenny would often describe it, she had "an amazing life" before the divorce. The couple had many friends, entertained frequently, and traveled around the world. One year ago, when the separation became "official," there was no alimony, and most financial support ended. Jenny then learned that the couple had "spent it as fast as they made it," and there was little money to share between them. She realized too late that she failed to plan for these changes in income and lifestyle.

Jenny's youngest daughter, Trisha, was 22 years old, and she had been living on her own but was forced to return home. She was part of a layoff from her employer who was restructuring. Trisha couldn't afford the payments on her condo and car, which her father had made before the divorce. Jenny's mother, Agnes, also moved into her home because her memory was failing, and she needed extra care. So, three generations were living under one roof.

Jenny had been employed at a popular housewares retail store called My Abode & More while married. She enjoyed the socialization from work. Jenny was one of three store supervisors and was fortunate to have flexible part-time hours, freeing her to participate in community activities. The job worked well for her lifestyle and provided an activity she enjoyed outside of her marriage and family life.

One year after the divorce, Jenny was offered a full-time manager's role at My Abode & More. She turned down the position as she had become disillusioned with her job over the past months. For example, Jenny couldn't afford the items at her store without her alimony. She also knew the physical stress of working a 40-hour week would be exhausting, especially with her new home worries and her mother's care needs. Jenny didn't have the same interest in socializing with the customers either because many had been wives of her ex-husband's friends, and these relationships dwindled after the divorce. Jenny wished she didn't have to work so hard and be on her feet most of the day.

Another issue was that her mother, Agnes, called her several times a day. Her boss was irritated with the numerous phone calls as it created many interruptions during customer sales transactions. Jenny's home and job lives were no longer aligned, so she decided she needed a job change.

Jenny instantly thought about working for Grand Teton Veterinarian, where her dog Buckley was boarded when she worked long days. She was introduced to the business when Buckley became ill with a rare skin infection and needed a special medicated cream compounded at Grand Teton's pet pharmacy. While there, Jenny was given a tour of the pet daycare facilities. It was very impressive, and the facility even had a pool with underwater therapy devices for dogs. Jenny switched Buckley to a veterinarian at Grand Teton that day.

A few weeks later, Jenny had an appointment for Buckley's rabies shot and inquired if they were hiring. She was delighted to hear they were. The open positions were for "Pet Techs," which were entry-level jobs. Jenny knew nothing about what the job would entail, but she thought that it would be fun and easy. However, she needed a job with a high enough income to support herself and her family. She inquired further and was told that they would also be looking for a new office manager in a few months. Their administrator, Wanda, would be moving out of state. They had not posted the position because they were focused on the immediate needs of technicians. The management opening sounded like a better opportunity.

During the dog visit, Jenny asked the veterinarian what qualities they were looking for in the manager. He indicated they needed someone organized, flexible, and optimistic. Primary responsibilities would be to ensure the business operated smoothly and efficiently, and knowledge of complex computer systems would also be necessary. At Grand Teton, the computer software was programmed to work as an integrated unit (i.e., appointments, billing, medical records, and prescription orders) for the best customer service. Jenny had no experience with computer systems, but since she was a fast learner, she thought she could "figure things out."

Within the month, Grand Teton called to ask Jenny if she was still interested in the manager's position, and they invited her to interview. Income was her priority. Therefore, Jenny asked questions about salary, merit pay, and timelines for pay increases. She was also concerned about health and retirement benefits. Jenny received little financially for her retirement from the divorce and was worried about saving for the future. She was relieved to learn that Grand Teton offered a 401(k) employer matching plan. Supporting her mother was taking its toll, so she wondered if they offered "elder care" reimbursement. Unfortunately, she was told their benefits covered the employee and not a parent. And finally, Jenny asked about time off and vacation. She wasn't sure how her mother's illness would progress and she wanted to plan for the unexpected.

Jenny decided the position was a good fit overall and inquired about a typical "day in the life" of a Grand Teton employee. Wanda shared that the company insisted that all employees enjoy pets and be an owner to identify with their customers. Jenny had both a French Mastiff dog and a Persian cat, so that was not a concern. Second, all new employees, regardless of background, position, or previous pet experience, participated in their standard training program to be educated in all aspects of the business. Third, Grand Teton required their employees to be "fast on their feet" and energetic as days could get jam-packed with their walk-in services. Finally, customer service was vital to retain repeat customers, and employees had to take a professional etiquette course. After interviewing with two of the veterinarians, Jenny was hired as the office manager, which included supervising six pet technicians. Her training started immediately.

Grand Teton had an online and virtual orientation program plus 5 days of onsite training at one of their seven locations throughout the city. This process provided variety yet consistency in their education about procedures to ensure that owners of pets received the same service and care at each site. It included intake (greeting, paperwork, pet history), exam room procedures, veterinarian assistance, pet care, grooming, pet education, medication preparation, phone etiquette, checkout (with billing), and cleaning. Jenny also met with Wanda. She discussed many of the management responsibilities, such as day-to-day office duties, hiring, and payroll. Nothing was discussed regarding the computer systems.

During her first few weeks, Jenny was very enthusiastic and willing to learn from her staff and other employees. The training was challenging because she had not been in a classroom since college—over 30 years ago!

Conversely, Jenny excelled at customer service and loved socializing with the pet owners and their pets. She made everyone feel welcome and special. She was pleasant with customers and was instantly a valued employee because of this trait. Customers liked Jenny, and they frequently complimented her. It was by far the best part of the job.

Because Grand Teton was always busy, everyone worked as a team, assisting one another. Sometimes, Jenny needed to work in the grooming room. Although she had a large dog herself, grooming pets was not a task she enjoyed and, she avoided it. Jenny would try desperately to get someone else to substitute in that area before she assigned herself. The smell of a wet dog bothered her, and Jenny was afraid she might injure a pet during the trimming process.

Regarding her official role as office manager, the veterinarians (Grand Teton owners) thought she was doing a good job. She was exemplary at taking care of customer issues. There were four positive online comments in the last month about Grand Teton, and they all noted Jenny's professionalism and customer service.

However, Jenny had an annoying habit. She made comments like, "another day at the grind," or "this is the longest day of my life," and "I need a vacation," which caused her employees to think she was unhappy at work. The veterinarians often overheard her mutter comments like these when she was filling in for a pet technician in the exam rooms, too.

Her feedback to her direct reports was irregular. It would consist of comments such as "I guess this is OK," or she would criticize employees for insignificant things such as checking a fitness watch for text messages during their break. When the Grand Teton owners finally asked Jenny about her performance evaluation of employees, she presented them with the following form:

JOB REVIEW

Employee Name: **Date:**

My impression of you:

The one thing you do well:

The worst customer complaint I have received about you:

The three things you need to do to improve:

Three things you can do to make my job better:

Another pattern of events also created discord with her direct reports. Jenny took calls from her daughter several times a day. Grand Teton had a policy of limiting personal phone calls to emergencies. One time her daughter called, said it was an emergency, and wanted to know if Jenny was bringing pizza home for dinner. Other employees could listen to the conversations because they worked in an "open" style office setting. When her mother called, which was often, it was disconcerting because the dialogue would be the same as it was an hour ago, and the hour before, and the hour before too! It didn't make for an enjoyable work environment. Her team, mostly her daughter's age, was not empathetic, and it wasn't easy to focus on their job and productivity because of her distracting calls.

After a couple of months had passed, Jenny met her best friend for lunch. She told her she felt like an outsider at Grand Teton and that other employees were "in a clique and stuck together like glue." Jenny said they didn't even say hello or acknowledge her when she arrived in the morning or say goodbye to her. Jenny couldn't understand why they would ignore her, since she was their manager. She tried to engage them in conversation, often about her past life, her daughter, her ex-husband, "how life used to be," and how successful she was at her old job. Her employees had no interest in listening to her brag about her past and didn't understand why she kept talking about it day after day after day. Unbeknownst to Jenny, the staff would often text back and forth at work commenting about her nonstop talking and their lack of patience with her. Neither Jenny nor her direct reports seemed to want to acknowledge their conflicts publicly.

Jenny felt she was at a crossroads again. Was she, or was this just a bump?

Discussion Questions

1. Describe Jenny's strengths and weaknesses. How did her personality traits help or hinder her job performance?

2. Job requirements "may include specific skills, types, and amounts of work experience, personal qualities, educational credentials, professional certifications or areas of knowledge" (Doyle, 2021, para. 1). What do you think are the job requirements for the office manager's job? Was that Jenny's job or was it something else?

3. In an interview, a candidate often asks questions about their "wants" to determine if the job is the right fit. For example, "I want a job that pays for three weeks of vacation. Do you offer this?" Or, "I want a job that has work hours of 11 a.m. to 7 p.m. Is this possible?" Jenny seemed resolute regarding her requirements for

the job at Grand Teton. Did the job at Grand Teton give Jenny what she wanted, or did the position give Jenny what she thought she wanted?

4. Demographers group and describe the U.S. population with specific characteristics and attributes based on birth year. Although there are differences in dates and names, these generally include the Greatest Generation (1925–1946), Baby Boomer (1946–1964), Generation X (1965–1984), and Millennials (1982–2004) (Colby & Ortman, 2014; Masnick, 2012; Sanborn, 2015). At age 57, assume that Jenny was born in 1963 (or the year President Kennedy was assassinated), making her a Baby Boomer. Also, assume that the technicians Jenny was supervising were Millennials. Based on your observations, what problems existed with Jenny's communication style in her direct reports?

5. Individuals returning to work at an older age often have an aging parent under their care. How did this impact Jenny's productivity and efficiency at work?

6. Would you want to work for Jenny? Why or why not?

7. Do you think the Grand Teton employees were intolerant of Jenny? If so, was there anything her direct reports could have done to improve their relationship with their supervisor?

8. How would you define ageism? Did you observe any instances of ageism against Jenny in the case scenario?

Assignments

1. Identify your strengths. List your five personal strengths. Now ask a close friend, relative, or parent to make a similar list. What did you learn about yourself? How can you use these strengths to find the right job for you?

2. Whether a job is a good fit is based partially on a person's ability to assess the potential job attributes with their personal needs. Completing a job map can quickly define what is most important and can focus on the job search. A job map is a graphic depiction of your career plan and goals broken down by crucial time elements of your life. Jenny's Job Map is listed here. Your task is threefold:

   a. Define the terms "financial values" and "personal values."

   b. Complete the available blanks on the grid.

   c. Explain the changes in Jenny's values over time and why they have changed.

3. Complete your personal job map using Jenny's graphic as a model.

Jenny's Job Map					
Age of Employment	Financial Life Stage*	Job Name	Financial Values	Personal Values	Hourly Pay
9 years	Early Childhood 6–12	Simple chores	Piggybank, candy money		$
13 years	Teen Years 12-19	Babysitting	Extra spending money for movies, shopping, and savings for college	Fun	$
21 years (graduated from college) 22 years (married)	Laying the Foundation 20-30	Waitress	Earnings for apartment living	Friends	$$
32 years (Trisha born) 40 years (starts working)	Early Accumulation 30–40		Education fund for children's college education	Social network, marriage, family, travel, high-society lifestyle	$$
48 years (separated from her husband)	Rapid Accumulation 40–50				$$ + Alimony
53 years (Divorced) 54 years (Present day)	Financial Independence 50–60	Office Manager			$$ + Rent by ex-husband

*The life stages listed in the chart are based on the Cambridge Financial Life-Cycle Model available at http://www.feeonlyadvisor.com/financial_lifecycle.html

4. Research the percentage of women in the workforce in 1940, 1960, 1980, 2000, and last year. For each time-frame you are researching, what is the primary motivation for women to work? Is it different by generation?

5. Research the top five reasons someone leaves their employer. Have these reasons changed over the last 10 years? Do they vary based on generation?

Additional Learning

- To learn more about your money values, complete the Financial Values Inventory at https://extension.usu.edu/utah/files-ou/Finance/Financial%20Values%20Inventory.pdf. Based on your responses, describe what motivates your spending and savings decisions.

Table 2.1: Adapted from Centers for Disease Control and Prevention, "Intimate Partner Violence and Associated Terms," *Intimate Partner Violence Surveillance: Uniform Definitions and Recommended Data Elements*, 2015.

References

Bump. P. (2014, March 25). Here is when each generation begins and ends, according to facts. *The Atlantic*. https://www.theatlantic.com/national/archive/2014/03/here-is-when-each-generation-begins-and-ends-according-to-facts/359589/

Colby, S., & Ortman, S. (2014, May). The baby boom cohort in the United States. Current population reports. U.S. Census Bureau. https://www.census.gov/prod/2014pubs/p25-1141.pdf

Daum, K. (2013, April 16). Define your personal core values: 5 steps. *Inc.* https://www.inc.com/kevin-daum/define-your-personal-core-values-5-steps.html

Dominus, S. (2016, February 25). Rethinking the work/life equation. *New York Times Magazine*. https://www.nytimes.com/2016/02/28/magazine/rethinking-the-work-life-equation.html

Doyle, A. (2021, October 22). What are job requirements? *The Balance*. https://www.thebalance.com/what-are-job-requirements-3928054

Hereford, Z. (n.d.). Have a personal value system. Essential Life Skills. http://www.essentiallifeskills.net/personalvaluesystem.html

James, K. (2020, January 15). The big pull: Going back to work after retiring. *Forbes*. https://www.forbes.com/sites/nextavenue/2020/01/15/the-big-pull-going-back-to-work-after-retiring/?sh=3556507a1851

Masnick, G. (2012, November 28). Defining the generations. Harvard Joint Center for Housing Studies. http://housingperspectives.blogspot.com/2012/11/defining-generations.html

National Endowment for Financial Education (2017.) Smart about money. LifeValues Quiz. https://www.smartaboutmoney.org/Tools/LifeValues-Quiz

NDSU Extension Service (n.d.). Financial services inventory. https://extension.usu.edu/utah/files-ou/Finance/Financial%20Values%20Inventory.pdf

Pilossoph, J. (2016, January 3). Tips for going back to work after divorce. *HuffPost*. https://www.huffpost.com/entry/tips-for-going-back-to-wo_b_8907252

Royal Financial Advisors (n.d.). Financial life cycle. http://www.feeonlyadvisor.com/financial_lifecycle.html

Sanborn, J. (2015). How every generation of the last century got its name. *Time*. http://time.com/4131982/generations-names-millennials-founders/

Strenger, C., & Ruttenberg, A. (2008, February). The existential necessity of midlife change. *Harvard Business Review*. https://hbr.org/2008/02/the-existential-necessity-of-midlife-change

U.S. Census Bureau. (2015, June 25). Millennials outnumber baby boomers and are far more diverse, Census Bureau reports. Release Number: CB15-113. https://www.census.gov/newsroom/press-releases/2015/cb15-113.html

Great Lakes Stock Exchange

Objectives

- Evaluate job applicants based on a written resume.
- Summarize best practices for the training of new employees.
- Explain the value of providing professional development opportunities for employees.
- Describe the advantages of embracing a diverse workforce.
- Summarize changes to the sex segregation of occupations in the 21st century.

Key Concepts and Words

career development, goal setting, job evaluation, key performance objectives, onboarding, professional development, severance, sex segregation of occupations, work culture, workforce training, workplace diversity

Overview

This case involves two women, Francie Morris and Mary Haines, whose education and professional goals set themselves on a career track in the financial services industry. Their backgrounds differ significantly, and although their education aligns, they find themselves in a work environment that doesn't result in the achievement and success they envisioned.

Scenario

Francie Morris was born and bred to be "in the money." Since she was a little girl, she had been surrounded by talk of finance, mergers, and acquisitions. Interestingly, when Francie was only 12 years old, she had amassed a portfolio of $28,000. She earned her start-up funds with money she made selling peanuts to baseball fans on their way to see the Chicago Cubs play at Wrigley Field.

Francie was a very competitive young lady, and the summer after high school, she participated in the 1996 Summer Olympics for the U.S. Equestrian Team. She was proud to have been chosen because it was one of the few Olympic sports where women competed equally with men (Waltemeyer, 2016). Francie's team missed winning the gold after she hooked a rail on the last jump. She could never forgive herself for the error. Francie was always trying to compensate for her failure and completed a daily "self-talk" to be and do her best.

Both her father and brother were alumni of Harvard's prestigious School of Finance, and she followed in their footsteps, attending college there. Francie's father was extremely successful in business and president of his family's brokerage firm in Chicago, Illinois. He started it more than 12 years ago. His firm serviced both U.S. and global clients. Although it was expected that Francie would join her family's business, she wanted to do things on her own. Because she was one of the few women in her graduating class (Bertrand et al., 2010), she was heavily courted by firms in Chicago, New York, and overseas. Her long-term goal was to open her own business specializing in investment strategies for single mothers and divorced women with annual incomes of $40,000 or less.

In contrast, Mary Haines was a young woman who struggled to earn a scholarship to a state college and had a dream of "making it big." She loved the movie *Wall Street* because of its contrast with good and evil, and it inspired her to seek a career in finance. Mary was determined to do great things in life, and she thought it required money. She wasn't the strongest student in her class, but she found a study group with the smartest students. She wouldn't admit it to others, but she felt she would have never done as well with her grades had it not been for her friends and study partners.

In January 2001, both women were hired in their senior year of college by the well-known Chicago banking firm EdRock Financial, which was part of the Great Lakes Stock Exchange. They would begin their career as summer interns immediately upon graduation. Francie and Mary were excited about this opportunity because EdRock had a good reputation on campus for hiring graduates. In fact, the *Men's Work Success Journal* hailed EdRock as one of the best banking firms in the Midwest, based on their employee benefit and compensation package.

BEST BENEFITS FROM TOP MEN'S EMPLOYERS 2000

- Generous vacation policy

- Discount gym membership

- Onsite fitness center

- Company tickets to sporting events

- Onsite child-care with extended hours until 11p.m.

- Employer sponsored baseball and basketball teams

- Casual dress

- Compressed work week

- Paid military leave

- 24/7 discounted meals in the company dining commons

- Carpool incentive program

Men's Work Success Journal (Master List), January 2000, Recognizing the Best Company Environments for Men.

Francie and Mary started their internships by shuffling paper, making photocopies, getting coffee, reorganizing the library, and reading and summarizing business portfolios. After a few weeks at EdRock, it was apparent to Francie that the internship was neither glamorous nor even close to what she had expected. She knew the details of the internship program at her father's firm, and the one at EdRock Financial was not equivalent. She called her father and told him she was "bored, and she wasn't learning a thing." (Unbeknownst to Francie, her father knew EdRock Financial's CEO, and he was updated on his daughter's progress frequently.) However, she did like that the job was "easy money," so she did what was expected.

In contrast to Francie, Mary thrived during the internship and appreciated the value of practical learning. After a few months, Mary was asked to work in the Emerging Markets group, led by Howard

Stockard. She thought this assignment confirmed that she had potential at the company. She excelled in this position and particularly at identifying errors in financial trends of annual reports.

Based on the demonstrated success during their internships, both women were promoted to permanent employees at summer's end and became floor traders at EdRock Financial.[1] Since their employment status changed, they received a pay increase and assumed their salary and benefits were comparable within the company and competitive to other Chicago financial firms.

Historically, the financial and investment field had been dominated by men (Ritholtz, 2016). This never scared Francie or Mary; instead, it created internal excitement and personally drove them to succeed. However, Francie and Mary often discussed privately that they felt they were not part of the "team." The two women were the first females who progressed to the Floor at EdRock Financial and had often felt like outcasts. For example, while the men went to the bar to celebrate a profitable day or discuss their heavy losses, Francie and Mary were never included. Francie cared about this, but not Mary. Mr. Stockard often asked Mary to work evenings, exploring historical trends and financial forecasting errors, like she had done during her internship. He depended upon her analytical skills and frequently used her charts to convince high wealth clients to invest additional funds at EdRock. She was so busy that she didn't have time for socializing.

One issue at work troubled both women. Francie and Mary noticed that their bids for buying and selling on the floor seemed to be ignored, which impaired their ability to make profitable trades and avoid client losses. With all the chaos on the floor, they witnessed their male counterparts seeking out other male colleagues to make trades, even though they were waving and ready to buy and sell for their clients. They watched their colleagues pump fists, shake hands, and jump when they completed a trade with each other. It was frustrating and depressing day after day. Francie had thought about going to Human Resources (HR) but felt it probably wouldn't help, and she feared retribution. Mary often thought

---

1   Although the majority of trading today is done through computers, in 2000 both Francie and Mary were employed when auction style trading (called open outcry) was the primary way of selling stocks for investors, and face-to-face interaction was necessary for the exchange.

about quitting, but her salary was $31,900 annually without a bonus, and she was forecasted to make over $60,000 that year.

In reality, Francie and Mary were not retaining clients like others, nor were the profits for their customers' portfolios doing as well as the average trader with similar dollar investments. They had been in their new role for 12 weeks with mixed performance when they both received written notification—it was time for their 90-day review. This performance review is common with employers, because it provides sufficient time to evaluate an employee's fit with the company and their overall capabilities and contributions.

John Freelman, a senior partner, was assigned the task to evaluate both women. He recognized that Mary had a dual role as a floor trader and as an investment advisor reporting to Mr. Stockard. However, upon completion of the performance review, he determined that both women's revenue contributions were significantly less than others who had taken the same position as floor traders for the same amount of time during the last 3 years.

Their inability to perform had many consequences. Two years before, John personally brought The Garcia Trust to the firm, and it was now assigned to Mary. Because of the most recent disappointing return on the family's money, Mr. Garcia left EdRock and took his investment to another firm.

Freelman was embarrassed and angered by losing the client. His boss, Andrew Paynes, had called John into the office for a weekly update and grilled him about losing the customer. Paynes was critical about the loss and reminded John that EdRock needed to retain and attract new clients to survive, meet payroll, maintain their reputation on the Exchange, and pay their six-figure bonuses to all partners. With the fiscal year ending in 3 months, these two employees affected the banking and investment firm in more negative ways than not.

To their detriment and Andrew's pressure, John decided it was necessary to terminate both women for their failure to meet financial targets and their loss of clients, who had portfolio values over $9 million.

John completed the exit paperwork with HR, dismissed both Francie and Mary, and provided each with a severance pay equal to their last 3 months' salary. Their exit documents required that the employee could not disparage or sue EdRock Financial after their departure. Francie refused to sign and requested 24 hours for her father to review the documents. Her father did not seem surprised by the dismissal and told Francie there was a place waiting for her in his firm. She sighed, scheduled a pedicure for herself, and signed the paperwork a few days later.

Mary immediately signed the document. With her head held high she happily deposited her check. She already had an offer from a competing firm, the Carter Lennox Group.

On her first day at Carter Lennox, Mary's schedule included an appointment with a familiar name: The Garcia Trust. This was the same Garcia Trust that left EdRock, and they appeared on her calendar as a potential new client. She had remembered the analysis she completed for Mr. Stockard and John, and it had conservatively forecasted double-digit returns. She asked the Garcia family why they passed over this advice, and they were shocked to learn that John never presented her portfolio review.

She asked herself why John would not have discussed her analysis with them. It occurred to her that her firing was not about performance but a grudge that John held against her for creating a plan to save the account. He hadn't been able to increase the earnings of the Garcia portfolio to their satisfaction for over a year, and Andrew and Mr. Stockard were berating him weekly. Perhaps it should have been John who was fired for non-performance, and not her!

She quickly calculated the total sum of money The Garcia Trust would have gained in the last 12 months had they followed her recommendation. Guess who they have as a financial advisor now? Yes, it is Mary Haines and 1 month later, she was promoted to a wealth management analyst for her excellent performance.

Francie's life took a different direction. She is a mother of a newborn baby and living in Switzerland.

Discussion Questions

1. At the beginning of the women's internships, were there any signs that EdRock Financial stereotyped its employees based on gender? Discuss.

2. Are there examples from the case that suggest the women's careers may have been affected negatively based on their gender? Describe these and debate the impact.

3. Were Francie and Mary performing their duties at the level expected by the company? How can you make that determination? Are Francie and Mary responsible for their inability to perform? Why or why not?

4. Do you think gender played any role in their termination? Explain.

5. Why are Francie and Mary both being treated the same and getting dismissed? Do you believe Francie and Mary should have been given more time to demonstrate positive performance?

6. How does one's childhood experiences influence their career choice and success in life? Respond using Francie and Mary as an example.

Assignments

1. Assume you will be interviewing both women and reviewing their resumes. List on a sheet of paper the differences between Francie and Mary. Based on your review alone, which individual would you hire? Would you hire both? Provide reasons to support your decision.

FRANCIE MORRIS

11113 Wells Parkway Naperville, IL 85251   312 (111-1113)

Franmorisme13@aol.com

CAREER SUMMARY

Energetic, competitive, and analytical individual seeking opportunity in the Financial Industry. Demonstrated expertise in:

Financial Knowledge	Sales	Entrepreneurism
Project Management	Investment Strategies	Communication

EXPERIENCE

Northstreet Investment Club

President & Founder

- Established a neighborhood investment club with returns between 8–22% on average
- Recruited 7 day traders and 21 long-term investors

AMA Country Club

Waitress

- Recognized for outstanding customer service

AMA Stables

Equestrian Coach

- Coached and trained Junior and Children riders on all aspects of competition jumping

Amagansett Beach, NY

Lifeguard

- Volunteered to watch and guard beach during Special Olympics Games

Entrepreneur

Peanut Saleswoman

- Earned start-up funds for future investment club by selling peanuts to baseball fans. Evaluated traffic patterns and attendance of baseball games (demand based on match-ups) to ensure best opportunity for success

EDUCATION

Bachelor in Finance, Harvard School of Finance, 2001

SELECTED TRAINING

Excellence in Speaking Seminar

Managing Multiple Priorities Workshop

Economic Value Add (EVA) Conference

Best of Best Sales Presentation Course

LICENSES

Series 7 and Series 63 stockbroker exams completed. License in process

SOCIAL ACTIVITIES

Roving Rowing Club 2000–1997

Northstreet Investment Group 1998–1995

Chicago Cavela Chess Society 1995–1994

Harvard Swim Team 2000–1998

Summer U.S. Olympic Equestrian Team 1996

MARY HAINES, BS

206 E. Kenilworth, #12 • Springfield, IL 62796 • 313.302.9299 • MHaines@hotmail.com

Education

Illinois State University, Normal, IL

Bachelor of Science with Honors, Finance, GPA 3.95 (Expected May 2001)

Presidential Scholarship Recipient

Telecom École de Management, Évry, France

Study Abroad: Banking and Finance in the European Union (Summer 2000)

Washington High School, Washington, IL

High School Degree, Rank 5/1228 (May 1997)

Experience

Illinois State University, Normal, IL

Tutor, Athletic Department, Student-Athlete Support Services (January 1998–current)

- Tutored student-athletes in finance fundamentals, telecommunications, and writing courses
- Increased students' proficiency in Microsoft Suite products: Access, Excel, Publisher, and Word

Research Assistant, Honors College (September 1999–December 2000)

- Analyzed and categorized techniques in textbooks for active and passive learning used in high school and college textbooks

Washington Credit Union, Washington, IL

Student Coop (September 1995–August 1997)

Served as student account liaison with Washington High School students

Language Proficiency

French: Reading and writing fluency   **Italian:** Travel fluency

Volunteering and Leadership

Assistant Coach, South Oakland A's 12U/13U Travel Baseball (March 1998-August 2000)

- Coached travel team, directed tournament scheduling and player development

Club President and Manager, Illinois State Baseball Club (August 1999–May 2001)

- Managed club finances, secured donations, scheduled team operations and activities, and performed manager responsibilities

2. Use the social network LinkedIn to locate and evaluate the resumes of five investment brokers. Then evaluate the resumes that both women submitted to EdRock Financial. What elements would you recommend Francie or Mary change if they were submitting their resume today? Based on your review of their resumes, create and submit a 1-page resume for yourself, using a format you have located online.

3. Francie and Mary could not achieve goals as quickly as EdRock Financial anticipated, resulting in several negative consequences for the company. Often, new employees are hired on a probationary basis. Locate two competing companies in the same industry, and compare their policies for probationary hires.

4. Define "at-will employment." Research the dismissal laws in California, Virginia, and Illinois. How does the definition differ from state to state? Is there any uniqueness between states? Is there a federal "at-will" law? How do these laws impact the employer and employee?

5. Review Morgan Stanley's (2016) article, "Why It Pays to Invest in Gender Diversity" located at https://www.morganstanley.com/ideas/gender-diversity-investment-framework. Create a short paragraph to convince the CEO of EdRock Financial to keep one or both women employed. If you choose one or both, support your recommendation based on facts within the case.

6. Jump forward to present day. Review the article "Wall Street wants more female traders, but old perceptions die hard, (Irrera, 2018) at https://www.reuters.com/article/us-banks-trading-gender/wall-street-wants-more-female-traders-but-old-perceptions-die-hard-idUSKBN1JA0DF. The article discusses the "boys' club." After reading the article, do you think the outcome would be different for Francie and Mary if a similar situation took place today?

Additional Learning

- What is the right career for you? Take the Myers–Briggs personality indicator and see how your personality can support or challenge your career choice. Visit http://www.humanmetrics.com/cgi-win/jtypes2.asp to determine your personality indicator.

References

Bertrand, M., Goldin, C., & Katz, F. (2010). Dynamics of the gender gap for young professionals in the financial and corporate sectors. *American Economic Journal: Applied Economics, 2*(3), 228–255. doi: 10.1257/app.2.3.228

Forbes Coaches Council. (2019, March 5). 13 things every new employee should do in their first 90 days on a new job. *Forbes.* https://www.forbes.com/sites/forbescoachescouncil/2019/03/05/13-things-every-new-employee-should-do-in-their-first-90-days-on-the-job/?sh=6665e8be5a21

Irrera, A. (2018, June 14). Wall Street wants more female traders, but old perceptions die hard. *Reuters.* https://www.reuters.com/article/us-banks-trading-gender/wall-street-wants-more-female-traders-but-old-perceptions-die-hard-idUSKBN1JA0DF

Jaekel, A., & St-Onge, E. (2016, October 25). Why women aren't making it to the top of financial services firms. *Harvard Business Review: Global Business Digital.* https://hbr.org/2016/10/why-women-arent-making-it-to-the-top-of-financial-services-firms

Johnson, J. (2020, September 16). What should happen in the first 90 days of new employee orientation? Business.com. https://www.business.com/articles/new-employee-orientation/

Jung Typology Test. (n.d.). http://www.humanmetrics.com/cgi-win/jtypes2.asp

Lucas, S. (2017, September 29). The right way to conduct a 90-day performance review. *Inc.* https://www.inc.com/suzanne-lucas/right-way-to-conduct-a-90-day-performance-review.html

McGeehan, P. (2007, September 23). Next to downsize on Wall Street? The exchange floor. *The New York Times.* http://www.nytimes.com/2007/09/23/nyregion/23exchange.html

Morgan Stanley. (2016, May 11). Why it pays to invest in gender diversity. https://www.morganstanley.com/ideas/gender-diversity-investment-framework

Ritholtz, B. (2016, February 24). Where are the women in finance? *Bloomberg.* https://www.bloomberg.com/view/articles/2016-02-24/why-don-t-more-women-hold-top-jobs-in-finance

Scutts, J. (2016, April 16). Unsung women: The woman who kicked down Wall Street's doors. *Time.* http://time.com/4297571/muriel-siebert-wall-street-history/

Stone, O. (Director). (1987). *Wall Street* [Motion picture]. 20th Century Fox.

Waltemeyer, C. (2016). Equestrian 101: The basics. NBC Olympics. http://www.nbcolympics.com/news/equestrian-101-basics

Vision 2020

Objectives

- Describe one's management philosophy and when and how it needs to change.
- Evaluate leadership styles and the benefits of one style versus another.
- Assess the change in communication style between a supervisor and employees during a conflict.
- Identify workplace challenges that COVID has created for managers and their direct reports.
- Explore the impact of stress on performance and personal well-being.

Key Concepts and Words

business planning, coach, collaboration, communication, crisis management, downsizing, employee empowerment, FMLA, hands-off, laissez-faire, leadership style, management philosophy, people skills, prioritizing, proactive, quota, reactive, revenue, vertical promotion, vision

Overview

This case takes the reader through the calendar year 2020 with Monica Lee, a district sales manager for a global pharmaceutical company. She manages through uncertainty after the global discovery of COVID-19 (AJMC, 2020). It forces her to reflect and evaluate her coaching and leadership styles. As COVID changes the workplace environment, Monica questions her ability to provide direction to her sales representatives with confidence and credibility.

Scenario

Preamble

Eyesight 20/20. Perfect, clear vision, near and far. My name is Monica Lee, and when I had eye surgery about 17 years ago, I was able to drive a car and read signs in the distance shortly after the procedure. I could swim laps without glasses at the local YMCA pool and enjoyed living without the burden of wearing glasses. No more reaching for my glasses in the morning before getting out of bed; no more searching for a pair so I could read my laptop or a magazine. I felt I was experiencing a new level of freedom and happiness.

What if life could be like 20/20 eyesight? You would have a perfect, clear vision of your life. You would experience each day to its fullest and see into the future. Well, a 20/20 life is not possible, and no year could demonstrate this better than the calendar year 2020. The United States was changed by a virus known as COVID-19 (Coronavirus Disease 2019), first discovered in China. (AMJC, 2020). Every infant, every child, and every adult has been touched in some way. The impact for me was most significant in my job as a district sales manager for a pharmaceutical company.

While senior leadership was evaluating how to keep the business profitable in March 2020, I was concerned with the security of my job, the health of my family, and how I would teach my children (8 and 11 years old) math, English, and history. Prioritizing my personal life without losing focus on my career was something I never needed to worry about before this year.

My job has been to lead a group of six pharmaceutical sales representatives. Their job has been to visit doctors in medical offices and discuss the benefits of three medications. If the doctor is convinced, they write a prescription, and the patient takes it to the pharmacy to be filled. That's how we achieve our sales goals.

Our employer, WELALTZ, is based in Gdansk, Poland, with U.S. offices and manufacturing facilities in Tempe, Arizona. For years, the primary operations were outside of San Francisco. In 2004, it moved closer to other companies that focus on the discovery of novel medications to treat neurological disorders. The flagship drug is called Parkitz, and it is recommended for patients who suffer from Parkinson's Disease. This is the primary drug that my team has been responsible for selling.

My Background

In 2015, I jumped at the opportunity to join WELALTZ as a district sales manager with the goal of eventually becoming the national sales director of the movement disorders division. Over 4 years, I advanced with titles of senior and master sales manager, but a promotion to the national role continues to be outside of my reach. I enjoy what I do, and just when I thought the opportunity would present itself for a vertical promotion, COVID covered the globe. My career advancement drew to a screeching halt.

In 2020, my management and leadership skills were tested and continue to be. In the past, dealing with change was easy. After managing several teams with five to 14 employees, I learned that every person accepts change differently. Some move into the unknown without a thought, and others fear it. As a leader, I have envisioned my job as the captain of a ship. I plan where we are going and how we will arrive at our destination safely and successfully. Fog is not a problem; darkness is not a problem, nor will a sudden storm put my team and me off course. Obstacles, like those, have been viewed as opportunities, and we have been successful regardless of the challenge. I also empower and trust my sales representatives to accomplish their work and contact me when they need help. They are self-sufficient. This management style has been effective, and I have thrived.

My goals have been to provide clear and practical direction, support, and confidence when needed. For 4 years, my district has led the country in sales of new Parkitz prescriptions. With consistent motivation, my sales representatives have achieved their goals, and as a result, we have earned a healthy monetary incentive. But this year is different. The appearance of COVID created a change in my work environment that I never anticipated. It has been difficult.

As the sales in my district have plummeted throughout the year, my representatives have struggled personally and professionally. Looking back in my work journal, I wonder if I did everything I could for WELALTZ and my team. Did I let them down? Did I let myself and my family down? Am I just being too hard on myself?

The following are my direct reports:

	Sales Representative Roster	
First	**Performance Level (previous year)**	**Tenure**
Phyllis	Meets	3
Jasmin	Low Meets	6
Ron	Exceeds	4
Dijon	N/A	<1year
Kathryn	Exceeds	3
Cheryl	Meets	2

Life During COVID

MY WORK JOURNAL—MARCH 2020 ENTRIES

3.1.20

Dear Journal: There is talk on the news of a virus called COVID-19 spreading throughout the United States. New York City has reported a few cases, and there have been several deaths in a nursing home in Seattle, Washington. We have had similar things occur in the past like SARS (severe acute respiratory syndrome). It is probably just an isolated issue.

3.2.20

Dear J: Today, my Washington state representative (rep), **Ron,** sent me an email. He is frightened to visit his physicians because of the high number of diagnosed COVID patients in his territory. His job is to meet with doctors, educate them, and sell Parkitz. I replied to his email and told him I understand the situation, but patients depend upon him. He must do his job to get paid. I feel a bit guilty for being so business driven.

Ron was concerned that COVID is contagious, and he may expose his son if he contracts the virus. He has been a great rep and is a first-time dad to a newborn just 4 months old. From what I have been reading, Washington state is a "hot spot" for this disease, and a state of emergency has been declared in Seattle (Baker & Weise, 2020). The news says that children and infants aren't getting infected, so he really shouldn't be worrying. Or should he? I am not sure. All the information in the news is so conflicting.

3.4.20

Ron emailed me a second time, saying he is scared! He reminded me that his doctors treat an older patient population, and this age group appears to be "getting" COVID more commonly than others. I told **Ron** he must talk to his customers in person. Demonstrating to the physician how the drug works with a 3D brain model is essential to convey its uniqueness. This can only be accomplished in the physician's office. So, I am not sure how he will do his job if he refuses to visit customers. He has been a top performer for the last 3 years. I don't understand what he thinks I can do about this.

3.9.20

Dijon is my new sales rep, and his hire date was today. His training has started virtually from his home. In the past, all new hires would go to the office headquarters for training, but WELALTZ has an airline travel restriction due to COVID. **Dijon's** orientation is based on videos, online tests, and an assortment of other activities such as phone calls with his peers on my team. I am not sure how effective virtual training will be, but I need him up and running as soon as possible to meet our sales and prescription quotas. His territory has the highest potential in my district.

My boss, **Beth Ann,** and the company have not said a word about COVID except for travel. Aren't the reps exposed every day by going to see doctors? I emailed **Beth Ann** to discuss this. Her secretary replied for her; she is too busy. I am very irritated with her.

3.18.20

Cheryl emailed me and asked about job security. I told her sales = job security. Isn't this common sense? **Dijon** also emailed me after reading the WELALTZ webpage that referred to the company's history of retaining employees, even in hard times. He asked if he made the right decision to join WELALTZ. He declined a competitive offer from another company to join us. I assured him that he did make the right decision and to focus his time on learning. Maybe I was too direct in my response?

3.23.20

Jasmin emailed that her son got into a car accident this morning. He is in the hospital because of his injuries. She is taking 3 days off from work and asked if she should quarantine. Quarantine? What is this all about? I guess she was allowed to visit him in the hospital for only a few minutes (because of COVID) and may have become exposed to the virus unknowingly. I emailed my boss to let her know. AND no response again. What is more important than the salespeople?

I haven't heard too much from **Kathryn.** I am glad she is a top performer and only calls when she needs my advice. Come to think of it, I have not heard from **Phyllis** either.

3.27.20

I need some help! **Ron** tested positive for COVID. Why didn't he call me by phone with something so important instead of emailing me?! I am really worried about him, but I also wonder if he could sue the company and me personally? He told me he was scared of getting COVID and what if his son gets it?

I called **Beth Ann.** She said that all sales reps must see doctors in their offices and keep her updated on **Ron.** With him getting sick, WELALTZ should really rethink the policy of selling to doctors personally. Maybe I should have been more understanding with **Ron** earlier when he first emailed me. I knew he was scared.

I just read that "37 states in the U.S. have closed their public schools" (Regan et al., 2020, para 2). And "(t) he White House has advised people not to gather in groups of more than 10" (Regan et al., para 4). A few people are wearing masks in public, but the CDC does not think that they help curb transmission of the virus. That doesn't make sense to me. Don't surgeons wear masks in surgery so they do not transmit germs? This is baffling. Frankly, I need masks for my family. I wonder if I can buy them on the Internet?

3.28.20 1:14am

My Fitbit showed I slept an average of 5 hours per night this month. No wonder I am so tired, but I can't stop thinking about work and COVID. I am glad sales are good, but with **Ron** and **Jasmin** off work, April may not be a good revenue month.

FIGURE 1.1   Monica's Professional Profile
(March 2020)

MY WORK JOURNAL—APRIL 2020 ENTRIES

4.1.20

Management still doesn't quite get it! WELALTZ informed us, all employees are required to visit doctors' offices but they are giving the employee the option of working from home. Sales goals will remain the same. I sent an email to my team with this information. Then, I was bombarded with emails! I think a conference call is in order. My reps wanted to know: "How can they speak with doctors when they are at home?" It's a good question.

4.2.20

I had the call, and it did not go well. Everyone said that many of their doctor offices have shut down access to drug sales representatives and medical vendors. They are not scheduling appointments by phone either. If the sales reps can't talk to the doctors, how can they sell? One rep asked, how is it possible that WELALTZ won't decrease the sales targets?

At that point, it occurred to me that we might all lose our jobs. Being unemployed is the more significant issue. They should be asking what more they can do to protect their job, rather than asking for a drop in their quota goal. While the call was going, **Ron** sent an email to everyone letting them know he got COVID. Everyone is upset and worried about him. I had to end the call. The team was completely distracted after they received it.

This evening, my husband **Jerod,** told me he wanted to quit his job. He is a sales manager in the luxury eyewear industry. You have got to be kidding, "Seriously? I asked him. How do you propose we pay our bills with one salary?" Working is tough right now, and he needs to plow through it like I am.

4.5.20

I talked to my niece today, and she said that everybody does Zoom calls these days and texts. She says her manager has been doing Zoom meetings for about 6 months. I think I should learn how it works. I know nothing about Zoom other than my car goes very fast ... zoom!

4.16.20

My boss, **Beth Ann** emailed me and wanted to know what is going on with two of six territories that are "way off track" in making their revenue target for April. Now, she calls me about sales. Where was she before when

I needed her? She completed an analysis that showed meetings with doctors are down 52% vs. February. She must think I am an idiot. Of course, visits are down. Doctors are not allowing the reps into their offices. I will text **Jasmin** and **Cheryl** tomorrow about their low numbers. **Beth Ann** did not even ask about **Ron** or even contact me with everything going on. I am really disappointed in her.

4.17.20

Not a good day. Both **Jasmin** and **Cheryl** were upset that I sent a text to the entire team about low sales and specifically mentioned them. Not only should I not have called them out on a group message, but I should not have "texted" bad sales news. I should have called them individually. What was I thinking? I wasn't.

I need to work this weekend. With so much going on, I have had zero time to analyze the sales performance. How can I manage if I am not reviewing the numbers? I feel like I am a psychologist and not a sales manager with the events of the last 6 weeks. I wish I could sleep in. Ugh. I am mentally exhausted.

4.23.20

My first Zoom meeting was today.

- Two of the sales representatives had their video going, and I felt a sense of connection. I saw their reaction to what we were discussing.

- The other three were "off-camera" and they complained they prefer email communication. A heated discussion ensued, and the team was divided.

- **Dijon and Kathryn** use video conferencing with their families and think Zoom is an effective way to communicate.

- **Cheryl** was off-camera and felt Teams (SoftwareONE, 2020) is a much better platform.

- **Jasmin's** husband was walking around behind her without a shirt.

My frustration grew until I ended the call abruptly. We should have been talking about business! Immediately, I sent a text to everyone apologizing. That was not professional or supportive of everyone's view. I am trying to be understanding, but this is hard.

Beth Ann sent me another email about sales. It was snarky. It's a good thing I worked last weekend and looked at the business. I sent her a response, but I am not sure it will answer her questions about performance.

4.30.20

The second Zoom call for the month took place today. I asked everyone to have their camera on so we could see each other.

- **Kathyrn** and **Jasmin** quickly emerged.

- **Cheryl** looked like she just woke up and was in her car. I am wondering if that was true.

- **Phyllis**'s background revealed a sandy beach. I don't recall her asking for vacation, and there is no beach in her territory.

- **Kathryn** had on a blazer and looked professionally dressed for customer visits.

- **Jasmin** had a small child crying and running in the background with no diaper. This is weird because she does not have any children.

I have never questioned what my reps do during their day. However, I am feeling uneasy. Are they working?

Cheryl sent me a text, and I found out why she was in her car. Her twin brother had been diagnosed with COVID and she had just dropped off food on his doorstep. Immediately, I responded that I was available to talk at any time. I told her I hoped her brother's illness was mild and sent prayers her way. Later this week, we have a scheduled business phone conference. Then I thought, she knew about her brother before the Zoom. Why didn't she communicate this before?

Jasmin emailed me too. Her sister-in-law has COVID, and she is taking in her niece and two nephews (age 2, 4, and 14 years old) because they cannot be home with their mother while she is sick. Now, I understand who the little boy was. She told me she is not sure how she will care for the children and work at the same time. I told her that her family is her priority now, but work objectives aren't going away. However, I didn't want to make her feel bad and tell her that I am concerned about her sales. That means mine too! (Where is **Jasmin**'s brother? Why isn't he taking care of his kids?)

Journal: Help me please! I got a migraine today for the first time in my life. Too much is going on. The public-school Board of Education sent an email that my kids need to be "home schooled." I have no idea what this means. I called my neighbor to get her perspective. Starting next week, I have to rework my calendar to help my daughter and son get on their computers for online school at home. How am I going to fit the school curriculum in my regular workday? I am starting to panic. There are parts of the courses that I need to teach them too. Math was not my strongest subject, and I failed geometry in high school. You know, my husband needs to turn it up a bit and help me with the kids instead of thinking about quitting his job.

I have gained 5 pounds since this COVID thing started. Sigh.

MY WORK JOURNAL—MAY 2020 ENTRIES

5.4.20

HAPPY MAY! But I am not happy. It was **Dijon's** first day to visit doctors in person, and it was a bust. No doctors were willing to see him. He emailed me that he is angry and frustrated. I encouraged him but think I should call him on his cell phone. **Ron** returned to work and I am relieved. Bad news, though; he is not 100% recovered and still tired. **Cheryl** was a "no show" for our business call.

5.5.20

Dijon dialed me before I had a few free minutes to call him. We reviewed a conversation he had with an important neurologist by phone. I was excited about his win and hope this experience encourages him—finally, something positive to tell you.

Cheryl called and apologized for missing several of her work appointments and our business call yesterday. I did not pick up my mobile phone because I was on my boss's weekly conference call, ironically discussing **Cheryl**. She knew I was booked because my calendar was blocked with meetings all day. Why didn't she call at another time?

5.8.20

Cheryl and I connected after three days of back-and-forth messages. We had a long discussion about her brother, the job, COVID, her kids, and her husband, Harry. She seemed back on track, but I am not sure. I suggested a weekly phone call to review her business and her successes.

Called **Dijon**. The rest of the week was not good. No doctor or nurse was willing to see him. I am not surprised because he has no relationships with anyone. None of the physicians' offices would allow him to make appointments either. They said everything is too uncertain with COVID. How is he going to sell if he can't talk to the doctors? It is the same question that keeps coming up time and time again. I reassured him; things will improve and to "hang in there." I asked him to buddy up with **Phyllis** for peer support. She is always positive. TGIF (thank goodness it's Friday), Journal!

Saturday 5.9.20

I basked in the sunshine today and did nothing. :)

5.13.20

The Zoom call went well today. Everyone participated on video. I shared the sales results for the previous month, April. Unfortunately, sales are dismal. I knew it and should have done something earlier to turn sales around. How can my team have been so successful and now, poof—sales are so poor?

5.25.20

Ron continues to have times throughout the day that he gets exhausted, a long-term issue some COVID patients experience. He is not sure he can do his job. He asked me about taking more time off from work under FMLA. "Absolutely! His health should come first."

My husband got laid off today, and I cried. His sales dropped as well as the entire eyeglass market. I guess most people try on several pairs to find the shape, style, and color that appeals to them. That experience isn't possible because of potential COVID transmission. We will have to create a family budget, but I don't have time to do it. I barely have time to do the budget for work. I am concerned about paying the bills, but I think my husband will get unemployment.

5.26.20

Dijon requested to take off the rest of the week. He was upset about the death of George Floyd, a man who was arrested and died while in the custody of the police (New York Times, 2020). **Dijon** and his girlfriend were peacefully protesting yesterday, and his shoulder was injured. Thank heavens, it wasn't a more serious injury. I sent him a card and a small care package to "get well" fast.

My boss scheduled a 1-hour conference call tomorrow to discuss district business and lagging performance %#*! The migraines started again.

5.27.20

It was our second monthly Zoom conference call today for May. I asked how everyone was doing and asked about each person's family.

- **Phyllis** immediately referenced the George Floyd tragedy, and everyone chimed in.
- Just like **Ron, Dijon** emailed his peers and told them why he was off work. I really wish he would have let me know before he did that. Everyone on the call was bothered. The topic consumed the

entire meeting, and no business was discussed. However, our time was well spent discussing how this situation was impacting everyone.

- **Ron's** wife appeared to be breastfeeding their new baby on the couch behind him.

- **Kathryn's** college-age daughter was talking on the phone behind her.

I thought, "How about some Zoom meeting etiquette?" **Beth Ann** canceled my conference call. "Is she giving up on me? Am I giving up on me?"

MY WORK JOURNAL—JUNE 2020 ENTRIES

6.9.20

Kathryn quit. She was the district's most successful representative with the highest sales over the last 2 years. I was so surprised and had no indication she was unhappy. **Kathryn** remarked on occasion that her salary was low, but WELALTZ was paying the industry average. This last quarter, she earned the highest total compensation because she excelled in sales. What did I do wrong? **Beth Ann** is going to be angry—very, angry. I barely have **Dijon** up and running, and now this? How will I explain losing the representative who brought in the most business? And **Ron** isn't working at full capacity either, and **Jasmin** is occupied with her niece and nephews. Oh my gosh, I forgot about **Cheryl's** twin brother with COVID.

Phyllis phoned to volunteer and cover **Kathryn's** territory while looking for a replacement sales representative. That was nice of her. Does she think she will also get **Kathryn's** bonus besides hers? To Do: Call Human Resources tomorrow.

6.10.20

Some bad news. My grandmother was diagnosed with pneumonia and possibly COVID. No visitors are allowed at her senior living complex. My kids are home for summer vacation now. Both astrology and swim camps are canceled. I got on the scale this morning. I gained 4 more pounds! Now, I am up 9 pounds.

6.15.20

Beth Ann sent an email. WELALTZ is not allowing any hiring because of COVID. Therefore, I will need to lead my team and act as the sales rep in the open territory due to **Kathryn's** departure. Anything else that can ruin my month?

Yes! Company sales are lagging due to COVID, and WELALTZ has had to cut costs. **Beth Ann** was going to tell me I had to downsize my team by one person, but since **Kathryn** quit, that will count as my one employee to lay off. What a horrible thing to happen during this difficult time. However, it got worse. The company is decreasing base salaries by 15% through December because sales are down. After phoning everyone, I was mentally drained. We all kept our jobs, but my reps are disillusioned and feel very insecure. Me too.

6.16.20

This month is June Gloom! Sales have not improved, but I have some ideas to turn it around. I need to get my ideas down on paper quickly, so I can formulate a plan.

6.18.20

I submitted for 2 weeks of vacation starting June 26! The whole family is going to spend it at a log cabin, "off the grid." The kids aren't excited, but I think they will like it once we get there. I can't handle anything else happening.

Phyllis got a St Bernard puppy; something to smile about. I saw a picture. He is soooo cute, and she named him Bear.

6.22.20

Today, I asked **Beth Ann** if I could present a business plan for increasing sales for the rest of the year. I have decided that she responds to me only if the topic is business! She needs to get some people skills. She said she was starting to lose faith, but I restored it with goals and steps to improve performance. I hope that this puts me back on track for a promotion. Not sure I want it, though. I have never worked harder than this year. However, I am blessed that I have my job. Many people don't.

MY WORK JOURNAL—JULY 2020 ENTRIES

7.4.20

Hello J! Drove back home today. The fireworks over the holiday weekend were amazing. I feel relaxed and refreshed. The vacation worked, and **Jerod** and the kids loved roughing it. I am focused on managing better. Zoom calls with every sales representative individually are at the top of my list instead of phone calls. I can gauge how the rep is doing if I can see them and hear them. I also need to communicate with them more frequently. Hands-off management doesn't seem to be the best approach, and maybe it's one reason sales dropped.

Another thought—I need to help my team find a better way to contact their customers and discuss Parkitz from home. One of my colleagues told me to ask my reps to try Facetime with their doctors. It is worth a try.

Friday, I am planning a Zoom district call to celebrate the first half of the year wins. It's time to recognize each person's achievement for the last 6months. Even though sales are not where I want, we did have successes. Maybe a change in mindset is needed. Imagine, Believe, and Achieve! That is going to be the vision. Wish me luck, Ms. Journal!

FIGURE 1.2   Monica's Professional Profile (July 2020)

MY WORK JOURNAL—AUGUST 2020 ENTRIES (NOTHING)

MY WORK JOURNAL—SEPTEMBER 2020 ENTRIES (NOTHING)

MY WORK JOURNAL—OCTOBER 2020 ENTRIES (NOTHING)

MY WORK JOURNAL—NOVEMBER 2020 ENTRIES

11.26.20

Hi J: It is Thanksgiving Day. There is good news; a COVID vaccine is on the way, and sales have improved. Catch you soon.

MY WORK JOURNAL—DECEMBER 2020 ENTRIES

New Year's Eve Day (7:12 am)

Dear J: I am sorry I have not written recently. I have not had the energy. I have been collaborating with my sales reps and working that open territory. It has paid off. Sales got better over the last few months. My team is optimistic, too, and we created their 2021 business plans together. However, this was still the worst sales year of my entire career.

New Year's Eve Night 2020 (11:58 pm)

With a glass of champagne in hand, I toasted my husband just before the stroke of midnight. "May we never experience another year like this. But if we do, we know we can survive! Cheers!" My internal self, asked "Did I survive, or did I thrive?" **Jerod** can almost read my mind and knows I am reflecting as I write to you. He says, Babe, you did your best. Go to sleep. XOXOXO

Discussion Questions

1. Define the major management challenges with Ron, Dijon, Jasmin, Cheryl, and Monica's boss. Discuss why the challenges exist.

2. Describe how Monica's leadership style and interactions change over time. What was the impact on her employees at the beginning of the story and end?

3. How does Monica communicate differently from the beginning of the case until the end of the year 2020? How much of the change is necessary because of the COVID pandemic?

4. If you are employed, would you prefer to communicate with your boss by email, text, phone, or video conferencing over the web? Why? Describe the advantages of one method over another.

5. Define appropriate attire and behavior during video conferences.

6. Monica is surprised when Kathryn submits her resignation. Were there any signs Kathryn was not happy in her job? Is Monica to blame? Discuss.

7. Does Monica's personal situation with her children influence her commitment to her career? Support your position.

8. Monica decides to take a vacation from work as a method of dealing with stress. Debate the benefits of vacation time to employees during stressful events and times of success. Are there other ways she controlled her emotions at work? What actions/activities would you suggest to decrease stress?

9. Monica writes almost daily in a "work journal." Discuss the benefits of this activity and expression of thoughts to use for personal and professional reflection.

10. Does Monica survive or thrive? Support your position.

Assignments

1. Share how COVID has changed you professionally and personally. Create two columns with headings of positive and negative impact in your life in the year 2020. Share if you feel you survived or thrived and why.

2. Many YouTube videos feature managers discussing how their leadership style changed in 2020. List the most common five behaviors cited. Choose one and provide a review of an actual situation that includes the job role and industry. Summarize why these changes were necessary.

3. Review the article "Pros and Cons of Laissez-Faire Leadership" (Cherry, 2020) (https://www.verywellmind.com/what-is-laissez-faire-leadership-2795316) on laissez-faire leadership, and summarize the advantages and disadvantages of the style.

4. Thousands of businesses have been impacted by COVID. Research which industries have been affected most negatively. Explain what these businesses did to stay afloat and, in many cases, became more profitable than before COVID.

5. The author reinforces meeting with customers personally to discuss Parkitz. Research the top three most impactful sales techniques used with customers in 2020. Discuss if and how sales methods have changed because of COVID.

6. Name a person you admire from the year 2020 who demonstrated managing their personal life and career successfully during the COVID pandemic. Explain why you admire them.

7. If you were employed in 2020, describe the relationship with your manager, if it changed and how.

Additional Learning

- Read the book, *The Four Life Agreements* for personal inspiration by Don Miguel Ruiz.

References

AJMC Staff. (2020, November 25). A timeline of COVID 19 developments in 2020. https://www.ajmc.com/view/a-timeline-of-covid19-developments-in-2020

Baker, M., & Weise, K. (2020, March 2). "When is it going to end?": Where coronavirus has turned deadly in the U.S. *New York Times.* https://www.nytimes.com/2020/03/02/us/coronavirus-washington-state.html

Centers for Disease Control and Prevention (2020). How to protect yourself and others. https://www.cdc.gov/coronavirus/2019-ncov/prevent-getting-sick/prevention.html

Cherry, K. (2020, July 2.) Pros and cons of laissez-faire leadership. VeryWell Mind. https://www.verywellmind.com/what-is-laissez-faire-leadership-2795316

New York Times. (2020, November 5). What we know about the death of George Floyd in Minneapolis. https://www.nytimes.com/article/george-floyd.html

Regan, H., Yeung, J., Renton, A., Wagner, M., Hayes, M., & Guy, J. (2020, March 17). March 17 coronavirus news. CNN. https://www.cnn.com/world/live-news/coronavirus-outbreak-03-17-20-intl-hnk/index.html

Ruiz, D.M. (2018). *The four life agreements*. San Rafael: Amber-Allen Publishing.

SoftwareONE. (2020). Microsoft Teams vs. Zoom. https://www.softwareone.com/en-za/blog/articles/2020/09/21/microsoft-teams-vs-zoom

YouTube About. (2020). Brand resources. https://www.youtube.com/about/brand-resources/#logos-icons-colors

Gender and
Work

2

Chinese Spinning Plates

By Deborah deLaski-Smith

Overview

Organizations and business units within companies frequently downsize for various reasons. This case study explores a "survivor's" life when her colleagues are terminated, and she and her colleagues' workloads double (or more) due to a corporate change. Combining the stressful work event with Betsy's personal life creates sadness, anxiety, and havoc, yet she prevails with commitment, determination, prioritizing, and flexibility. It is reminiscent of a precision balancing technique in which Chinese women spin plates, working hard to keep them all moving without crashing to the floor.

Scenario

Betsy is 38 years old and has worked 8 years for the technology-marketing firm, 2Gather, in Boston, Massachusetts. The organization had an executive director, director, associate director (Betsy), sub-category managers, and administrative support staff. The company worked with demanding clients who wanted their products advertised in print, on the web, and in television and cable commercials.

Objectives

- Discuss the impact of task reassignment during a company's reorganization and downsizing.
- Explain the stress of redefining employee roles and procedures.
- Discuss how job and work changes impact personal lives and friendships with those who have been let go and are now unemployed.
- Explore why the assignment of multiple roles more often goes to female employees rather than males.
- Evaluate how gender or personality differences foster varied reactions to changes at work.

Key Concepts and Words

change management, communication, multitasking, prioritizing, reorganization, retaining employees, work overload

Several clients backed out of their contracts to hire 2Gather for marketing projects. As a result, the company was auditing its financials and reducing its expenses to make sure it met its obligations and profits for the year. Two active contracts had major due dates in the next quarter, and 2Gather was preparing for television and cable spots to be recorded. As Wednesday morning work began, the director, John, let Betsy know that he had a meeting shortly with the executive director, Noel Mercy. This was routine for them to meet, so she continued working on the details of a TV shoot. Betsy reported to John, who reported to Noel.

John returned from his meeting and told Betsy that Noel wanted to meet with her immediately. Betsy entered Noel's office and was directed to have a seat. The meeting conveyed that Betsy's supervisor, John, was being let go due to 2Gather's financial constraints. Betsy would assume John's duties and responsibilities along with her own, with no additional pay. Noel referred to this as "flattening the organization," as Betsy would now be reporting to Noel. Noel and Joel also had an administrative assistant, Pearl, and she would be informed next of her termination.

Betsy was asked to keep the news quiet and was told other downsizing changes would be taking place. One was within the two media departments, which would combine Print and Media Relations' managerial roles. The senior-most employee, Stella Starr, would take on Print and Media since she had some experience in both areas. She would be told shortly. Other managers and support staff would soon lose their positions as well.

Betsy returned to her desk shocked but tried to convey on her face that things were okay because all the news would be communicated later that day. Looking around the room, it became clear that the new skeleton crew would be all females (excluding the executive director, Noel). All workloads would double or more, and 2Gather would recruit college student interns or other free/inexpensive labor. However, the pressure was on to complete work on existing projects. At the same time, it was equally important to find time to secure agreements with new clients, remembering that the reorganization was due to financial issues.

Following the afternoon meetings, corrugated boxes were obtained so leaving staff could pack up their desks. These events took an emotional toll on those terminated and those lucky to remain employed.

The next day Betsy arrived early at the office after having had a restless night. She knew her work was critical to the current clients. As the new director, she needed to bolster her teams' morale so others would handle the routine work and look ahead to pending tasks. It was challenging to know what to do first. The phone was ringing, and Pearl, their previous administrative assistant, was not there to answer and direct calls to the correct recipient. A client review of the storyboards for a commercial/TV spot was moments away. Betsy looked at the empty coffee pot and knew she needed to make the brew to appease staff and the clients, who would arrive shortly. She and her remaining colleagues were not prepared for the additional amount of work.

At about 11 a.m., Betsy found herself in the restroom breathing heavily and in a cold sweat. "How am I going to keep up this pace? How am I going to keep others calm and focused when my world is crumbling?" she muttered to herself. Her friends had been laid off. Some were single mothers. Her heart ached for their situation. "Will it be awkward to connect with them or post anything good on Facebook?" she thought. Betsy had not told anyone about her mother being ill and her cat had thrown up all night. Her husband was on edge, and their continuing attempt to have a family was not going well. "How would all of these issues get resolved?"

… Six months later, Betsy scanned the office. She noted the two empty chairs where colleagues once sat but had found employment at competitive firms. That day, she interviewed three candidates to replace one position. 2Gather had taken on two interns, which sometimes was more work than doing things herself. The company had finished the project for one influential client and recently landed a new account. Betsy's mother's health had stabilized. The cat was well and trying to conceive a baby remained an emotional roller coaster with no success. With each day, Betsy felt stress about work and her personal life, and an annoying eye twitch reminded her of all the challenges that persisted. She routinely found herself seeking refuge in the restroom for an emotional reprieve. Betsy wondered whether loyalty to 2Gather was worth the effort and the toll on her.

Following a few deep breaths, a smile came over her face. She was thinking about a variety show she recently saw on TV, where a tiny Chinese woman had ceramic plates that she set up on sticks and began to spin them. As the woman set into position a new plate, she would return to the first few and give them a spin. With time, she had many plates spinning while she ran back and forth. Betsy fortified herself to leave the restroom, determined to keep plates spinning so happy clients would give referrals, and the firm would continue a successful path. The goal was to push forward so 2Gather would grow, and no one else would be terminated.

Discussion Questions

1. Did Betsy have an obligation to agree to take on the additional work? What other options might she have considered?

2. Was there another way for the executive director to handle the terminations or was his process a good one? Should he have stepped down to save the most money or have taken a pay cut?

3. Do the employees have any recourse to return to work or file for unemployment? In this case, both men and women were let go, but overall, with corporate downsizing more women and minorities lose positions (Kalev, 2016).

4. What strategies could Betsy consider to ease the workload? How could Betsy modify the work tasks of others to address these changes?

5. What reactions from the remaining employees will Betsy have to address as time goes on? How might negativity impact the organization internally and externally? What toll might reorganization and downsizing have on employee absenteeism and physical and mental health?

6. Do you think there are specific gender characteristics about females that can assist with taking on additional roles/workload? Provide reasons for your thinking.

7. Should Betsy stay in touch with those who were let go? If yes, in what way?

8. What role, if any, did the type of company (advertising) factor into which employees remained on the job (women except for Noel)? Would this be the case for downsizing in other industries? Would it differ for a nonprofit business?

9. Why would Betsy, who is overworked with so many personal challenges, want to remain employed? Was it for the paycheck regardless of added responsibility? Was it about proving oneself for future promotion?

Could Betsy have been thinking about the near-term future and hoping to get recruited to a client's company who notices how hardworking she is? Why would you stay?

Assignments

1. How can you as a manager make termination/layoff due to downsizing (not poor performance) less traumatic for the individual? Are there known methods to diffuse emotion like body language or tone of voice? Describe.

2. All companies go through change and life is moving every second, every minute. Business articles cover the topic of change and speak about it being a constant. Companies that undergo massive reorganization often use consultants to assist with transition. The book *Leading Change*, by John P. Kotter, stresses the need for communication, information sharing, and listening well. Using Kotter's book, explain why listening is important when conveying "bad" news to an employee.

3. Prioritizing is critical to be successful at many jobs and in personal life. It becomes even more critical when employees face work overload. One technique to solve for the extra responsibilities is creating daily "to do" lists and prioritizing tasks. Identify the benefits of daily lists to an employee and employer and one's personal life. Reference articles and best practices from your research.

4. Locate two articles/readings/YouTube videos discussing how a person should evaluate staying in their job or departing. Describe the advice given. Did you find the advice differed for men and women? If so, define how.

5. Read the Marques et al. article (2014), listed in References, on innovative behaviors and downsizing. What role does job insecurity play on innovative/creative behavior?

6. List two strategies Betsy might use to keep the remaining employees engaged in their work for the future of 2Gather. Why would these strategies help?

Additional Learning

- For fun, watch this YouTube video of learning how to spin plates by the National Circus Project (https://www.youtube.com/watch?v=YdEd3-Yq_hc). Try doing it yourself.

References

Aneil K., Mishra, A. K., & Spreitzer, G. M. (1998). Explaining how survivors respond to downsizing: The roles of trust, empowerment, justice, and work redesign. *Academic Management Review, 23*(3), 567–588.

Fatemi, F. (2016). 5 roles men project on women in the workplace. *Forbes.* http://www.forbes.com/sites/falonfatemi/2016/09/30/5-roles-men-project-on-women-in-the-workplace/#64ce18112ccc

Kalev, A. (2016). How "neutral" layoffs disproportionately affect women and minorities. *Harvard Business Review.* https://hbr.org/2016/07/how-neutral-layoffs-disproportionately-affect-women-and-minorities

Kim, H.-S., (2009). Examining the role of informational justice in the wake of downsizing from an organizational relationship management. *Journal of Business Ethics, 88*(2), 297–312.

Klehe, U.C., Zikic, J., Van Vianen, A., & De Pater, I.E. (2011). Career adaptability, turnover and loyalty during organizational downsizing. *Journal of Vocational Behavior, 79*(1), 217–229.

Kotter, J. (2012). *Leading Change.* Brighton: Harvard Business Review Publishing.

Marques, T., Galende, J., Cruz, P., & Ferreura, M. P. (2014). Surviving downsizing and innovative behaviors: A matter of organizational commitment. *International Journal of Manpower, 35*(7), 930–955. http://www.emeraldinsight.com/doi/full/10.1108/IJM-03-2012-0049

Schiro, J. B., & Baker, R. L. (2009). Downsizing and organizational change survivors and victims: Mental health issues. *The International Journal of Applied Management and Technology, 7*(1), 91–121.

Stroh, L. K., & Reilly, A. H. (1997). Loyalty in the age of downsizing. *Sloan Review: Summer 1997 Research Feature.* http://sloanreview.mit.edu/article/loyalty-in-the-age-of-downsizing/

Vahtera, J., Kivimäki, M., Pentti, J., Linna, A., Virtanna, M., Virtanna, P., & Ferrie, J. E. (2004). Organisational downsizing, sickness absence, and mortality: 10-town prospective cohort study. *British Medical Journal, 328*(7439), 555. https://www.ncbi.nlm.nih.gov/pmc/articles/PMC381046/?tool=pmcentrez

Zeinab A. K-S. (1999). *Organizational downsizing, discrimination and corporate social responsibility.* Quorum.

Intent vs. Perception

By Melina Carlson

Overview

This case focuses on company policies and situational work environments. It involves a young employee who makes two decisions she believes are correct, but her department manager disagrees. One choice involves her understanding of the company dating policy. The second is a potential misinterpretation of the dress policy.

As you read this case study, evaluate the employee's choices and decisions. Note the behavior of her manager and coworkers. Decide if the employee violated any company policies and determine if the decisions made by both the employee and management were appropriate.

Scenario

Alicia Cummings graduated from the University of Texas with a bachelor's degree in accounting. She landed her first job as an accounts payable analyst working for the prestigious accounting firm Nicolls, Penny & Sense (NP&S). This was her second year on the job. Alicia loved her work, and she was a confident, hard worker. Alicia received a "meets expectations" review during the past year, meaning she earned

Objectives

- Explain the business rationale behind dating and fraternization policies.
- Describe why a company institutes a dress code and personal grooming policies.
- Define proper business attire.
- Evaluate what responsibilities employees have regarding company policies and procedures.

Key Concepts and Words

business and professional attire, hierarchal romance, intent, lateral romance, perception, workplace policy a good performance rating and an encouraging evaluation from her supervisor. She hoped that her solid work ethic and personal motivation would support her career advancement within the firm. There were many positions available to her, and Alicia's personal career goal was to become the accounting manager. For her to move up the career ladder, she would need at least 5 more years of experience and be required to return to school to obtain her certified public accounting (CPA) license.

Alicia was well-liked and cordial to her colleagues. A few peers didn't want to socialize with their co-workers, but the company's employees were generally friendly and collaborative.

Alicia's manager, Brandon Coiner, was the lead administrator of the Accounts Payable department. Brandon had been with the company for 7 years. The majority of senior managers were gender-mixed, with the managers' ratio of 60% male to 40% female. With this ratio, Alicia was encouraged that long-term opportunities existed for promotion into upper management.

Alicia recently met another associate at her office. His smile and sense of humor attracted her, and they started to date. His name was Eric Johnson, and he worked in the payroll department. Eric had been with NP&S for 4 years and was due for a promotion at the end of the fourth quarter. He was very social, and everyone at NP&S seemed to know who he was. Eric had a good reputation with his co-workers and management.

According to the company policies, dating was permissible if it wasn't between a supervisor and their employee. Alicia believed it was acceptable to date Eric because his position was in the payroll department, and he was not her immediate supervisor.

Alicia and Eric planned to go out this evening, and she was preparing to bring a change of clothes to work for their date. As she was selecting her clothes, Alicia made a quick decision to find work and date attire that would suit both situations. Today was "Casual Friday" attire, so she thought it would be easy to accommodate both. She wanted to be comfortable and casual for their date, so Alicia chose a green and pale blue sleeveless shirt, jeans, and low-heel sandals. Alicia believed that the clothes she had selected to wear for work and the evening were appropriate.

She arrived to work 5 minutes early and headed toward her desk to begin the day. Alicia's co-worker, Rebecca, greeted her to say "hello." After a few minutes of catching up, she suggested to Alicia she might get cold at her desk wearing a sleeveless shirt. There was a small conversation between the two women, but after several more minutes, Alicia mentioned to her friend, she needed to begin reviewing her "list" for the day.

Later that morning, Alicia's manager, Brandon stopped by her cubicle. Brandon had been the payroll manager in the accounts payable department for the past 5 years. He was Alicia's manager for a year. He offered a quick "good morning" greeting and dropped off some work files with instructions on what needed to be processed. Brandon left Alicia's cubicle, only to return after 10 minutes. He stood in the doorway of her cubicle and announced that her clothes were inappropriate for the workplace. He informed her that her outfit did not follow the company's dress code policy. Brandon's voice became increasingly loud as he reprimanded Alicia for her appearance. He finally asked, "Why did you choose to wear such a skimpy top to work? Your shirt is inappropriate. Tank tops are not allowed according to company policy." Alicia replied in a relatively soft-spoken manner, "My top doesn't have a low neckline and isn't tight fitting. I didn't realize that it was against the dress code policy."

Alicia explained that she chose the attire because of a date planned after work. Brandon then asked her, "Who are you going out with?" Alicia shared that she was seeing Eric, who worked in payroll. At that point, Brandon lost his temper. He angrily stated, "Now, you have broken the company's dress code policy and the dating policy, too. I have no other option but to send you home until further notice. You will also be docked pay for the hours missed today." Brandon's scolding was loud and embarrassing to Alicia. She was devastated by her mistake but did not understand how she had violated the dating policy with Eric.

Alicia gathered her personal belongings and quickly left the building without talking to anyone. She went home feeling humiliated by the incident, ashamed and canceled her date with Eric. She received a phone call later that day from Brandon's administrative assistant, Kashie. Alicia was directed to report to work at the regular time on Monday, and she had a meeting scheduled with Brandon at 9 a.m.

When she arrived on Monday, she went directly to Brandon's office for their appointment. Alicia was nervous about the meeting. She was worried and afraid that Brandon would be angry and again raise his voice. She was hoping there would be additional managers sitting in on the meeting. As Alicia approached

Brandon's office, she noticed the doorway was open. Brandon saw her and motioned her to enter. He then directed Alicia to have a seat; no other manager was present. He closed the office door and reiterated the dress code violation explaining this was a formal verbal warning. If she received another warning due to any office issue, she would be given a written notification of the violation. The written documentation would go in her personnel file, and if a third violation occurred, she could be terminated.

The last point Brandon brought up was the NP&S's workplace dating policy. Alicia felt Brandon's voice became angrier in tone when he discussed who Alicia was dating. Brandon stated, "Eric is due to receive a promotion this coming year. Do you realize by continuing to date him, he would violate the company dating policy and it could be held against him?" The meeting lasted approximately 30 minutes, and Alicia felt once again humiliated like a child disciplined by a parent. All Alicia wanted to do was return to her desk and work. She hung her head low as she hurriedly walked back to her cubicle and sat down without looking up. She tried not to make eye contact with any of her co-workers. The day ended with no embarrassing office gossip or acknowledgment of the previous incident. Alicia was relieved she could go home at 5 p.m.

The next day Alicia was still feeling uncomfortable about the dress code incident and how Brandon loudly reprimanded her in front of the other office workers (cubicles were not private). The day began without anyone saying anything regarding the incident. It was as if Alicia were invisible. The environment seemed stressed, and Alicia was happy when it was nearing the close of business again.

Rebecca stopped on her way out of the office to say good night. She wanted to share her thoughts about consensual relationship agreements and suggested Alicia contact Human Resources for assistance. Rebecca indicated the company might accept this type of relationship with Eric. She encouraged Alicia to review the workplace policies another time because she felt Alicia was not breaking the policy. Rebecca tried to make Alicia feel better since she had overheard everything from her cubicle located next to Brandon's office.

Alicia stated she didn't want to discuss the situation any further. She was already debating whether she should contact Human Resources to discuss the way Brandon handled her clothing and dating issue.

Although Alicia continued to feel unsettled about the warnings; she wanted to stay employed and enjoyed her job. The company's work attire and dating policies are detailed below.

DRESS CODE POLICY: NICOLLS, PENNY & SENSE

Business personnel will often have contact with the public, and your appearance helps create a positive image for the Company. Therefore, you should dress in a manner appropriate for a work environment. Your dress and grooming should be consistent with your job's physical, safety, and comfort requirements. If you report for work improperly dressed or groomed, your supervisor may ask you to return home to change clothes or make grooming adjustments. Employees are encouraged to ask their supervisor in advance if they have any questions regarding the propriety of their dress to avoid being sent home to change their clothes and/or missing pay for time out of the office.

A. Business Attire Policy: Business Casual

Business casual dress is a lesser standard than formal business attire and typically requires slacks and a collared shirt for men and the equivalent attire for women. It does not include jeans, tennis shoes, flip-flops, and the like.

B. Business Attire Policy: Casual Friday's Dress Code

Every Friday, NP&S associates may dress casually, unless they are acting in a representative capacity for NP&S on that particular day and are required to wear Business Casual attire, as described above in section A. On Casual Fridays, NP&S associates may wear jeans, shirts without collars, and sneakers, but they may not wear inappropriate dress. Refer to page 6 in the Employee Handbook for details on inappropriate dress. We encourage our employees to dress comfortably for work and in casual dress on Fridays. However, even on casual Friday, you cannot wear anything that other employees might find offensive or deemed in poor taste. This could be clothing that displays profanity or clothing that promotes areas that include, but are not limited to, politics, religion, sexuality, race, age, gender, and ethnicity.

Every day of the week, employees are expected to demonstrate proper judgment and professionalism. Note: Casual days are every Friday unless directed otherwise.

C. Inappropriate Attire

The following items are not considered appropriate business attire and should not be worn to work:

- T-shirts, including logo t-shirts (including profanity or offensive wording or logos)

- Cutoffs

- Athletic wear, sweatpants, and jogging suits

- Dirty sneakers, flip-flops of any kind

- Jeans that are ripped, tattered, or have holes

- Tank tops, tube tops, halter tops with narrow straps, off the shoulder tops, midriff length tops

- Beachwear

- Provocative attire, including mini-skirts, Spandex, or Lycra (e.g., bicycle shorts)

D. Appropriate Attire for Men

For men, appropriate business attire includes:

- Blazers, suits, or sports coats

- Dress slacks, chinos, or Dockers

- Ties

- Dress shirts with buttons and collars

- Sweaters or vests

- Dress shoes

E. Appropriate Attire for Women

For women, appropriate business attire includes:

- Dresses

- Blouses (but not see-through or low cut)

- Polo shirts

- Sweaters

- Slacks or skirts

- Dress capris or ankle dress pants

- Stockings or nylons

- Dress shoes

F. Enforcement

Department managers/supervisors are responsible for monitoring and enforcing this Dress Code:

1. Managers will meet with the employee they deem to be dressed inappropriately to help the employee understand what they did wrong and ensure that the mistake isn't repeated.

2. If the violation is deemed flagrant, the manager will hold the discussion with the employee and ask him/her to go home, change, and return to the office in appropriate attire. The returning employee's timetable will be at the discretion of the manager. (The employee) will not be compensated for the time necessary to do so.

3. Violations in this policy that are repeated will result in disciplinary action and may include termination.

G. Requests for Accommodation

Enforcement of the Dress Code will be consistent, but in a way that respects each employee's personal circumstances, including their race, religion, gender, physical/mental condition, nationality, family status, etc. Employees may request exemptions or accommodations to their Dress Code on these and other grounds by asking their department managers. All requests for accommodations will be considered on an individual basis.

DATING AND FRATERNIZATION POLICY

A. NP&S encourages the development of friendships and relationships within the Company. We do not expect that these friendships or relationships prove to have a negative impact on the work environment. Any relationship that interferes with the Company's teamwork, or productivity of individuals, will not be tolerated and will be addressed by managers or by a Human Resources department representative.

B. **The NP&S's policy concerning dating or sexual relationships between managers and supervisors, managers, and employees within the same department, is prohibited.** A manager or someone holding a supervisory role needs to understand that personal relationships with employees who report to them may perceive such treatment as favoritism, misuse of authority, or even sexual harassment. If a situation arises where an employee becomes a supervisor of a relative due to a promotion, change of position, marriage, or other circumstances, the affected department shall take action to resolve the conflict as soon as possible. This would require one of the employees to move from their department under conflict.

C. Relatives shall not be selected, appointed, or assigned to a position in the Company in which one relative may directly or indirectly control or influence the work or employment of the other relative.

D. Fraternization is defined as dating, romantic involvement, and sexual relations. Fraternization between any employee who directly reports to the manager or who receives from the manager/supervisor pay raises, promotions, evaluations, and job advancement is prohibited.

E. NP&S does not encourage dating between a manager and supervisor or with employees in the same department. This type of romantic relationship could promote complicated situations or problems within our organization's work environment. Relationships among managers and employees can affect the careers of both employees concerning advancement or career choices within the Company. These types of relationship can consequently impact our service to customers or productivity within the Company.

F. The Human Resource representative should be contacted if a manager is seeking a close relationship with an employee. The Company will decide what actions are necessary with regard to assignments and current positions. NP&S does not support **any manager to date, become romantically involved with, or have sexual relations with an employee that directly reports to that manager.**

G. NP&S recognizes that employees have different opinions and understandings about the definition of a close relationship, friendship, or romantic involvement. The Human Resource department is available for clarification in these matters. If you have questions or need further guidance, please contact the Human Resources department. One of their goals is to see that our policies are conducted consistently and fairly and to help inform your choices.

H. NP&S encourages employees to develop friendships and teamwork spirit both in the workplace and outside of work. It is not the Company's goal to interfere with the growth of employee friendships and relationships. This policy's intention is to identify when personal relationships are appropriate, and when they are not.

I. This policy informs employees of the potential consequences if the policy is violated. This Company's goal is to encourage a positive work environment for the employees and customers, and this dating or fraternization policy is developed to discourage any possibility of sexual harassment claims.

J. Employees who disregard this policy will receive disciplinary actions, which may include employment termination.

Discussion Questions

1. Some companies have informal employee policies, while others have all policies in writing. Why would a company choose to have written policies for dating and attire?

2. What are some personal and workplace ramifications for breaking a company policy?

3. Based on NP&S's written policy, did Alicia violate the dress code requirements? Defend your rationale.

4. Based on NP&S's written policy, did Alicia violate the dating rules? Support your answer by referring to language in the company policy.

5. Discuss the potential need for changes or improvements to the NP&S dress code and dating policies. For example, are they biased to favor one gender over another? Justify your perspective.

6. If Alicia meets with a Human Resource (HR) manager, what complaints can she report? Would you consider these complaints "just" cause to meet with HR? Explain why.

7. How would you rate Brandon's handling of the situation? Factor in the reasons why Alicia was being scolded and not Eric.

8. Assume Eric and Alicia continue to date. If Eric becomes a manager for the accounts payable department, what decisions would Eric and Alicia have to make concerning the work environment and their personal situation? (Remember, Alicia currently works as an analyst in accounts payable).

9. Is the Company wrong to have a dating policy? Isn't a romantic relationship at work a private matter?

10. It is often said you should dress for the job you want. Discuss if this is true in today's workplace?

Assignments

1. If you had the role of the manager, describe how you would handle the dress code violation, from the initial identification of the violation and any subsequent follow-up actions or meetings. Be detailed in supporting your opinion.

2. Locate two workplace dress policies online and compare them to the NP&S policy. Develop a list of common features from all three. What are the differences? Explain why you think there are differences between the three corporations.

3. Research three different workplace dating policies, using NP&S as one of them. Describe your results, noting similarities and differences.

4. Why do you think more workplaces are accepting "casual dress" as appropriate? Do you agree with this trend? Why or why not? Conduct research on the topic of casual dress in the workplace. Do your research findings support your response?

5. Explore common practices for workplace policy violations. What are the common steps or procedures that management implements with the employee who is at fault?

6. Locate the federal law that includes content covering discrimination for clothing attire in the workplace. Explain what is covered under this section of the law.

Additional Learning

- Open your closet and review your clothing. Ask yourself, do you have the appropriate attire for your current job if you are employed? If not, determine one to three items that you can purchase and mix and match with some of the clothes you own. If so, congratulations for recognizing the importance of the accepted dress for your position and work environment!

References

Business.com. (2020). Dating in the office. What is the best policy? https://www.business.com/articles/office-dating-policy/

Clivilez-Wu, I. (2016, June 1). Dangerous liasions *[sic]*: How dating a co-worker can ruin your reputation and career. *Forbes.* https://www.forbes.com/sites/isabellaclivilezwu/2016/06/01/dangerous-liaisons-how-dating-a-co-worker-can-ruin-your-reputation-and-career/?sh=288229363bbd

FindLaw. For Legal Professionals. (2017). Regulating work place romances. http://corporate.findlaw.com/litigation-disputes/regulating-work-place-romances.html

Krasny, J. (2016). Survey: More workplaces have casual dress code. ABC Action News. http://www.abcactionnews.com/news/national/casual-dress-codes-now-more-common-in-workplace-survey-shows

Leonard, K. (2019, February 6). Meaning of professionalism and work ethic. *Houston Chronicle.* http://smallbusiness.chron.com/meaning-professionalism-work-ethic-746.html

Miller, B. (2015, January 7). Can an employer prohibit employees from dating one another? *HR Daily Advisor*. http://hrdailyadvisor.

blr.com/2015/01/07/can-an-employer-prohibit-employees-from-dating-one-another/

Spors, K. (2017). *Top 10 dress code violations*. Smallbiz Ahead—The Hartford. https://sba.thehartford.com/managing-employees/

employee-dress-code-violations/

U.S. Equal Opportunity Commission. (n.d.). Prohibited employment policies/practices. https://www.eeoc.gov/prohibited-employment-

policiespractices

U.S. International Trade Commission. (2002). Administrative announcement: Dress policy. https://www.usitc.gov/employment/

dress_policy.htm

Workplace Fairness. (2020). Your rights dress codes and grooming—questions and answers. https://www.workplacefairness.org/

grooming-codes

Zandan, N., & Lynch, H. (2020, June 18). Dress for the (remote) job you want. *Harvard Business Review*. https://hbr.org/2020/06/

dress-for-the-remote-job-you-want

Volenti Citrus

The reader is advised that this case contains sensitive or disturbing content. For those that may be experiencing domestic violence, you are encouraged to seek assistance at the National Domestic Violence Hotline: 1-800-799-7233 or http://www.thehotline.org.

Overview

Josephina Tucker is a lawful permanent resident residing and working in Florida. She is successful, happy, and the mother of one daughter. She dreams of a great life for her child. Josephina found a well-paying job for her skill set and is satisfied with her employer, which offers health benefits and a matching retirement savings plan. Unfortunately, Josephina is a battered woman who arrives at work with signs of abuse. This violence by her boyfriend extends into the workplace. The employer takes some action to protect Josephina, yet the outcome is a disaster.

Objectives

- Define and describe domestic violence and the differences between emotional and physical abuse.
- Explain how an employer can create an environment of trust when an employee experiences a personal crisis affecting work performance.
- Discuss how an employer should acknowledge and react to an employee's sensitive, highly personal, and confidential situation.
- Define and describe workplace violence.
- Explain an employer's legal and ethical obligations to provide employees with a safe and protected environment from workplace violence.

Key Concepts and Words

domestic violence, home-family conflict, intimate partner violence, safe working conditions, trust at work, workplace violence

Background

Table 2.1 describes four types of intimate partner violence (IPV) recognized by healthcare and legal professionals. These include "physical violence, sexual violence, stalking, and psychological aggression (including coercive acts) by a current or former intimate partner" (CDC, 2015, p. 11). Please use the following information as a reference as you read through the facts of this case.

TABLE 2.1   INTIMATE PARTNER VIOLENCE TYPES AND DEFINITIONS

Physical violence	The intentional use of physical force with the potential for causing death, disability, injury, or harm. Physical violence includes, but is not limited to, scratching; pushing; shoving; throwing; grabbing; biting; choking; shaking; aggressive hair pulling; slapping; punching; hitting; burning; use of a weapon; and use of restraints or one's body, size, or strength against another person. Physical violence also includes coercing other people to commit any of the above acts. (p. 11)
Sexual violence	<ul><li>This type of violent behavior is divided into five categories. Any of these acts constitute sexual violence, whether attempted or completed. Additionally, all of these acts occur without the victim's freely given consent, including cases in which the victim is unable to consent due to being too intoxicated (e.g., incapacitation, lack of consciousness, or lack of awareness) through their voluntary or involuntary use of alcohol or drugs.</li><li>Rape or penetration of victim—This includes completed or attempted, forced or alcohol/drug-facilitated unwanted vaginal, oral, or anal insertion. Forced penetration occurs through the perpetrator's use of physical force against the victim or threats to physically harm the victim.</li><li>Victim was made to penetrate someone else—This includes completed or attempted, forced or alcohol/drug-facilitated incidents when the victim was made to sexually penetrate a perpetrator or someone else without the victim's consent.</li><li>Nonphysically pressured unwanted penetration—This includes incidents in which the victim was pressured verbally or through intimidation or misuse of authority to consent or acquiesce to being penetrated.</li><li>Unwanted sexual contact—This includes intentional touching of the victim or making the victim touch the perpetrator, either directly or through the clothing, on the genitalia, anus, groin, breast, inner thigh, or buttocks without the victim's consent.</li><li>Noncontact unwanted sexual experiences—This includes unwanted sexual events that are not of a physical nature that occur without the victim's consent. Examples include unwanted exposure to sexual situations (e.g., pornography); verbal or behavioral sexual harassment; threats of sexual violence to accomplish some other end; and /or unwanted filming, taking or disseminating photographs of a sexual nature of another person. (p. 11–14)</li></ul>
Stalking	A pattern of repeated, unwanted, attention, and contact that causes fear or concern for one's own safety or the safety of someone else (e.g., family member or friend). Some examples include repeated, unwanted phone calls, emails, or texts; leaving cards, letters, flowers, or other items when the victim does not want them; watching or following from a distance; spying; approaching or showing up in places when the victim does not want to see them; sneaking into the victim's home or car; damaging the victim's personal property; harming or threatening the victim's pet; and making threats to physically harm the victim. (p. 14)

| Psychological aggression | This is the use of verbal and nonverbal communication with the intent to harm another person mentally or emotionally, and/or to exert control over another person. Psychological aggression can include expressive aggression (e.g., name-calling, humiliating); coercive control (e.g., limiting access to transportation, money, friends, and family; excessive monitoring of whereabouts); threats of physical or sexual violence; control of reproductive or sexual health (e.g., refusal to use birth control; coerced pregnancy termination); exploitation of victim's vulnerability (e.g., immigration status, disability); exploitation of perpetrator's vulnerability; and presenting false information to the victim with the intent of making them doubt their own memory or perception (e.g., mind games). (p.15) |

(CDC, para. 11–15)

Scenario

Josephina Tucker was a young mother and a lawful permanent resident (also known as a "green card" holder) working at the Volenti Citrus factory in Glenville, Florida, near the Panhandle area. She had a three-year-old daughter, Justina, who came with her to the United States. Josephina was a hard worker, very social, and loved her daughter dearly. She also sent money back to her family in Central America to support them while giving her daughter the best life she could. Josephina often volunteered to work overtime, and she saved that money for her daughter's college education. She was saving to purchase a new computer as well.

Josephina enjoyed a simple life, and one reason for coming to the United States was to escape a volatile relationship with an obsessive boyfriend, Stephan, who was Justina's father. Josephina often cried to her mother that her partner was belittling and verbally combative when living back home. Her mother frequently asked her about being physically abused, and like many battered women, Josephina denied any violence between them (CDC, 2015). Josephina often wore long sleeves and pants to work to hide her injuries, even though temperatures in the summer often exceeded 90 degrees with high humidity in her homeland. When questioned about the unusual clothing, Josephina would respond she wore long sleeves to avoid sunburn.

When Josephina and her daughter moved to Florida, her routine changed. Her mother was sent photos of them at the beach smiling and looking very happy in their swimsuits. She told her mother she was amazed at the smell of orange and lemon blossoms on the trees in the spring. Summer in Florida was just as hot and humid as home. Josephina's mother missed her daughter and granddaughter tremendously; however, she was happy that they were safely living in the United States.

Josephina's family had kept quiet about her leaving home, but word spread, and Josephina's boyfriend learned that she had moved to the United States. Stephan was angry that she had left without telling him. He found his way to the United States, then to Florida, and after a few months, he had located Josephina at her residence. She was stunned, afraid and told her friends at work he showed up where she lived. She didn't know what to do. One week later, he appeared at Volenti Citrus during Josephina's lunch hour, bringing her a sandwich and flowers. Her friends thought he was a nice guy. He was well dressed and often complimented Josephina during his visit. Her friends were perplexed. Josephina said she feared him, yet he was polite, well-spoken, and Josephina appeared to enjoy her time with Stephan. He even drove her to work every morning and was waiting for her every day at the end of her 4 p.m. shift. Josephina used to get up early in the morning to take the bus to the factory, so her friends were happy she could now sleep in.

There was another difference, though. Josephina's daughter often cried when she left for work, and Josephina feared that Stephan might be yelling at Justina as he had in the past. Justina always ran into her arms when she got home, and she only wanted to spend time playing games with her mother. Her daughter would hug her tightly for long periods of time. At night, Justina only wanted Josephina to read her a bedtime story. Josephina loved this routine since she could spend solo time with her daughter. But she had noticed this was a change in Justina's behavior. Before Stephan had arrived, her daughter's bedtime habit was to flip through the colored pages of books and then quickly fall asleep. Josephina also thought she was becoming shy, especially around Stephan.

Later that week, Josephina arrived at work with a bruised and broken lip. She told her friends that Stephan had hit her because she didn't introduce him to them properly. Josephina's supervisor, George, asked about her injury. Because she was embarrassed, she told him she had slipped on the wet kitchen floor and hit the counter. In the coming days, Josephina returned to wearing long sleeve tops and pants in the plant. Her friends noticed this and asked if something was wrong. "Do you feel OK? It's almost 94 degrees in the factory, and you are wearing long sleeves and sweating." Josephina said that she was suffering from the flu and a cold, and she was working through a fever. Once, she almost passed out and lemons from several crates scattered to the floor. Her friends thought she might be pregnant and were secretly excited for her.

Josephina also started sending letters instead of using Skype[1] to communicate with her mother. But, before the letters and change in communication, her mother had noticed that she was back to wearing long sleeve shirts. When asked, Josephina gave her the same story she told her colleagues at work. Josephina did not mention that Stephan had located her and had moved into her apartment with their daughter. She knew her mother would worry.

Over the next couple of months, Stephan continued to visit Volenti Citrus. However, he seemed more demanding and asked about Josephina's working conditions and why she could not leave her job precisely at 4 p.m. He told her supervisor George, over lunch one day, "she must be home by 4:30 p.m. to make dinner for him and their daughter. She was a great cook," and he "appreciated that she made food that reminded him of home." Her boss didn't think his comments were unusual as Josephina was paid hourly and saw she clocked out on time. However, George noticed that Stephan was picking her up at exactly 4:01 p.m. daily, and she wasn't volunteering for overtime as she had in the past. He thought that they must be spending more time with their daughter.

Josephina always embraced and kissed Stephan when he arrived, and she was sure to include her friends while they ate lunch. One day, though, Stephan arrived at Volenti mid-morning and demanded to see Josephina. The receptionist asked if this was an emergency, to which he responded no. However, she was alarmed by his demeanor and tone and immediately called Josephina's supervisor, George, who was also the foreman on the lemon crate production line. George was annoyed he was being phoned. He was focused on a shipment deadline to a large grocery chain, and Volenti Citrus had already worked seven days in a row. "I cannot let Josephina take a break to see her husband. We are backed up, and the crates have to be loaded on the trucks in time for departure." Stephan was angry and threatened the receptionist. He then yelled, "If you don't let me see Josephina, you are going to regret it!" The receptionist became frightened and pushed a button under her desk that called security. Stephan was immediately escorted off premises. This enraged him more. "I am going to get you all for this!" he screamed at the receptionist.

---

1   Skype Brand Elements and Skype and the authors and publisher are not affiliated, sponsored, authorised (sic) or otherwise associated by/with the Skype group of companies.

WHAT IS WORKPLACE VIOLENCE?

"Workplace violence is any act or threat of physical violence, harassment, intimidation, or other threatening disruptive behavior that occurs at the work site. It ranges from threats and verbal abuse to physical assaults and even homicide. It can affect and involve employees, clients, customers and visitors.

However it manifests itself, workplace violence is a major concern for employers and employees nationwide." (OSHA, 2002)

The next Monday morning, Josephina did not show up to work, nor did she the following day. She came to work on Wednesday, and Stephan brought her to the factory, but he never left the parking lot all day. Josephina was very quiet and rushed off quickly at the end of her 4 p.m. shift. On Thursday morning, Volenti Citrus security approached Stephan's car and told him he could not remain on the premises all day. He yelled, "Josephina is my wife, and I will wait here if I want to!" and so he waited and did the same on Friday. When leaving for the weekend, Josephina asked for a week off and was scheduled to return the following Monday. But she did not return to work. George said she called and requested two more days off because her daughter was sick.

One of her friends was worried and went over to her apartment. She found Josephina almost comatose in a living room chair. After several minutes, Josephina finally uttered some horrifying and shocking news.

The company announced shortly that a terrible incident occurred with one of their employees. Josephina's three-year-old daughter had been brutally beaten and died. Her boyfriend was the suspect.

Josephina did not come back to work at Volenti Citrus. She disappeared after the traumatic and incomprehensible death of Justina. Her friends thought she moved back home, or she was committed to a psychiatric hospital. Perhaps, she changed her name and is living near a beach with fond memories of her daughter building sandcastles, and the pain of lost happiness.

Discussion Questions

1. The U.S. Department of Labor (DOL) lists several indicators that an individual may be experiencing abuse in their life either on the job or outside of the workplace. These are detailed below. As Josephina's manager, what behaviors did she exhibit that were clues she was being abused?

PERFORMANCE/CONDUCT INDICATORS

"Being aware of performance and/or conduct problems which may be warning signs of potential trouble is good prevention strategy. These signs may show up in perpetrators of violence, those who are victims, and those involved in domestic violence. Although it is possible that only one of these indicators will occur, it is more likely that a pattern will occur or that they will represent a change from normal behavior. **Remember that the presence of any of these characteristics does not necessarily mean a violent act will occur. They may be indicators of another type of problem such as being ill, depressed, bereaved, etc.** Some examples of performance and/or conduct indicators are listed below (listing is not intended to be all inclusive):

- **attendance problems**—excessive sick leave, excessive tardiness, leaving work early, improbable excuses for absences;

- **adverse impact on supervisor's time**—supervisor spends an inordinate amount of time coaching and/or counseling employee about personal problems, re-doing the employee's work, dealing with co-worker concerns, etc.;

- **decreased productivity**—making excessive mistakes, poor judgment, missed deadlines, wasting work time and materials;

- **inconsistent work patterns**—alternating periods of high and low productivity and quality of work, inappropriate reactions, overreaction to criticism, and mood swings;

- **concentration problems**—easily distracted and often has trouble recalling instructions, project details, and deadline requirements;

U.S. Department of Labor, Selection from "DOL Workplace Violence Program," DOL.gov.

- **safety issues**—more accident prone, disregard for personal safety as well as equipment and machinery safety, needless risks;
- **poor health and hygiene**—marked changes in personal grooming habits;
- **unusual/changed behavior**—inappropriate comments, threats, throwing objects;
- evidence of possible drug or alcohol use/abuse;
- evidence of serious stress in the employee's personal life—crying, excessive phone calls, recent separation;
- **continual excuses/blame**—inability to accept responsibility for even the most inconsequential errors; and/or **unshakable depression**—low energy, little enthusiasm, despair." (DOL, n.d.)

2. If you were Josephina's colleague, would you have gone to her supervisor and alerted him that Josephina may be having problems at home? Why or why not?

3. Josephina's friends and supervisor created their own explanations for her changes in behavior. Do you believe they did not recognize her behavior as strange and unusual? Or, did they not want to get involved in her personal life?

4. Establishing a trusting relationship with employees is important for a manager. It creates a healthy environment for dialogue. Do you feel Josephina's supervisor had a good relationship with her? If so, why? If not, how would you create a solid and trusting working relationship with Josephina?

5. The U.S. Department of Labor, Office of Safety and Health Administration under the "General Duty Clause" of the Occupational Safety and Health Act (OSHA) of 1970, requires employers to provide employees with a safe work environment "free from recognized hazards." This includes workplace violence (sec. 5(a)). Stephan's threats appeared to have "crossed the line." What should Volenti Citrus have done to assure employees it had zero-tolerance for workplace violence?

GENERAL DUTY CLAUSE

"(a) Each employer—

(1) shall furnish to each of his employees employment and a place of employment which are free from recognized hazards that are causing or are likely to cause death or serious physical harm to his employees;

(2) shall comply with occupational safety and health standards promulgated under this Act.

(b) Each employee shall comply with occupational safety and health standards and all rules, regulations, and orders issued pursuant to this Act which are applicable to his own actions and conduct."

(OSHA, n.d.)

Assignments

1. You have decided that Volenti Citrus must create employee safety awareness through a flier about workplace violence. As noted above in the definition for "Workplace Violence," OSHA has listed four types of workplace violence: threat of physical violence, harassment, intimidation, or threatening disruptive behavior. The pamphlet should cover each of the four types of workplace violence and encourage employees to come forth and seek help. Search the internet and create a 1-page flier. Ask two or three individuals (outside of the classroom) to provide feedback. Your flier should be easy to understand and make employees feel comfortable coming forth to ask for their employer's assistance. If not, make changes before submitting to achieve this goal. See https://www.osha.gov/OshDoc/data_General_Facts/factsheet-workplace-violence.pdf.

2. Most companies offer an Employee Assistance Program (EAP) as a health benefit. A sample program at the United States Postal Office can be accessed at https://www.magellanassist.com/mem/default.aspx. What type of assistance is offered? What specifically may have helped Josephina? Why did her manager not provide her access to an EAP program?

3. Research the impact of domestic violence on the workplace. Include statistics of lost days worked, productivity costs, and healthcare implications (refer to Table 2.1).

4. There are hundreds of articles written about how to build trust with employees. Stephen Covey (2009) is a well-known author and expert on leadership and management principles. After reading an excerpt of his numerous publications, would his advice have helped Josephina's supervisor build trust with her? See https://www.shrm.org/resourcesandtools/hr-topics/organizational-and-employee-development/pages/leadersbuildtrust.aspx.

5. What is the Violence Against Women Act, which was signed by President Clinton in 1994? How does this law protect victims of domestic violence? See https://www.justice.gov/ovw.

Additional Learning

- Volunteer at a local domestic violence shelter. Inquire about the types of activities where help is needed and the time commitment involved. Prior to your phone call, write down your skills and evaluate how you could be of value. Ask a friend to volunteer with you if possible.

References

Centers for Disease Control and Prevention. (2015). Intimate partner violence surveillance. Uniform definitions and recommended data elements. https://www.cdc.gov/violenceprevention/pdf/ipv/intimatepartnerviolence.pdf

Centers for Disease Control and Prevention. (2020). Preventing intimate partner violence. https://www.cdc.gov/violenceprevention/intimatepartnerviolence/fastfact.html

Covey, S. (2009). How the best leaders build trust. https://www.shrm.org/resourcesandtools/hr-topics/organizational-and-employee-development/pages/leadersbuildtrust.aspx

National Center for Injury Prevention and Control, Division of Violence Prevention. (2016). Prevention. Intimate partner violence: Definitions. https://www.cdc.gov/violenceprevention/intimatepartnerviolence/definitions.html

Occupational Safety and Health Act of 1970, 29 U.S.C. § 651 et. seq.

OSHA. (n.d.). Workers' rights. https://www.osha.gov/Publications/osha3021.pdf

OSHA. (n.d.). Workplace violence enforcement. https://www.osha.gov/SLTC/workplaceviolence/standards.html

OSHA Fact Sheet. (2002). What is workplace violence? https://www.osha.gov/OshDoc/data_General_Facts/factsheet-workplace-violence.pdf

Pickert, K. (2013, February 27). What's wrong with the Violence Against Women Act? *Time.* http://nation.time.com/2013/02/27/whats-wrong-with-the-violence-against-women-act/

U.S. Department of Justice. (n.d.). Office on Violence Against Women. https://www.justice.gov/ovw

U.S. Department of Labor. (n.d.). DOL, Workplace violence program. https://www.dol.gov/oasam/hrc/policies/dol-workplace-violence-program.htm

U.S. Department of Labor. (n.d.) Workplace violence overview. https://www.osha.gov/workplace-violence

U.S. National Library of Medicine. (2020). Domestic violence. Medline Plus. https://medlineplus.gov/domesticviolence.html

Lights, Camera, Action

Objectives

- Describe the social and business challenges men and women experience in the workplace specific to gender.
- Explain the changes that have taken place in the workplace in the past 40 years in terms of gender.
- Explain one's responsibility for improving workplace dynamics and equality between men and women.

Key Concepts and Words

- #MeToo, benevolent sexism, female intensive occupations, gender differences, gender roles, gender stereotypes, male intensive occupations, quid pro quo sexual harassment, societal norms

Overview

This scenario showcases the employment of a secretary and her husband, Hal, who both work within the movie business. It is a "Then and Now" perspective from Hal, a friend of the authors' dad, who discusses his challenge with the accepted ways of interacting with women. He wonders if the treatment of women is vastly different today and whether women are experiencing a better workplace. The reader should ask themself the same question.

Background

Turner Classic Movies (TCM), Disney Studios, Jennifer Lawrence, Steven Spielberg, Robert Pattison, Emma Stone, and Adam Sandler. These are companies and people associated with the movie industry and Hollywood. When you ask anyone to identify their favorite movie, the list is unbelievably long and includes classics like *Casablanca*, *The Godfather* series, and *Star Trek*. Action-packed films such as *Goldfinger* (007), *Terminator*, and *Ocean's Eleven* rock to the top. Others like *Wall Street*, *Lord of the Rings*, and *Good Will Hunting* and the comedies

Animal House, Caddyshack, and *Bill & Ted's Excellent Adventure* have been films nominated during the Academy Awards and Oscar ceremonies. The best of the best are recognized for their performance, and the awards are coveted by many.

The film industry began in the 1890s, and the first movies were called silent movies (Filmsite, 2020). The movie itself was shown on screen, but there was no sound matching the actors' and actresses' movement. Although the film was silent, the earliest ones were shown with musicians playing in the theater or someone narrating the story. Technology continued to improve by adding sound, talking, color, and animation. In the 21st century, the industry continues to explore and develop techniques to excite the viewer and create continuous interest. After all, it is a very profitable business.

Going to the movies is a treat, a date night, or can be a special child's event. Children who experience the wonder and magic of *The Polar Express* hold the memory deep into adulthood. The movies have the ability to transform you to another dimension or let you dream and laugh. Historical documentaries can startle, intrigue, or teach you about events in time. Frequently, special cuts are created to give you a glimpse of the making of the movie behind the scenes.

Scenario

Martha was a secretary who worked behind the scenes in the 1980s for Hollywood producer Bruce Shiner. Martha's husband, Hal, was also in the movie business and discovered up and coming actors and actresses. Hal and Martha were friends of my dad, and they frequently had interesting stories about Hollywood when they were over for dinner. Hal was my immediate first choice when I was looking for someone to provide a perspective on women in the film industry. After interviewing him, I was astonished to learn what a woman's role in the workplace was and wondered if a woman's "place" was better before than it is today.

Hal started by saying, "It was a different time. Men did not work with women, and everything was done separately." I wasn't sure if he was apologizing or reflecting with nostalgia.

The Coffee Girl

Hal continued. Secretaries did clerical work, got us (the "men") coffee, typed letters and memos, wrote in shorthand,[1] and answered phones. We called them "girls" as a rule.

When my colleagues and I left the office for lunch, we would sometimes go for the entire afternoon. Lunches were often at a strip club or an elegant restaurant, and sometimes, we drank into early evening. Cell phones didn't exist. Therefore, my secretary had to call the restaurant or get in the car and find us if something important happened. Bruce, Martha's boss and a colleague of mine, wouldn't talk to me about business or look at the menu until his third martini. By then, he was drunk, and that was either a good thing since he would agree to the lead actress I was suggesting, or he would not agree to anything at all. These lunches were a widespread occurrence, never less than three times a week. Work was enjoyable.

Today, my secretary, Yolanda, is called an "administrative assistant." She has the same responsibility for office tasks, but she uses a computer, and she expects me to know how to send her emails and respond to hers. I make changes to Excel spreadsheets and PowerPoint presentations too. I was never taught to type. Therefore, I use the two-finger method, and it takes me a long time to craft a message.

Most of the time, I give up and call Yolanda on the phone or ask her to come by my office. It seems to me that talking to a person is a better way to communicate anyway. There used to be errors upon errors in my emails until my son turned on the "check spelling" feature. He joked this was a good idea, so I would not make an idiot out of myself misspelling a word like "cat."

I would say that my work has increased several-fold from when Bruce and I worked together. I maintain my own calendar and appointments, and Yolanda does NOT get me coffee. She does stop at Starbucks in the morning on her way to the office and brings us coffee. I am grateful, and I pay for both hers and mine.

---

1   "Shorthand is any system of rapid handwriting which can be used to transcribe the spoken word. Shorthand systems use a variety of techniques including simplifying existing letters or characters and using special symbols to represent phonemes, words and phrases" (Omniglot, 2021, para. 1).

High Heels

My wife, Martha, worked for Bruce for 6 years, and he frequently complimented her on how "nice" she looked, which never surprised me. She is a beautiful woman. She and the secretaries always dressed nicely and wore dresses or skirts with heels. Their hair was always done up and never unkempt. The ladies always wore lipstick too. Any man had to be blind not to appreciate how pretty they looked. I thought they just woke up looking that way since Martha did.

I know better now. Martha helped me understand how important it was to portray a certain image. This is true today as well, and the acceptance of women beyond their physical appearance has grown leaps and bounds. I think this is a good thing.

Yolanda, my secretary (I still like using the old word, but I am told it is sexist) always looks nice, but I don't think she has worn a skirt since she started working for me. She looks pretty, but I cannot tell her. Human Resources (HR) scolded me several months ago when I was walking down the hallway. They overheard me telling Yolanda that I liked her hair. She had gotten it cut and colored over the weekend and was showing it off to another secretary. HR said that the "recipient may not be open to your feedback and to refrain from similar comments." Doesn't every woman want to be complimented? I asked Martha, and she told me I could flatter her anytime, just not the ladies in the office.

Another time, I was saying something similar to a writer we had just hired. I caught myself and apologized. Fortunately, she said she appreciated that I noticed, and I was relieved. Frankly, it is very hard to understand this new way of treating women. I do not know when it is OK to talk to them and when it is not. My son, who is a cinematographer, feels the same way I do. He says he sometimes feels it's better to avoid working with women because he is not sure what is acceptable or not.

And what about doors and elevators? Do I open a door for a woman? Do I let her walk into the elevator first? Am I sexist if I do these things, or do I still do them to be polite?

Off Limits

Both Martha and Hal shared there was a lot of "action" at work. Martha was "off limits," but Bruce fraternized with the other "girls" in the office.

It was common for him to court the secretaries. He was not discreet, and Martha often booked dinner and movie dates for Bruce. It created havoc for the work environment. Sometimes in the breakroom, the secretaries' cold shoulders toward one another were beyond frigid. One year, Bruce asked Martha to buy holiday gifts for two secretaries, Samantha and MaryLou. It was perfume. Bruce mixed up the gifts because he got drunk, and that is how they found out that he was cheating on them. Martha had a hard time with these kinds of requests, but she was his secretary, and maintaining his schedule was her job.

Bruce's behavior went beyond dating subordinates. He often told me that he just loved women, loved everything about them. He also believed that they loved him. He was and still is a handsome guy, but that does not mean there is always a "love connection."

Leading ladies were hired and paid by Bruce and his studio. He expected that the actresses attend the many fancy events that promoted the film before production. This is where Bruce got friendly with the women as the liquor flowed.

Once the movie started filming, marketing parties were less frequent. However, it was not uncommon for Bruce to request lunch with an actress to celebrate production milestones. Martha scheduled these too, and the Beverly Hills Grandly Hotel, "The Grandly", was a common location as well as an actress's dressing room on the studio lot. Martha suspected that something "funny" might be going on, but nothing was ever said to her by any actress.

I am sure this stuff happens today and the #MeToo (Dastagir, 2019) movement has brought attention to the mistreatment of women, really any employee in the workplace (Fortin, 2017). Martha and I don't read much about the #Me Too movement these days. I wonder if that is because women's treatment in the workplace has progressed or that the topic has lost significance with the media. Have women's rights and treatment regressed or improved? I do not know, but Martha says things have gotten better.

But I am thinking, everyone is called an "actor" now regardless of their gender. No one uses the word "actress," and I don't understand why or when this change happened. Isn't getting rid of the word, "actress" a negative for the women's movement?

Roses Are Red …

I like to tell a good joke. Let me rephrase, I *liked* to tell a good joke. A guy walks into a bar … STOP!

When I was young, the recognition of class clown went to me. I was proud that I could make people laugh and bring happiness to their day. Nothing made me happier than to watch people cry over a hilarious joke. I was sarcastic, too, and my personality was often incorporated into the punchline. It's how I found my way to the movie business and met Bruce Shiner for the first time. There was an ad in the paper for a comedic writer, and he hired me immediately after I told him a joke about a cowgirl and a horse. (I will skip the joke details for the sake of political correctness.) After the gig was over, he invited Martha and me out for dinner, and that is how she got hired as his secretary.

Often, I would pick up Martha for lunch, and Bruce always asked to hear another joke. His favorite topics were politics, religion, and women—the three topics I avoided unless I was with a small group of guys and never with Martha. I would tell the joke to him in his office. Martha told me that Bruce repeated the joke to everyone, without regard, over the next couple days. She got so angry that she threatened to divorce me if I did not "clean" it up. My problem was Bruce. He expected this performance, and if I stopped, I wondered if Martha's job would be affected. When I asked her, she conceded that things should probably stay the same.

Today, I don't tell jokes at work ever. I started to say "Roses are red, violets are blue…." and my colleague, David, shook his head. It was not a joke, but I saw fear in his expression, anticipating how I would finish the rhyming poem. Last year, he had a sit-down with our boss. The topic was the appropriateness of sending jokes through email, and he was given a warning to stop. I do not recall anything offensive he ever wrote, but his gesture signaled me to "cease and desist." Mine was an impromptu "Roses are red, violets are blue, may I help and carry that for you?" to a lady janitor struggling with a heavy garbage bag. I don't think she would have been insulted had I completed the melody. I am still angry I did not offer her a hand. David assured me that not helping was the "safe" choice. Where is the balance between common courtesy and the risk of offending someone?

Gifts Galore

Gift-giving to my secretary was a common occurrence. It was expected I fund or contribute to her birthday and Christmas gifts and the other secretaries in the office as well. All secretaries were excluded from the Christmas company party (referred to as a holiday party now) just like lunches, and none of us thought anything about it either. Until this day, I do not remember seeing my secretary open her Christmas gift or know what she received. If any of the guys squawked about contributing, they would have been fired. A buddy of mine complained one time, and my boss said, "Don't you have an expense account? Figure it out." To me, that was fraud, but it is what some did to cover their contribution.

Over the last couple of years, gift-giving guidelines have changed. I received a memo from Human Resources this year, which was sent to all employees. It said, "Gift-giving is not acceptable for any employee. However, a holiday card can be given with a small token of appreciation of 10 dollars or less." I do not agree with this, but Martha said it's the thought that counts. She never told me what she received from Bruce, and I never asked either.

What Now?

Hal and Martha have two grandsons, 16 and 17 years old. I asked Hal what advice he will give them as they enter the workforce. In short, he shakes his head and ponders. "The work environment is so different. It is hard to say. But, if there is any question of impropriety, you are always presumed guilty."

Discussion Questions

1. Explain your perspective regarding the shift of women's treatment in the workplace over time.

2. Hal refers to the "girls" and the "men." He switches during his narrative and uses the word "ladies." Do you feel that this substitution demonstrates a positive change in interacting with women or is there still an underlying condescension (or inequity)?

3. As above, analyze how this verbiage may have a different impact if used with a supervisor and a direct report vs. peers at the same level.

4. Discuss why "administrative assistant" is the more accepted term for "secretary" since the role and responsibilities remain the same.

5. Martha sacrifices her ethics because she agrees that Hal should continue telling Bruce jokes even though she is offended. Why would Hal agree to this decision?

6. Hal asks the reader about common courtesy after the incident with the female janitor. What stopped him from helping her?

7. Hal's final comment makes a strong comment about the workplace. Do you agree or disagree with him? Why?

8. Share your opinion of how you can play a role in changing societal norms that you believe are unacceptable regardless of gender.

Assignments

1. Describe a conversation you have heard between a supervisor and their direct report (differing gender) or that you have personally experienced which you felt was inappropriate or offensive. Offer a better version of the interaction.

2. Discuss how employers manage appropriate content for joke-telling. Secondly, discuss how it is monitored through emails on the company server.

3. Write a summary of your work environment. Explain your views of the treatment of women. Identify changes that you believe should be made and why.

Additional Learning

- *Mad Men*, a popular television series (2007–2015), is about Don Draper, an executive for an advertising agency in the 1960s. Watch the first three episodes (https://www.imdb.com/title/tt0804503/) and compare Don Draper's 1960 experience to Hal's 1980 and present-day experience.

References

Covert, B. (2017, September 2). The best era for working women was 20 years ago. *The New York Times.* https://www.nytimes.com/2017/09/02/opinion/sunday/working-women-decline-1990s.html

Dastagir, A. (2019, October 28). It's been two years since the #MeToo movement exploded. Now what? *USA Today*.https://www.usatoday.com/story/news/nation/2019/09/30/me-too-movement-women-sexual-assault-harvey-weinstein-brett-kavanaugh/1966463001/

Filmsite (2020). Silent films. https://www.filmsite.org/silentfilms.html

Fortin, J. (2017, October 10). The women who have accused Harvey Weinstein. *New York Times*. https://www.nytimes.com/2017/10/10/us/harvey-weinstein-accusations.html

Guilder, G. (1986). Women in the work force. *The Atlantic*. https://www.theatlantic.com/magazine/archive/1986/09/women-in-the-work-force/304924/

Hauser, S. (2012). The women's movement in the '70s, today: "You've come a long way, but".... Workforce.com. https://www.workforce.com/news/the-womens-movement-in-the-70s-today-youve-come-a-long-way-but

IMDb. (2021). *Mad men*. https://www.imdb.com/title/tt0804503/

Omniglot. (2021). Shorthand. https://omniglot.com/writing/shorthand.htm

Smith, A. (2018, February 16). How to accommodate "gender-nonbinary" individuals—neither men nor women. Society for Human Resource Management. https://www.shrm.org/resourcesandtools/legal-and-compliance/employment-law/pages/gender-nonbinary-individuals.aspx

U.S. Bureau of Labor Statistics. (2003, October). Women at work: A visual essay. *Monthly Labor Review*. https://www.bls.gov/opub/mlr/2003/10/ressum3.pdf

Zambron, V. (2020, November 5). What are some different types of gender identity? *Medical News Today*. https://www.medicalnewstoday.com/articles/types-of-gender-identity#types-of-gender-identity

Equality, Inclusion, and Diversity

3

TIMELINE OF IMPORTANT EEOC EVENTS

1963	Congress passes the Equal Pay Act of 1963, which protects men and women who perform substantially equal work in the same establishment from sex-based wage discrimination. The Department of Labor is given authority to enforce the new law.

1963
Congress passes the Equal Pay Act of 1963, which protects men and women who perform substantially equal work in the same establishment from sex-based wage discrimination. The Department of Labor is given authority to enforce the new law.

1964
President Lyndon B. Johnson signs into law the Civil Rights Act of 1964. One section of the Act, referred to as Title VII, prohibits employment discrimination based on race, sex, color, religion, and national origin. The Act applies to private employers, labor unions, and employment agencies. The Act also creates the Equal Employment Opportunity Commission (EEOC) to enforce Title VII and eliminate unlawful employment discrimination.

1965
EEOC opens its doors for business on July 2, 1965—one year after Title VII becomes a law. EEOC has a budget of $2.25 million and approximately 100 employees.

1966
EEOC opens its first field office in Dallas, Texas. By year's end, the office is relocated to Austin, Texas. Three other field offices open this year—Atlanta, Chicago, and Cleveland.

1967
Congress passes the Age Discrimination in Employment Act of 1967 (ADEA) protecting individuals who are between 40 and 65 years of age from discrimination in employment. Originally, the Department of Labor—not the EEOC—has enforcement responsibility.

1968
Although EEOC cannot file lawsuits directly against employers, the agency begins to submit amicus or "friend of the court" briefs in cases brought by individual employees.

1972
Congress gives EEOC the authority to file lawsuits against private companies. It also applies Title VII to the entire federal government and to all state and local government agencies with at least 15 employees.

1973
Congress passes the Rehabilitation Act of 1973. Section 501 prohibits the federal government from discriminating against qualified individuals with disabilities.

1978
Congress amends Title VII by passing the Pregnancy Discrimination Act of 1978 to make clear that discrimination based on pregnancy is unlawful sex discrimination. In the same year, President Jimmy Carter transfers responsibility for enforcing the Equal Pay Act and the Age Discrimination in Employment Act from the Department of Labor to EEOC.

1990
President George H. W. Bush signs into law the Americans with Disabilities Act of 1990 (ADA). EEOC is given responsibility for enforcing Title I of the ADA which prohibits private employers, state and local governments, unions, and employment agencies from discriminating against people with disabilities in employment. Title I does not become effective until 2 years after the president signs the bill (July 26, 1992).

U.S. Equal Employment Opportunity Commission, "Timeline of Important EEOC events," *Youth at Work*.

1991
Congress passes the Civil Rights Act of 1991 (CRA) to overrule several decisions by the United States Supreme Court that had made it more difficult for employees to prevail in job discrimination lawsuits. The Act gives employees the right to request a jury trial in Title VII and ADA lawsuits and allows successful plaintiffs to recover compensatory and punitive damages in intentional employment discrimination cases under Title VII and the ADA. The CRA also expands Title VII's protections to include congressional and high-level political appointees.
2008
President George W. Bush signs into law the Genetic Information Nondiscrimination Act of 2008. EEOC is given authority to enforce Title II of the Act, which prohibits employment discrimination based on genetic information. President George W. Bush signs into law the Americans with Disabilities Act Amendments Act of 2008. The Act makes important changes to the definition of the term "disability" that make it easier for a person to establish that they have a medical condition covered by the ADA, as amended.
2009
President Barack H. Obama signs into law the Lilly Ledbetter Fair Pay Act of 2009. The Act addresses when pay discrimination charges can be filed with EEOC. This Act was the first bill signed into law by President Obama.

Reference

U.S. Equal Employment Opportunity Commission. (n.d.) Timeline of important EEOC events. https://www.eeoc.gov/youth/

timeline-important-eeoc-events

My Grandma's Diary

Overview

This case takes place during WWII and involves a young woman by the name of Esther Morgan. As an infant, Esther is abandoned at an orphanage in Alabama and raised by the members of a religious charity. In 1941, at the age of 20, Esther enlists in the U.S. Army Nurse Corps (AN or ANC). When asked about her race on the application, she indicates she is a Caucasian woman. However, due to an unusual series of events, she learned that information might not be the truth.

Objectives

- Explain the racial inequity in the workplace in the 1940s.
- Describe the Civil Rights Act of 1964 (Title VII), its reason for existence, and its impact on today's work environment.
- Define and distinguish the terms "equity" and "inclusion" as they apply to work.
- Explain the difference between cultural appropriation and racial identity.

Key Concepts and Words

cultural appropriation, diversity, equity and inclusion (DEI), racial and ethnic segregation of occupations, racial discrimination, racial identity, Title VII of the Civil Rights Act of 1964

THE CIVIL RIGHTS ACT

"Title VII of the Civil Rights Act of 1964 protects individuals against employment discrimination on the basis of race and color as well as national origin, sex, or religion.

It is unlawful to discriminate against any employee or applicant for employment because of race or color in regard to hiring, termination, promotion, compensation, job training, or any other term, condition, or privilege of employment. Title VII also prohibits employment decisions based on stereotypes and assumptions about abilities, traits, or the performance of individuals of certain racial groups.

Title VII prohibits both intentional discrimination and neutral job policies that disproportionately exclude minorities and that are not job related.

Equal employment opportunity cannot be denied because of marriage to or association with an individual of a different race; membership in or association with ethnic based organizations or groups; attendance or participation in schools or places of worship generally associated with certain minority groups; or other cultural practices or characteristics often linked to race or ethnicity, such as cultural dress or manner of speech, as long as the cultural practice or characteristic does not materially interfere with the ability to perform job duties." (EEOC, 2021, para. 1)

Scenario

Part 1: The Diary

I loved my Grandma Esther. She raised my three brothers and me. My parents were killed in a car accident when I was 5 years old, and Grandma and Gramps took over as our parents. It was always just the six of us (Grandma, Gramps, my brothers, and me) since my mother was an only child. Gramps died when I was 25, and Grandma passed away this year. Amazingly, she was 98 years old and "as sharp as a tack," she would often say.

My name is Anna. As the oldest, I handled Grandma's estate, such as making arrangements for her funeral and selling her house. When I was cleaning out her things, I came across a diary she had written. She wrote it while she was a nurse with the U.S. Army Nurse Corps in World War II and stationed overseas. She never mentioned the diary or much about her WWII experiences. I know that is not unusual with veterans, but I was curious what I might read.

Before I opened it, I smiled, remembering what a good woman Grandma Esther was. She gave her heart and soul to us and worked as a nurse into her 60s. I looked again at the old, worn book and thought about the experiences that journal might hold. I hesitated and wondered if it was meant to be found. After all, it was hidden underneath a box of old photos and tied with a perfect bow of string. I thought and thought. Then I opened it and started reading.

I read the entire diary. Not only did I learn about the horrors of war, but I uncovered some surprising information about myself that I am still trying to reconcile. I think I know why she did it, but now I feel confused inside.

Part 2: Esther's Beginnings

As a newborn, Esther was abandoned and left at the Alabama Orphanage and Maternity Home in Grassy Lake, Alabama, run by a community of Catholic religious sisters. When she was a young child, Esther was befriended by one of the sisters by the name of Sister Mary. Sister Mary was like a mother to Grandma Esther, and she was a patient and loving woman. I believe it was one of the reasons Grandma was so caring and giving. Two weeks before Grandma's 18th birthday, Sister Mary became deathly ill. Grandma stayed at her bedside and took care of her day and night. On the eve of Esther's 18th birthday, Sister Mary told her she had something important to give to her. Esther was told to go into the bottom drawer of her bureau and find a small package with a few photos tied together. Then she asked her to open the package and take out a piece of paper written in pencil. Esther opened it slowly with some trepidation. It was difficult to read but said:

> *My dearest baby daughter Esther,*
>
> *I am so sorry I cannot be with you today, but I know you are now a beautiful and loving woman. Eighteen years ago, I left you in good care with Sister Mary. I am very sad I could not keep you. You see, I was a farmworker and orphan myself and became pregnant by a neighbor boy. I was so ashamed. Then I met Sister Mary when she was distributing food and water to the workers in the fields. She saw me praying and she was kind to me. She let me live*

at the orphanage when I was pregnant, and I helped the cook make meals for the children.

When you were born, I gave you to Sister Mary to keep. I had no way to take care of you.

Please forgive me.

Love always,

Your Mamma Evelyn

Grandma Esther wrote in her diary that when she read the letter she cried and cried. Sister Mary explained that her mother (my great-grandmother Evelyn), desperately wanted to keep her. However, she was incredibly young, had no family, no money, and no place to live permanently.

Esther asked Sister Mary about her father. She said she had met him once, and he was a gentle man. He was the son of the local preacher, and then Sister Mary handed Grandma a picture of her father (my great-grandfather). He was a handsome man too. Esther looked again at the photo and quizzed Sister Mary. "Yes," said Sister Mary. "Your father was a fair-skinned African American man. And your mother too." Sister Mary died 3 hours after she gave Grandma the letter.

I stopped. I took a deep breath. Did I read what I just read? African American woman? Wait ... Grandma looked white. I was white. We are white. Now I am reading my great-grandma was of a different race. I tried to catch my breath. Who am I? What am I? Does it matter?

Part 3: Esther's Career Decision

When World War II started in September 1939, Grandma Esther was 18 and ready to go out on her own. She was a kind and nurturing person, and she often helped take care of the younger children at the orphanage. She loved feeding and bathing the babies, and she would cuddle, hold, and rock them for hours at a time. From the age of 12, Esther dreamed of being a nurse. When she left the orphanage, she got a job taking care of an older woman in the local town.

In December of 1941, when the Japanese bombed Pearl Harbor, the need for nurses soared, and Esther saw her opportunity to enlist in the Army Nurse Corps. She wanted to leave the South, travel the world, and thought the Army was the way. It was. She was trained in nursing procedures and specialized in the care of severely wounded soldiers with head injuries.

At that time, all branches of the U.S military were segregated (Delmont, 2017). WWII nurses were assigned duties and patients based on their race. African American nurses were allowed to care only for African American service members (in segregated Army hospital wards in the South). However, they were also assigned to look after the Italian and German POW prisoners held in the U.S. camps in places such as Arizona (Clark, 2018). These POW medical camps were the worst assignments. The nurses often experienced harassment and verbal abuse from the German POWs as their cruelty was a part of the Nazi indoctrination (Clark, 2018). The African American nurses hated these assignments. Because they were not helping American servicemen, it felt like the U.S. government was being disloyal to them (Clark, 2018). These women also lived in segregated quarters, and often, the African American nursing officers were refused salutes by male officers, both black and white. (PBS, n.d.). Esther had heard the religious sisters talking about the African American nurses at the orphanage. She prayed with them for their strength. Esther agreed the treatment those nurses endured was terrible.

After Sister Mary died, Esther grew to understand that "as a white woman," she did not experience the discrimination and segregation that many blacks in her Alabama community did. For instance, as a young teen, she would sit at the front of the bus with the white folks, while black riders had to sit in the back. She would use the "white only" bathrooms at the local department store and drink at "white only" water fountains. No one ever challenged her. After all, she looked like a Caucasian teenager.

The life experienced by dark-skinned Americans made Esther sad, but she wasn't exposed to it much. She spent most of her time at the orphanage, and everybody did chores, ate meals, and sang songs together.

When it became time to meet the Army recruiter and fill out paperwork for enlistment, Esther told the recruiter she didn't have a birth certificate (a lie), but she had a religious record from the orphanage. He accepted the paper, which made no mention of her race. When she had to complete the application, there were only three choices of race (White, African American, or Native American). Esther's skin coloring was light in color, she had blue/green eyes, and she was socially treated as white. Even though she now knew she was African American, she listed her race as white on the application.

She likened her decision to those who lied about their age to join the service. What difference did it really matter, she rationalized to herself. She looked Caucasian, always identified as a white person, and was going to accomplish her dream of becoming a nurse to help many soldiers. However, she was a bit afraid that someone would find out that she had not been truthful. What would Sister Mary think?

Grandma Esther had a long career in the Army, rose through the ranks, and was nominated to lead the European Nursing Corp in England as her first overseas assignment. Her best friend, Deborah, was a Lieutenant Colonel in the Corp and part of the committee who selected her for the promotion. She was grateful to Deborah for her mentorship.

Esther was sent to North Africa during the Rommel campaign and worked with General Bradley. Her next transfer was to Sicily where she worked as an operating room nurse. When she returned to the States, she became an administrator at Walter Reed National Military Medical Center in Washington, DC. She was bestowed with the rank of Colonel for her exceptional leadership of the entire nursing unit.

She was a fabulous nurse, but her lie haunted her daily. What if someone found out? Would she be court-martialed? Would she have to spend time in prison?

Part 4: Life Before Title VII

While at Walter Reed, she met my grandfather, James Alexander. He was a captain in the Army who suffered severe war injuries. For his bravery, he received two Purple Hearts and a Bronze Star. He was at Walter Reed for over a year, 6 months recovering from injuries and 9 months in the psychiatric ward. While he was recovering from injuries, Esther would often take him outside for fresh air on the grounds. It was there that she fell in love with him. It started with an affair that was inappropriate for many reasons. First, Esther had a higher rank than James. That was an Army fraternization violation. Second, nurses were not allowed to have a relationship with a patient.

In mid-1947, Esther left the Army. The need for nurses was dramatically reduced because the war had ended 2 years earlier. Esther and James married 3 months later after he was released from the hospital with an honorable discharge. My grandmother Esther eventually got a master's degree in nursing from

Johns Hopkins University and continued to work in the field. When my parents died, she retired at age 62 to take care of my brothers and me.

But Esther was not the only nurse with a secret romance during the war. In her diary was a newspaper article from *Stars and Stripes,* the military newspaper. The clipping was about an African American nurse, Bessie Fields. While an Army nurse, Bessie had an affair with a patient named Gunther Müller, a German POW, who was white[1]. She secretly married the POW right after his discharge from the hospital and prior to him being sent to a European prison. Bessie received a dishonorable discharge from the Army for the affair when the Army discovered the relationship. Her offense was that her relationship was not only with a patient, but it was with someone who was the "enemy." What Esther did was no different than Bessie, yet Esther lived a good life, while Bessie forever had a scarlet letter on her face.[2]

Esther constantly felt guilty about lying on the application, but she was able to see and travel the world. She would never have been able to rise through the ranks had she not "passed"[3] as a white woman. She experienced discrimination during wartime (and many females still do in the military), but this was gender and not racially based.

There was one final secret revealed in my grandma Esther's diary. My grandfather James was white, born and raised in Virginia, and she never told him she was an African American woman. Since the late 1600s in Virginia, interracial couples were not allowed to get married, and anti-miscegenation laws outlawing racial intermarriage existed in many states. This was eventually changed in 1967 by the U.S. Supreme Court in the case of *Virginia v. Loving*, but when Grandma and Gramps were married in Virginia, their marriage, unbeknownst to Gramps, was illegal. Grandma never told Gramps she was of mixed blood. She lied again and said her family had died in a barn fire before she joined the military. My blue-eyed mom, Ellie, was born into a white, middle-class family, as was I and my brothers, and there was no reason anyone thought differently. Grandma kept the secret of her heritage to her death. She referenced her guilt over and over again in her writings. She lied to the Army, she lied to my Gramps, and she lied to the world.

---

1   This is based on actual events during WWII, with Elinor Powell a, black Army nurse and a white German POW.

2   A scarlet letter applies to a symbol of shame, as used in the classic novel *The Scarlet Letter* by famed author Nathaniel Hawthorne.

3   Passing refers to a person representing themselves to being a different race or having a different ethnic background.

Part 5: My Life

Today, I know there is the Civil Rights Act to protect individuals from discrimination and poor treatment. Yet, the media report mistreatment of individuals from all walks of life for many reasons. And, now I am experiencing the same decision my grandmother, Esther, had to make over 80 years ago.

Ironically, I am applying for a new job, and the application asks to input race. After I read Grandma's journal, I had a DNA test that confirmed what I learned. An option for race is "other," but I am conflicted. I have identified as white all my life, but now I know I am a different race and proud to be either. It doesn't change who I am inside, and it doesn't matter to me. It may to the world, but that is not important.

Discussion Questions

1. How do you define race? Is it genetic-based, identity-based, or determined by social context (Albuja, Sanchez, & Gather, 2018)?

2. The case study takes place in a different time and age. As you have read, Esther had been told her parents were African American. Using the 1940s as a timeframe, did Grandma Esther lie on her application? Did she compromise her position in the Nursing Corps during World War II?

3. Is there ever a justification to lie on a job application or during an interview?

4. Do you think the impetus for Esther saying she was Caucasian, when there was evidence of African American ancestry, was to avoid the sharply segmented racial division in the Army? Or was it something else?

5. Discuss the Civil Rights Act of 1964 (Title VII), its reason for existence, and its impact on today's work environment. See https://www.eeoc.gov/prohibited-employment-policiespractices for more information.

Assignments

1. In 2020, Jessica A. Krug, an associate professor at George Washington University, who was an expert on Africa, Latin America, the diaspora, and identity, confessed she was White and not Black-Latina. She resigned from her position at George Washington University. Should she have resigned? Or is an apology of her cultural misappropriation of a Black Caribbean identity enough? In other words, on a scale of 1 to 10, what type of lie is this? Is it similar to lying about a criminal record on a job application?

2. Federal and state laws have identified certain questions that are illegal and cannot be asked by a prospective employer. These include age, race, ethnicity or color, gender or sex, country of national origin or birthplace, religion, disability, marital or family status, or pregnancy. (See https://www.eeoc.gov/prohibited-employment-policiespractices). Have you ever been asked an illegal question in an interview? If so, how did you handle it? Did you answer the question?

3. The U.S. Census Bureau (2018), in its 2020 questionnaire, asks a person to identify their race. "(C)urrent race categories 'reflect a social definition of race … not an attempt to define race biologically, anthropologically, or genetically.'" (p. 11) Possible answers now include "White; Black or African American; American Indian or Alaska Native; Chinese; Filipino; Asian Indian; Vietnamese; Korean; Japanese; other Asian; Native Hawaiian; Samoan; Chamorro; other Pacific Islander; some other race" (United States Census 2020, para. 6). However, when it comes to gender, the question asks the respondent to identify their sex. The choices are male or female and do not account for someone's sexuality, presentation, or gender. If you worked for the U.S. Census Bureau, would you rewrite the question? If so, what changes would you make and why?

References

Albuja, A., Sanchez, D., & Gaither, S. (2018). Fluid racial presentation: Perceptions of contextual "passing" among biracial people. *Journal of Experimental Social Psychology, 77*(7), 132–142. https://doi.org/10.1016/j.jesp.2018.04.010

Bates, K. (2018, May 27). What happens when two enemies fall in love? PBS. Retrieved from https://www.npr.org/sections/codeswitch/2018/05/27/555619978/what-happens-when-two-enemies-fall-in-love

Clark, A. (2018, February 15). The Army's first Black nurses were relegated to caring for Nazi prisoners of war. *Smithsonian Magazine.* https://www.smithsonianmag.com/history/armys-first-black-nurses-had-tend-to-german-prisoners-war-180969069/

Commegna, P. (2020, February 19). Changing race and ethnicity questions on the U.S. census form reflect evolving views. Population Reference Bureau. https://www.prb.org/changing-race-and-ethnicity-questions-on-the-u-s-census-form-reflect-evolving-views/

Delmont, M. (2017, August 24). Why African-American soldiers saw World War II as a two-front battle. *Smithsonian Magazine.* https://www.smithsonianmag.com/history/why-african-american-soldiers-saw-world-war-ii-two-front-battle-180964616/

Eligon, J. (2020, June 26). A debate over identity and race asks, are African-Americans "Black" or "black"? *New York Times.* https://www.nytimes.com/2020/06/26/us/black-african-0american-style-debate.html

Felicianco, A., & Green, Z. (2018, June 17). "They didn't let racism win"—The story of an interracial couple on opposite sides of WWII. Transcript. PBS News Hour Weekend. https://www.pbs.org/newshour/show/they-didnt-let-racism-win-the-story-of-an-interracial-couple-on-opposite-sides-of-wwii

Harvey Mudd College. (n.d.). EEOC guide to pre-employment inquiries. https://www.hmc.edu/human-resources/wp-content/uploads/sites/23/2014/04/EEOC-Guide-to-Pre-Employment-Inquiries.pdf

Kesler, J. (2012). Military nurse ranks. *Military Nurse*. https://www.military-nurse.com/military-nurse-ranks.html

Linge, M. (2018, May 19). Army nurse and Nazi POW. *New York Post*. https://nypost.com/2018/05/19/the-secret-romance-of-a-black-army-nurse-and-nazi-pow/

National Women's History Museum. (2019). African American nurses in World War II. https://www.womenshistory.org/articles/african-american-nurses-world-war-ii#:~:text=Although%20African%20American%20nurses%20were,Army%20Nurse%20Corps%20(ANC).&text=April%201941%2C%20forty%2Deight%20African,nurses%20were%20assigned%20to%20camps

PBS American Experience. (n.d.). Battle of the Bulge. Nurses' tales. https://www.pbs.org/wgbh/americanexperience/features/bulge-nurse/

PBS American Experience. (n.d.). Race and the Army during World War II. https://www.pbs.org/wgbh/americanexperience/features/alaska-WWII/

U.S. Army Center of Military History. (2003). The Army Nurse Corps. CMH Pub 72-14. https://history.army.mil/books/wwii/72-14/72-14.HTM#:~:text=The%20Army%20Nurse%20Corps%20accepted,the%20number%20of%20black%20enrollments.

U.S. Census Bureau (2018). Questions planned for the 2020 census and American community survey. https://www2.census.gov/library/publications/decennial/2020/operations/planned-questions-2020-acs.pdf

U.S. Equal Opportunity Employment Commission. (2021). Facts about race/color discrimination. https://www.eeoc.gov/laws/guidance/facts-about-racecolor-discrimination

United States Census 2020. (2020). Questions asked on the form. https://2020census.gov/en/about-questions.html?cid=23759:us%20census%20questions:sem.ga:p:dm:en:&utm_source=sem.ga&utm_medium=p&utm_campaign=dm:en&utm_content=23759&utm_term=us%20census%20questions

Ward, M. (2020, November 19). An anti-racist's dictionary: 19 words on race, gender, and diversity you should know. *Business Insider*. https://www.businessinsider.com/words-on-race-gender-and-diversity-you-should-know-2020-7

Invisible Manager

Workhorse or Glass Ceiling?

By Dorothy McAllen

Overview

This study focuses on Lena, a manager in a large federal agency, the ABC Agency. Lena was promoted to her management position 2 years ago. While she mainly supervised 43 highly trained investigators, her boss has limited Lena's work to administrative duties, such as processing paperwork, drafting policies, and reviewing reports. Others at ABC Agency, all male, have been invited to participate in activities where they collaborate and network with other executives both inside and outside the organization.

Lena is now seeking to be promoted to an executive level in the organization; however, she believes she is hampered by her restrictive duties, lack of opportunity to collaborate with others in the agency, and her absence at executive events.

Objectives

- Outline the differences between the "concrete" and "glass ceiling."
- Explain how a manager can limit a person's job mobility based on the supervisor's definition of gender roles and personal biases.
- Define old-fashion sexism and its impact on an employee's career path and workplace environment.
- Define the elements to support a hostile work environment complaint.
- Identify the steps an employee should take to pursue a complaint about an unequal or hostile work environment.

Key Concepts and Words

age discrimination, concrete ceiling, gender differences, gender roles, gender stereotypes, glass ceiling, hostile work environment, modern sexism, networking, old-fashioned sexism

GLASS CEILING

"The term 'glass ceiling' is generally used to refer to instances where women and minorities have progressed within a firm but, despite their ambitions and qualifications, find it difficult to make the movement into key higher level management positions, or management positions at all" (EEOC, 2004, para. 1). "But the glass ceiling and the concrete ceiling, as its termed for women of color, are still in place" (Tan, 2016, para. 1).

Scenario

The ABC Agency is a large federal organization with approximately 10,000 employees specializing in certain areas of investigative expertise. An additional 800 clerical employees also work for the organization. Due to its historical hiring practices, there are only 253 female special investigators, or approximately 2.5%, in the entire organization.

Lena is a 45-year-old federal government employee who has worked for the ABC Agency for 18 years. She began working for the organization after graduating from college with a B.S. in business administration. While working full time and attending school part time, she obtained her M.B.A. in 5 years. Lena applied to the ABC Agency because of the challenging nature of the work, the variety of tasks, and due to its size and scope, the room for advancement within the organization.

Lena was one of the first women to be hired by the organization and soon realized that many men were uncomfortable with females "joining their ranks." Lena excelled in her various assignments, earning high marks on her performance reviews and receiving positive feedback from her managers. Despite the resentment of some male colleagues, Lena was respected by most of her coworkers, collaborated well and was selected to lead many group projects. In her first 10 years with ABC Agency, she received two commendations for outstanding work. She was also promoted twice to supervisory positions based on her experience in the organization, promotional exam scores, performance reviews, and recommendations by her managers.

Two and a half years ago, Lena was promoted to a senior management position to head up a group of 43 highly specialized investigators. She was the first woman to achieve this management level in the organization. Her promotion was based on seniority, previous work evaluations, and an interview process. Lena was confident in her ability to handle the job. Because her promotion was history-making for ABC, and it was a role highly sought after by many top candidates, she began her new position with a mixture of fear, trepidation, and excitement.

She met the investigators she would manage and her new boss, Richard, whom she previously knew just in passing. During her first week as a manager, Lena scheduled a meeting with Richard, and they reviewed her job responsibilities and expectations. Richard advised Lena of the standards to oversee 43 investigators' work to ensure all tasks were completed in a comprehensive and professional manner. He also expected Lena to keep him abreast of all activities weekly through email. If necessary, she was told to contact him immediately by telephone or text if there was an emergency or a particularly worrisome incident. Richard oversaw four other senior managers, and they all met at his biweekly staff meeting to update each other on their group's activities. Lena was collegial with her peers and interacted with them only at her boss's meeting.

Lena's group conducted excellent investigations, and she submitted the results of their work in a written memo, which she assumed, Richard shared with others in the organization. Richard also gave Lena the duty of updating the policies and procedures for all of his managers to make certain they were correct, compliant, and up-to-date.

At the end of her first year in the senior role, Lena received a written performance review indicating that she "met" or "exceeded" expectations in six of 10 areas of the evaluation. She was disappointed with the ratings. She felt she deserved the highest rating in eight areas and was transparent in telling Richard. He told her he was pleased with her overall work and to keep working diligently this next year. He reinforced her responsibilities to manage her investigators and guarantee the accuracy and timely submission of documents. Because of her stellar work on the policies and procedures, Richard delegated his own assignment to update the investigation protocol manuals for the entire investigative division to Lena. This included all the employees of his five senior managers, a total of 317 people.

During the second year, Lena continued to manage her investigators and completed the projects assigned to her; however, she noticed a change in the activity of Richard and his other four senior managers. At least once or twice a week, she saw Richard and her four colleagues leaving the office together. Lena observed that Richard included them, but not her, in various executive meetings or briefings. Some interactions were with ABC Agency executives, and other meetings included high-level officials from government or private sector agencies. Lena also discovered that her peers were accompanying him to luncheons and receptions. On at least three occasions, the four senior managers were invited to participate in golf outings sponsored by private companies working with ABC.

Lena felt she had a good relationship with Richard but was included only in the biweekly staff meeting. She found herself increasingly "in the dark" when Richard and the other managers discussed cases. These conversations were a "follow-up" from these frequent outside meetings and gatherings. Recognizing this trend, Lena wondered if this was intentional and personal. Was there a professional reason she was excluded from these important group activities? Lena knew she needed to speak with Richard to understand this behavior.

Lena also had hoped to apply for a promotion to an executive position in ABC Agency where she would oversee multiple managers, similar to Richard's role. She knew at least one other senior manager who worked for Richard would apply for the same executive position. She was excited about the opportunity, and she felt initially, she had the competitive edge over her colleague based on her past and current performance.

However, Lena realized that while she was knowledgeable about what was occurring within her team, she had been isolated from the rest of the associates in ABC Agency for the past 2 years. Besides overseeing her employees, her other responsibilities consisted of the administrative projects she completed on Richard's behalf. She had not been networking either and was unaware of the inner workings elsewhere in the organization. Also, she suspected that the ABC senior leadership team was familiar with her activities only through the written reports she submitted to Richard. She concluded she was an "invisible" manager.

Lena asked for a conference with Richard and shared her concerns. She communicated that she felt excluded from important meetings and social gatherings. Because of this, she could not make contacts with a wide variety of people both within and outside of the Agency. She was uninformed about events taking place or planned, and she wasn't able to participate in relevant discussions regarding active cases. Lena shared she was denied the opportunity for others to view her in different settings. She had not been speaking with other managers either about her cases and suspected that executive leadership did not know her beyond written reports. This was important because the same individuals would be on the interview panel for promotions.

Richard advised Lena that her duties were clearly laid out in her job description and that these other activities were not a part of the role. Who he invited to meetings was at his discretion. He further stated that he didn't think she should pursue the executive promotion because it was more stressful and required many additional hours of work. He felt she was at the highest level a woman had ever reached in ABC Agency. At her age, she should be proud of what she accomplished and be content to do a good job as a manager. Lena was appalled by his sexist and outdated view. Was he really suggesting she should be satisfied remaining in her current role because she was a woman?

Lena applied for the executive director position. However, it was awarded to the other senior manager in Richard's group. Lena now believed she was purposely not included in important meetings and events, relegated to only administrative duties, and these actions directly affected her ability to obtain the promotion.

Discussion Questions

1. Review the definitions of glass and concrete ceiling. Has Lena "hit a glass ceiling" in the ABC Agency? Why or why not? How does a "glass ceiling" compare to a "concrete ceiling"?

2. For the first time in history, the United States elected a female vice president who is both an African American and South Asian American woman.

   a. Are the terms "glass ceiling" and "concrete ceiling" applicable in light of the 2020 election results?

   b. Are the two terms generational (i.e., used by baby boomers) and outdated?

   c. Do you believe ceilings exist today in the workforce? Support your opinion within your discussion group.

3. Lena told Richard about her interest in applying for another position at ABC. Was that a mistake? Why or why not? Do you believe an employee is obligated to tell their supervisor about applying for another position in the Agency?

4. If you were Lena's manager, what criteria would you use to give her "permission" to move on to another role? Did she earn the right to be promoted?

5. Richard appears to have made certain assumptions about the role of female employees in the ABC Agency.

    a. Describe what roles he felt were appropriate for male and female employees.

    b. Does Richard stereotype Lena's competency based on her gender?

    c. Has he made any assumptions about her emotional, psychological, or physical traits to succeed?

    d. Define the word, sexist. Do you believe Richard was sexist?

6. Richard refers to Lena's age as a barrier to promotion. Is this comment alone sufficient to pursue a complaint on age discrimination? Or, is this a gender stereotype (meaning that women cannot handle the stress in certain types of jobs)?

7. In Lena's meeting with Richard, he alluded to the job duties listed on the position description. Does this list of job duties protect Richard's actions if they don't include language or actions that might apply to these outside meetings or events?

8. Networking is an asset in many corporations because being selected for promotion often involves other people beyond the hiring person.

    a. Did Richard have an obligation to include Lena in outside meetings or events?

    b. What steps should she have taken with Richard after sensing she had not been given the same opportunities for networking as her male colleagues?

    c. What could Lena have done differently to ensure she would be included?

9. Do you think its coincidental that she schedules a meeting with Richard at the same time of the promotion? For example, was she accepting of the exclusion behavior until it impacted her career?

HOSTILE WORK ENVIRONMENT

A hostile work environment is a type of work harassment. "Harassment is a form of employment discrimination that violates Title VII of the Civil Rights Act of 1964, the Age Discrimination in Employment Act of 1967, (ADEA), and the Americans with Disabilities Act of 1990, (ADA). Harassment is unwelcome conduct that is based on race, color, religion, sex (including pregnancy), national origin, age (40 or older), disability or genetic information. Harassment becomes unlawful where 1) enduring the offensive conduct becomes a condition of continued employment, or 2) the conduct is severe or pervasive enough to create a work environment that a reasonable person would consider intimidating, hostile, or abusive." (EEOC, 2020, para. 2)

"Petty slights, annoyances, and isolated incidents (unless extremely serious) will not rise to the level of illegality. To be unlawful, the conduct must create a work environment that would be intimidating, hostile, or offensive to reasonable people." (EEOC, 2020, para. 3)

"Offensive conduct may include, but is not limited to, offensive jokes, slurs, epithets or name calling, physical assaults or threats, intimidation, ridicule or mockery, insults or put-downs, offensive objects or pictures, and interference with work performance." (EEOC, 2020, para. 4)

10. If you were Lena, would you describe the work environment as hostile or a job with normal challenges? (Refer to the definition above for Hostile Work Environment.)

Assignments

1. Who is Roz Brewer, and what barriers in business has she overcome? See https://www.forbes.com/sites/ maggiemcgrath/2021/01/28/breaking-the-concrete-ceiling-roz-brewer-to-be-the-sps-only-black-female-ceo/?sh=7edebb19667b.

2. Define and distinguish these three terms: gender differences, gender roles, and gender stereotypes. Provide an example of each of these terms not previously reviewed in the discussion questions.

3. Does Lena have the basis to file a complaint for a "hostile work environment"? Why or why not? What information is missing from the scenario that would help determine whether Lena has a hostile work environment case? Use this link to the U.S. Department of Labor web page to assist you in answering this question: https://www. dol.gov/agencies/oasam/centers-offices/civil-rights-center/internal/policies/workplace-harassment/2012.

4. Using the link provided in Question 3, has Lena satisfied a basis for notifying her department about her complaint? Can Lena file a complaint in state and/or federal court before exhausting the agency's internal process for filing complaints?

5. Analyze the case study and identify what actions, words, or conduct comprise the totality of elements needed to support a formal complaint for unequal treatment.

6. Lena announced her desire for an executive position which would make her an "equal" to Richard. He responded negatively and was not supportive. Your assignment is to respond to Richard in a professional way to his advice (agreeing or objecting). In crafting your response, use the acronym SOAR (Stop, Oxygenate, Analyze, Respond). You can find an expanded definition of this acronym (SOAR, n.d.) with a quick Internet search. Do you believe his advice was sincere, and he was looking out for her best interest?

7. In cases of discrimination or creating a hostile work environment, rarely is there one specific incident that is the "smoking gun" or the proof needed to support the allegations. Rather, these types of cases are usually supported by the totality of the situation or circumstances. This includes the actions, words, conduct, or lack of action on the part of the players involved. Carefully review the case study. Complete the following chart by identifying the actions, words, conduct, or lack of action that would support Lena's complaint of a hostile work environment. Also include the players involved in those actions.

TABLE 3.1   SUMMARY OF LENA'S HOSTILE WORK ENVIRONMENT

Incident	Describe the action, words, conduct, or lack of action	Player(s) involved	How does this incident support a hostile work environment?

8. One of the elements necessary for showing a hostile work environment is that the hostility must seriously disrupt the employee's work, such as an employee's career progression. In this case study, list the elements that Lena could use to support her assertion that her boss interfered with her career progress along with the actions of her boss. Both should support her claim that she was a viable candidate for the executive position and her boss's and/or coworker's actions disrupted her career progression.

9. Locate a federal agency of your choosing and research the appropriate internal steps an employee must follow to file an internal complaint against a manager for unequal or discriminatory employment practices, particularly as it relates to promotional practices.

Additional Learning

- Read the article "Formal and Information Discrimination Against Women at Work: The Role of Gender Stereotypes." The authors, Brian Welle and Madeline Heilman (2005), assert that while most people are familiar with examples of blatant harassment in the workplace, there are many other forms of gender discrimination that are less visible but just as destructive. Visit http://dspace. mit.edu/bitstream/handle/1721.1/55933/CPL_WP_05_02_HeilmanWelle.pdf to learn more.

- The U.S. Equal Employment Opportunity Commission (EEOC) has guidelines specifically related to harassment in the workplace. Review this site carefully and note specific language or examples that reflect what happened to Lena. Visit https://www.eeoc.gov/harassment.

- The EEOC has written a document titled "Enforcement Guidance on Vicarious Employer Liability for Unlawful Harassment by Supervisors." This document outlines the obligation of both the employer and the employee in harassment-type cases. See https://www.eeoc.gov/laws/guidance/enforcement-guidance-vicarious-liability-unlawful-harassment-supervisors.

References

Bachman, E. (2020, August 11). The differences between workplace bullying and a "hostile work environment." *Forbes*. https://www.forbes.com/sites/ericbachman/2020/08/11/the-differences-between-workplace-bullying-and-a-hostile-work-environment/?sh=5b0f809b613f

Content Team. (2015). Hostile work environment. *Legal Dictionary*. https://legaldictionary.net/hostile-work-environment/

Doyle, A. (2019, November 23). How to identify and handle a hostile work environment. The Balance Careers. https://www. thebalancecareers.com/what-is-a-hostile-work-environment-2062007

McGrath, M. (2021, January 28). Breaking the "concrete" ceiling: Roz Brewer to become the S&P 500's only Black female CEO. *Forbes.* https://www.forbes.com/sites/maggiemcgrath/2021/01/28/breaking-the-concrete-ceiling-roz-brewer-to-be-the-sps-only-black-female-ceo/?sh=7edebb19667b

Muller, D. (2020, April 9). How to recognize and investigate a hostile work environment. Hracuity.com. https://www.hracuity.com/blog/investigating-signs-of-a-hostile-work-environment

SOAR. (2019, June 20). Leadership. https://soar.ucsc.edu/v2/leadership.html

Tan, J. (2016, April 20). For women of color, the glass ceiling is actually made of concrete. *HuffPost.* https://www.huffpost.com/entry/for-women-of-color-the-gl_b_9728056?guccounter=1

The Center for Leadership Studies. (n.d.). Situational leadership model. https://situational.com/situational-leadership/

U.S. Department of Labor (2020). What do I need to know about ... Workplace HARASSMENT. https://www.dol.gov/agencies/oasam/centers-offices/civil-rights-center/internal/policies/workplace-harassment/2012

U.S. Equal Employment Opportunity Commission. (2020). Enforcement guidance on vicarious employer liability for unlawful harassment by supervisors. https://www.eeoc.gov/laws/guidance/enforcement-guidance-vicarious-liability-unlawful-harassment-supervisors

U.S. Equal Employment Opportunity Commission. (2004, March 4). Glass ceilings: The status of women as officials and managers in the private sector. https://www.eeoc.gov/special-report/glass-ceilings-status-women-officials-and-managers-private-sector

U.S. Equal Employment Opportunity Commission. (2020). Age discrimination. https://www.eeoc.gov/age-discrimination

U.S. Equal Employment Opportunity Commission. (2020). Harassment. https://www.eeoc.gov/harassment

Welle, B., & Heilman, M. E. (2005). Formal and informal discrimination against women at work. The role of gender stereotypes. Working Papers. Center for Public Leadership. http://dspace.mit.edu/bitstream/handle/1721.1/55933/CPL_WP_05_02_HeilmanWelle.pdf

Jingle Bells

By Katrina Bezak

Overview

This case involves a college student who seeks a position as a waitress at a family-owned restaurant in her college town. Soon after her employment, the owners of the business changes the "family-friendly" restaurant to a sports bar, which is frequented primarily by male customers. Subsequently, a new restaurant manager imposes uniform and size requirements for the female servers only. The employee gains weight, requests a larger uniform, and the manager rejects her request. The server is terminated from her position due to her physical size.

Objectives

- Define sex discrimination in the workplace.
- Determine if weight restrictions can be considered sex discrimination.
- Describe the difference between sexual harassment and sex discrimination.
- Describe the types of behavior in the workplace that can be considered sexual harassment.
- Explain the applicability of the federal Pregnancy Discrimination Act to an employer as it relates to the employee's weight gain.

Key Concepts and Words

Federal Pregnancy Discrimination Act, pregnancy discrimination, sex discrimination, sexual harassment, weight discrimination

PREGNANCY DISCRIMINATION

"Pregnancy discrimination involves treating a woman (an applicant or employee) unfavorably because of pregnancy, childbirth, or a medical condition related to pregnancy or childbirth." (EEOC, 2021, para. 1)

Scenario

Molly Plumley is a 19-year-old college student who was salutatorian of her high school class. In high school, she participated in many school extracurricular activities such as National Honor Society (NHS), choir, and Future Farmers of America (FFA). Molly was very close with her family. She was religious and respectful of her faith, and her family regularly attended Shabbat together.

Based on her academics, Molly was fortunate to receive a 4-year college scholarship to a midwestern university. However, the scholarship did not include room and board. Like many students, Molly came from a modest family and sought employment to pay for her living expenses. She had no part-time job during high school, but she volunteered as a breakfast cook at a local shelter. Because of her limited work experience, Molly wanted to use her volunteer skills to seek a position in the hospitality/service industry. Molly began her search by checking the student newspaper. There, she eyed an advertisement for a local restaurant operated by the Jangle family. The posting read:

PART-TIME SERVER WANTED

Local family-owned restaurant looking for a waitress with good math skills and the ability to work well with the public. Apply in person from 9–11 a.m. at Jangle's, 3180 Caroline Drive, Mitten, Michigan.

Molly was excited about the opportunity, and she applied for the position that day. The owners were impressed with her volunteer experience, and coincidentally, the restaurant donated their extra daily meals to a community homeless shelter. The Jangle family thought she was a perfect fit, and she was hired on the spot! Molly was given a uniform, comprised of a white polo embroidered with the restaurant name, and a pair of comfortable black, knit pants. All employees, even the owners, wore the white polo and black pant attire on the job.

Once Molly began her job, she found that during the weekdays, the restaurant was very family friendly. Each Tuesday evening, a magician and clown visited the business to entertain the children. However, she gradually saw a change in weekend customers, which shifted from families to predominately male patrons. Customers started referring to her as "toots," "babe," "sexy lady," and "honey baby." She was asked out on dates by fellow college students and men old enough to be her father (and grandfather)! Molly usually worked weekdays and enjoyed the friendly families, but she accepted the annoyances of any weekend shifts solely because the tips were occasionally better.

After five months working at Jangle's, the owners Jane and Jim Jangle hired a new manager, Cliff Charles. Cliff immediately instituted changes to the operation of the restaurant. First, he ordered new uniforms for the female servers that replaced the white polo and black pants with a white tank top and red short shorts. The male servers, however, continued to wear white polos and black pants. Second, with the Jangle family's permission, Cliff changed the restaurant's name to Jingle Bells. Local families were immediately offended by the new name and uniform changes. Within a few short months, the restaurant environment changed from families sharing pizzas with their children to a sexually charged one with all-female servers and a mostly male clientele—even during the week.

Molly was uncomfortable wearing her new uniform. She felt it was very provocative and sexualized her. She was also frequently cold wearing the tank top and wanted to wear a sweater, which was not allowed. Overall, she decided she needed the money, the tips were good, many customers were appropriately sociable, and so, she continued to work. The verbal harassment, however, was unnerving, uncomfortable, and escalated. She was often propositioned for sexual favors and touched by customers on her buttocks. One inebriated patron even tried to pull down her tank top.

One month later, life became very stressful for Molly. Besides working at least 20 hours per week for Jingle Bells, she carried a full college course load of 15 credits. Her father became gravely ill, requiring expensive medical treatments that he could not afford. Molly thought about dropping out of school to care for her father, yet making money was necessary to cover those costs too.

About this same time, it was Molly's 6-month anniversary at Jingle Bells, and she was scheduled for her first performance review. During the evaluation with Cliff, Molly mentioned her discomfort with the constant customer harassment. He told her if she wanted the job to "deal with it." And "deal with it," was what she did.

In reaction to the severity of her father's illness, the stress caused by school and her job, Molly found eating as the outlet for her stress. She indulged in sweets, and in particular butter pecan ice cream. Consequently, she put on a few pounds. Those few turned to five, 10, and eventually 22 pounds.

It was clear to Molly she needed a larger uniform due to her weight gain. Because her employer provided the uniform, Molly had to ask her boss, Cliff, for a larger size. When she initiated the discussion with Cliff, he commented that she was getting a "bit pudgy." He told her that she needed to lose weight if she wanted to keep her job. Getting a larger uniform was not an option, he said. Molly was horrified at this unexpected response and walked away speechless from the meeting.

After reflecting for a few seconds, she turned around, walked back into Cliff's office and said, "There are many reasons people gain weight!" As she left the second time, Molly overheard Cliff calling her Molly Pudgy (instead of Plumley).

The stress in Molly's life continued, and she gained three more pounds. She was again forced to speak to Cliff about the uniform. He said:

> I told you to lose weight, and I am not interested in providing you with a new uniform. The uniform you were given was a size 10, which is the largest size I will purchase. It is your responsibility to have an attractive figure as a Jingle Bells waitress. It is very clear in the employee manual you must wear the company-provided uniform, and you have chosen to let yourself go.

One piece of information was missing from the conversation. Molly failed to inform Cliff she was also 3 months' pregnant, which she felt he did not need to know. She did not miss any work due to the pregnancy, and despite the constant customer harassment, her performance on the job was excellent.

After the second uniform discussion, Molly reflected on Cliff's comments. She was scared about losing her job and needed to work. She made a personal choice to come to work in other clothes that would fit: a white top that covered her midriff and red shorts. She chose similar-looking clothes with identical colors and thought her outfit would be acceptable. When Cliff saw she was not wearing her Jingle Bells uniform, he fired her on the spot for refusing to comply with the company uniform policy. Again, she never explained the weight gain and just listened to his haranguing.

Molly shared her story with her best friend, Chris. She described working at Jingle Bells as an "unwelcoming" work environment. Chris was a school friend who had just completed a "Women in the Law" course at their university. He told Molly she might have a lawsuit for sexual discrimination, sexual harassment, or pregnancy discrimination and that she should seek an attorney's services. He also told her that state and federal laws might apply to Jingle Bells's work issues.

Equal Employment Opportunity is THE LAW

Private Employers, State and Local Governments, Educational Institutions, Employment Agencies and Labor Organizations

Applicants to and employees of most private employers, state and local governments, educational institutions, employment agencies and labor organizations are protected under Federal law from discrimination on the following bases:

RACE, COLOR, RELIGION, SEX, NATIONAL ORIGIN
Title VII of the Civil Rights Act of 1964, as amended, protects applicants and employees from discrimination in hiring, promotion, discharge, pay, fringe benefits, job training, classification, referral, and other aspects of employment, on the basis of race, color, religion, sex (including pregnancy), or national origin. Religious discrimination includes failing to reasonably accommodate an employee's religious practices where the accommodation does not impose undue hardship.

DISABILITY
Title I and Title V of the Americans with Disabilities Act of 1990, as amended, protect qualified individuals from discrimination on the basis of disability in hiring, promotion, discharge, pay, fringe benefits, job training, classification, referral, and other aspects of employment. Disability discrimination includes not making reasonable accommodation to the known physical or mental limitations of an otherwise qualified individual with a disability who is an applicant or employee, barring undue hardship.

AGE
The Age Discrimination in Employment Act of 1967, as amended, protects applicants and employees 40 years of age or older from discrimination based on age in hiring, promotion, discharge, pay, fringe benefits, job training, classification, referral, and other aspects of employment.

SEX (WAGES)
In addition to sex discrimination prohibited by Title VII of the Civil Rights Act, as amended, the Equal Pay Act of 1963, as amended, prohibits sex discrimination in the payment of wages to women and men performing substantially equal work, in jobs that require equal skill, effort, and responsibility, under similar working conditions, in the same establishment.

GENETICS
Title II of the Genetic Information Nondiscrimination Act of 2008 protects applicants and employees from discrimination based on genetic information in hiring, promotion, discharge, pay, fringe benefits, job training, classification, referral, and other aspects of employment. GINA also restricts employers' acquisition of genetic information and strictly limits disclosure of genetic information. Genetic information includes information about genetic tests of applicants, employees, or their family members; the manifestation of diseases or disorders in family members (family medical history); and requests for or receipt of genetic services by applicants, employees, or their family members.

RETALIATION
All of these Federal laws prohibit covered entities from retaliating against a person who files a charge of discrimination, participates in a discrimination proceeding, or otherwise opposes an unlawful employment practice.

WHAT TO DO IF YOU BELIEVE DISCRIMINATION HAS OCCURRED
There are strict time limits for filing charges of employment discrimination. To preserve the ability of EEOC to act on your behalf and to protect your right to file a private lawsuit, should you ultimately need to, you should contact EEOC promptly when discrimination is suspected:
The U.S. Equal Employment Opportunity Commission (EEOC), 1-800-669-4000 (toll-free) or 1-800-669-6820 (toll-free TTY number for individuals with hearing impairments). EEOC field office information is available at www.eeoc.gov or in most telephone directories in the U.S. Government or Federal Government section. Additional information about EEOC, including information about charge filing, is available at www.eeoc.gov.

FIGURE 3.1   EEOC Employment Poster for Private Employers

With Chris's help, Molly went online to the federal Equal Employment Opportunity Commission's website, which provided information about sex discrimination, sexual harassment, and pregnancy discrimination under federal law. She learned that sex discrimination (Title VII of the Civil Rights Act of 1964) applied to "any aspect of employment, including hiring, firing, pay, job assignments, promotions, layoff, training, fringe benefits, and any other term or condition of employment." And according to the EEOC, treatment of employees could not simply be different; it must be unfair or not equal (EEOC, 2020, para. 2). She also learned that sexual harassment and pregnancy discrimination are types of sex discrimination. But interestingly, weight was not mentioned by the EEOC.

The website said that sexual harassment was a type of sex discrimination. It said that it included "(un) welcome sexual advances, requests for sexual favors, and other verbal or physical conduct of a sexual nature constitute sexual harassment when this conduct explicitly or implicitly affects an individual's employment, unreasonably interferes with an individual's work performance, or creates an intimidating, hostile, or offensive work environment" (EEOC, 2020, para. 2).

As far as Molly's pregnancy, she learned that the federal "Pregnancy Discrimination Act (PDA) forbids discrimination based on pregnancy when it comes to any aspect of employment, including hiring, firing, pay, job assignments, promotions, layoff, training, fringe benefits, such as leave and health insurance, and any other term or condition of employment" (EEOC, 2020, para. 3).

PREGNANCY DISCRIMINATION AND HARASSMENT

"It is unlawful to harass a woman because of pregnancy, childbirth, or a medical condition related to pregnancy or childbirth. Harassment is illegal when it is so frequent or severe that it creates a hostile or offensive work environment or when it results in an adverse employment decision (such as the victim being fired or demoted). The harasser can be the victim's supervisor, a supervisor in another area, a coworker, or someone who is not an employee of the employer, such as a client or customer." (EEOC, 2021, para. 4)

Molly was unsure what steps to take next, but she contacted her local law bar association for a referral to an attorney experienced in employment law for further guidance.

Discussion Questions

1. Describe Molly's work situation. Could she have approached Cliff differently with her concerns?

2. Are women judged more harshly than men for their physical appearance in a work situation? What about in society? Discuss.

3. Do you think it's acceptable for a company to impose weight restrictions on its employees, when weight is not a criterion for adequately performing job responsibilities? Should an employer be able to impose a uniform requirement that is specific to only one gender?

4. Did Molly have a legal, moral, or ethical obligation to notify Cliff about her pregnancy?

5. Referring to the text box within the case scenario, the EEOC states under the Pregnancy Discrimination Act (PDA) that "(d)iscrimination on the basis of pregnancy, childbirth, or related medical conditions constitutes unlawful sex discrimination under Title VII. Women affected by pregnancy or related conditions must be treated in the same manner as other applicants or employees who are similar in their ability or inability to work" (EEOC, 2020, para. 1). Using this definition, does Molly have any reason for a lawsuit against Jingle Bells for pregnancy discrimination based on the Pregnancy Discrimination Act? Do you think her failure to inform Cliff about her pregnancy reduces her chances for a successful lawsuit against Cliff or Jingle Bells?

6. Molly chose to continue to work at Jingle Bells knowing that she and the female servers were being sexualized. Does her acceptance negate any claim for harassment? Debate.

7. Did Cliff have a basis to fire Molly? Explain.

Assignments

1. How does the federal Equal Employment Opportunity Commission (EEOC) define sex discrimination from a legal perspective? Provide an example.

2. What is the difference in the legal standards between sex discrimination and sexual harassment? Review the EEOC's website (https://www.eeoc.gov/) for information on the differences. Should Molly pursue litigation

against Jingle Bells for sex discrimination or sexual harassment? Do you think she would be successful with a lawsuit against her employer? Explain.

3. There are two types of sexual harassment: quid pro quo sexual harassment and a hostile work environment. How does the federal EEOC describe the difference between these two terms? Which did Molly experience or neither? See https://www.sexualharassmenttraining.com/blog/detail/13/what-is-quid-pro-quo-and-hostile-work-environment-sexual-harassment.

4. In 1986, the sex discrimination case of *Meritor Savings Bank v. Vinson* was decided by the U.S. Supreme Court. It involved a sexual harassment claim against the male supervisor for a female employee. Why was this a critical case in the development of sexual harassment law? See https://www.oyez.org/cases/1985/84-1979.

5. Read this article on weight discrimination in the workplace particularly as it affects women (http://www.refinery29.com/2015/06/89803/women-weight-discrimination-at-work). Based on your reading, present an argument that the federal law should be amended to include weight discrimination.

6. In 2013, a group of female employees sued their employer in the New Jersey state court alleging weight discrimination. The court found that the employer's actions were legal (see http://nation.time.com/2013/07/26/too-big-to-cocktail-judge-upholds-weight-discrimination-in-the-workplace/). This is in contrast to a Michigan case (see http://www.candgnews.com/news/hooters-weight-discrimination-case-moves-arbitration) in which two Hooters waitresses sued their employer for placing them on a 30-day weight probation. Michigan is one of the few states that has a state law that makes it illegal to discriminate on the basis of weight (see https://www.michigan.gov/mdcr/0,4613,7-138-4954_4997-16288--,00.html). Compare and contrast the two decisions from New Jersey and Michigan.

7. The EEOC has provided employers with guidelines on pre-employment interview questions that are gender-based such as child-bearing plans. Go to the EEOC website at https://www.eeoc.gov/. Describe the types of types of gender-based questions that are acceptable and those defined as illegal. Provide examples.

8. Both state and federal laws cover different aspects of workplace discrimination. However, each state has different legal classifications covered in the workplace. Identify five states you would like to research, and using the Internet, locate either (1) the website for the civil rights department for each of your chosen states or (2) search the state's law through its respective state legislature. Then complete the chart here with a yes or no answer and include the link to the website used as a source. A sample entry for the state of Michigan is included.

TABLE 3.2   SUMMARY OF STATE WORKPLACE DISCRIMINATION

State name	Weight protection	Gender identity protection	Age	Other (describe)	Other (describe)
Michigan	Yes, weight is protected under the Elliott-Larsen Civil Rights Act 453 of 1976. http://www.michigan.gov/mdcr/0,4613,7-138-4954_4997-16288--,00.html	Pending	Yes, age is protected under the Elliott-Larsen Civil Rights Act 453 of 1976. http://www.michigan.gov/mdcr/0,4613,7-138-4954_4997-16288--,00.html	Yes, height is protected under the Elliott-Larsen Civil Rights Act 453 of 1976. http://www.michigan.gov/mdcr/0,4613,7-138-4954_4997-16288--,00.html	Yes, genetic information is protected under the Elliott-Larsen Civil Rights Act 453 of 1976. http://www.michigan.gov/mdcr/0,4613,7-138-4954_4997-16288--,00.html

References

Associated Press. (2020, October 14). Effort to ban LGBTQ discrimination moves ahead in Michigan. NBC News. https://www.nbcnews.com/feature/nbc-out/effort-bar-lgbtq-discrimination-moves-ahead-michigan-n1243347

Civil Rights Act of 1964 (Title VII), 42 U.S.C. § 2000e et. seq. (1964).

Cormier, S. (2011, July 13). Hooters weight discrimination case moves to arbitration. *C & G Newspapers*. https://www.candgnews.com/news/hooters-weight-discrimination-case-moves-arbitration

Meritor Savings Bank v Vinson, 477 U.S. 57 (1986).

Mertens, M. (2015, June 26). The workplace problem that no one is talking about. https://www.refinery29.com/en-us/2015/06/89803/women-weight-discrimination-at-work

Michigan Civil Rights Commission. (2021). For victims of unlawful discrimination. Rights to equal employment opportunity. https://www.michigan.gov/mdcr/0,4613,7-138-4954_4997-16288--,00.html

Miller, B. (2014, September 3). Sexual harassment in the workplace: Quid pro quo versus hostile work environment. HR Daily Advisor.

https://hrdailyadvisor.blr.com/2014/09/03/sexual-harassment-in-the-workplace-quid-pro-quo-versus-hostile-work-environment/

Pregnancy Discrimination Act, 42 U.S.C. § 2000e-2(a) (1978).

Sanborn, J. (2013, July 26). Too big to cocktail? Judge upholds weight discrimination in the workplace. *Time*. https://nation.time.

com/2013/07/26/too-big-to-cocktail-judge-upholds-weight-discrimination-in-the-workplace/

U.S. Equal Opportunity Employment Commission. (2021). Facts about sexual harassment. https://www.eeoc.gov/eeoc/publications/

fs-sex.cfm

U.S. Equal Opportunity Employment Commission. (2021). EEO is the law poster. https://www.dol.gov/agencies/ofccp/posters

U.S. Equal Opportunity Employment Commission. (2021). Pre-employment inquiries and gender. https://www.eeoc.gov/

pre-employment-inquiries-and-gender

U.S. Equal Opportunity Employment Commission. (2021). Pregnancy. https://www.eeoc.gov/eeoc/publications/fs-preg.cfm

U.S. Equal Opportunity Employment Commission. (2021). Pregnancy discrimination. https://www.eeoc.gov/pregnancy-discrimination

U.S. Equal Opportunity Employment Commission. (2020). Types of discrimination. https://www.eeoc.gov/laws/types/sex.cfm

Figure Credit

Fig. 3.1: Source: https://www.laborposters.org/federal/81-equal-employment-opportunity-poster-english-poster.htm.

Pinnacle Pop

Overview

Clara Andrews is a middle-aged female supervisor for a manufacturing facility in a coal mining town in southwestern Pennsylvania. She develops her management skills without any formal training and only through work experience. Jamie, one of her direct reports, is a young man excited to experience life with aspirations to leave his hometown, move to New York, and make a career on Broadway. Both grew up in a small city where opportunities were limited.

Jamie is trying to find the right balance for his personal and professional goals. He leaves the company where he is competent, excels, and is respected by his manager, because he feels the employer does not provide him with the proper support to retain him.

Objectives

- Determine what actions a company or manager should take, if any, upon learning that an employee is gender transitioning.
- Describe how an employer can support its trans employees while meeting its obligations to all employees.
- Explain the responsibility of a supervisor to respond to workplace bullying of a direct report.

Key Concepts and Words

bullying, employee health, gender identity, gender transitioning, microaggression, social issues, Title VII of the Civil Rights Act of 1964, transgender (trans), transgender rights, unconscious bias

GENDER IDENTITY

"Gender identity means one's inner sense of one's own gender, which may or may not match the sex assigned at birth. Different people choose to express their gender identity differently. For some, gender may be expressed through, for example, dress, grooming, mannerisms, speech patterns, and social interactions. Gender expression usually ranges between masculine and feminine, and some transgender people express their gender consistent with how they identify internally, rather than in accordance with the sex they were assigned at birth." (OPM, 2015, p. 2)

Scenario

Jamie Forrestor is a 26-year-old male employee of Pinnacle Pop, a soda pop manufacturing facility located in Latif, Pennsylvania. The company has been in business for 67 years and is still employee owned. The town where Pinnacle Pop is located is caught in the past with little city development. However, Pinnacle Pop has modernized its facilities and even added a full exercise facility to promote health and wellness.

Jamie's father was a coal miner, and his mother was a waitress at the Blue Eagle, a local diner downtown. Jamie often came to work with his mother as a child, and he helped clean tables for a few dollars a week. The owner also let him eat for free and do his homework in one of the red vinyl booths in the corner, where it was quiet and rarely needed for a customer. There wasn't much to do in town, so children created their own fun with games like skipping between the train tracks, playing cards, and listening to music. There were few options for work in Latif, Pennsylvania, and anyone looking for employment as an adult was often hired where their parents had worked. After having several part-time jobs, Jamie asked his dad about his employer, Pinnacle Pop. He wanted to earn and save money to move to the east coast and make his lifelong wish to be a professional dancer come true. Jamie applied and was hired to work on the assembly line filling green glass pop bottles. He also did some custodial work at night.

After five and a half years at Pinnacle Pop, he was promoted to foreman, managing five manufacturing lines while supervising 21 women. All his direct reports liked Jamie, and he often took a break with his employees who worked the assembly filling line. They conversed about many things, mostly their kids, the movie playing at the town theater, and cooking. Jamie was well respected by his boss, Clara, and the other foremen, too. Clara was the only female manager at Pinnacle Pop, and she reported directly to the president, Harvey Wallace.

At the beginning of his sixth year working for Pinnacle, Jamie confided in a friend that he no longer felt authentic and wanted to disclose to his boss, Clara, that he was gender transitioning. He wasn't sure how she would react, but they had a solid working relationship. He decided he would take a chance. When he confided in Clara, he asked her to now call him Frankie, which was his preferred name and to refer to him by a female pronoun. Clara said she would do her best, but it was company policy to only refer to him by his legal name, regardless of his request.

Two days after Frankie's preferred name request, Clara, Frankie, and several other employees were taking a scheduled break when Clara inappropriately blurted out that Jamie was now Frankie. Frankie wasn't happy that Clara broke her trust and shared her personal information with the group.

Frankie had planned to tell her direct reports about her life changes and had been waiting for the right moment. Clara knew she had erred in breaking confidentiality, but the "news was out," and she really didn't want to know any more about Frankie's personal life. She said to herself, "I am not getting involved in this situation. I will do what Jamie asked, but no more. I felt it was my responsibility to tell the team on the line, and that's all I am going to do." Clara did not feel there was any reason to say anything to upper management as Frankie came to work as always and continued to be an excellent forewoman.

Soon after, Frankie's external physical appearance transformed. She took on the characteristics of a female and changed her clothing to appear more feminine. Frankie let her hair grow longer and highlighted it. Her employees noticed an alteration in her voice and pitch.

One late afternoon, a few of the foreman were still at the manufacturing facility, and Clara was approached by two of them. They asked, "What's happening to your shining star or shall we say starlet? Who's planning the next girl's night out? Be sure to invite Jamie, or is it Frankie?" And, sometimes when Clara went down on the floor to review a pop filling line, she heard a snicker when she and Frankie walked past.

Frankie was unnerved by the comments and mentioned this to Clara. She asked her about the company's code of conduct policy, but Clara told Frankie this was just normal workplace bantering. Clara again thought to herself, "No need for me to get involved." But she felt badly that Frankie was being harassed by her colleagues.

Within the next month, there were subtle changes in Frankie's demeanor, but her team's performance was even more robust. The lines were consistently filled beyond quota, meaning more bottles were filled per hour with soda pop versus their goal. And, if the team's work exceeded their monthly target, Frankie continued her tradition of treating the women on the line with a "pizza and pop tunes" break.

Frankie began using the women's locker room in the company gym after work for changing clothes. Several female employees mentioned this to Clara in passing, and one woman in particular went to Human Resources (HR). She told them that she felt uncomfortable undressing in front of Frankie and asked HR to direct her to the men's locker room. Similarly, the men "barred" Frankie from entering the men's locker room saying to Human Resources she made *them* feel uncomfortable and that she was wearing women's workout clothes. Frankie asked management for some help because she did not know what to do and was feeling embarrassed and intimidated. At first, HR told her she should use the men's locker room. After a couple of weeks, Frankie realized their directive wasn't working for her, as the sarcastic remarks continued while becoming more emotionally hurtful. She continued to overhear harassing comments from her coworkers. Frankie went to HR again.

Human Resources finally called a meeting with Clara as Frankie's manager. Clara told the HR director, "I don't know what to do. Frankie's work performance is solid. In fact, her group by far is the strongest of my four teams. Frankie did confide that she was transitioning, and she started wearing different clothes that were more feminine. Basically, she comes to work on time and continues to do a great job managing the filling line. Frankie's direct reports respect her as their forewoman. There are no problems except for the locker room issue."

Clara was nervous having this discussion and kept fidgeting with her hands. She continued saying, "I know she uses the women's restroom during the day, so I frankly have no idea what to tell her or her colleagues about the gym after work. She is a guy after all! All I know is that she wanted me to call her Frankie, and that's what I am doing. You are the experts. You figure it out."

After 1 month, Frankie went on short-term medical leave, which extended to long term. After several months into her long-term leave, Pinnacle Pop decided that they did not want to extend health benefits to her anymore (it had been over a year). The Human Resources department was getting ready to challenge her doctor for her return to work. Frankie told her doctor she had no plans to return to the company and be subjected to the same harassing work conditions. When Clara found out, she was relieved.

Frankie, however, was disappointed. While she packed her bags for the airport, she started singing the famous song, "New York, New York" by legendary, Frank Sinatra, and her mood lifted. Next on the playlist was "Beautiful" by Christina Aguilera as Frankie danced out her front door. Broadway was waiting for her!

(Note: In a historic decision made on June 15, 2020, the U.S. Supreme Court ruled in *Bostock v. Clayton County, Georgia* and *Altitude Express, Inc. v. Zarda* that the 1964 Civil Rights Act protects gay, lesbian, and transgender employees from discrimination based on sex.)

Discussion Questions

1. Clara might have known that Jamie had a personal life event happening before he confided in her. What obligation does a manager have to ask an employee about their personal life? If performance was declining, would it alter your opinion?

2. Clara said to herself that "she wasn't getting involved." What do you think she meant?

3. Do you think Clara was uncomfortable managing Frankie? Support your opinion.

4. When Frankie complained to Clara that she "felt harassed by her colleagues," what was Clara's responsibility as a manager?

5. Was Clara empathetic with Frankie? What evidence supports this?

6. Bullying is a common term used to describe how individuals feel when faced with adversity in the workforce. How does one define normal disagreement in the workplace versus bullying versus gender discrimination? Are the lines "blurred"?

7. When Clara remarks that she is "relieved," do you think her comment is about herself or Frankie?

8. In their employee handbooks, many companies state that any employee, transitioning or not, can use the restroom of the gender of which they identify. However, "coworkers uncomfortable with a transgender

employee's use of the same restroom or locker room should be advised to use separate facilities" (Human Rights, 2015, p. 7). Do you agree with both guidelines? Why?

Assignments

1. Many colleges and universities have adopted "preferred name policies," which allow students to identify themselves in campus information systems by a name different from their legal name. What about businesses? Research this topic in the business and corporate sector. What did you find?

2. Most corporations have guidelines on managing employee interactions appropriately and professionally. Find two company policies and compare and contrast, specifically paying attention to employee name and bathroom use policies.

3. Describe the EEOC's position on "Bathroom/Facility Access for Transgender Employees." Was Pinnacle Pop in compliance with that policy? Why or why not? See https://www.dol.gov/asp/policy-development/ TransgenderBathroomAccessBestPractices.pdf.

4. In 2012, the EEOC issued a ruling in *Macy v. Holder* regarding discrimination and transgendered individuals. Research the ruling. Did Pinnacle Pop comply with the *Macy* case? Why or why not? What about compliance with the 2020 U.S. Supreme Court case *Bostock v. Clayton County, Georgia* and *Altitude Express, Inc.*? (See References for link information.)

5. Go to the EEOC website (http://www.eeoc.gov). Based on federal guidelines, do you believe Frankie should have filed a claim against Pinnacle Pop for gender identity discrimination? Why or why not?

BACKGROUND

- "Transgender" refers to people whose gender identity and/or expression is different from the sex assigned to them at birth (e.g., the sex listed on an original birth certificate). The term transgender woman typically is used to refer to someone who was assigned the male sex at birth but who identifies as a female. Likewise, the term transgender man typically is used to refer to someone who was assigned the female sex at birth but who identifies as male. A person does not need to undergo any medical procedure to be considered a transgender man or a transgender woman.

TITLE VII OF THE CIVIL RIGHTS ACT OF 1964 AND TRANSGENDER INDIVIDUALS

- In addition to other federal laws, the U.S. Equal Employment Opportunity Commission (EEOC) enforces Title VII of the Civil Rights Act of 1964, which prohibits employment discrimination based on race, color, national origin, religion, and sex (including pregnancy, gender identity, and sexual orientation). Title VII applies to all federal, state, and local government agencies in their capacity as employers, and to all private employers with 15 or more employees.

- In *Macy v. Dep't of Justice*, EEOC Appeal No. 0120120821, 2012 WL 1435995 (Apr. 12, 2012), the EEOC ruled that discrimination based on transgender status is sex discrimination in violation of Title VII, and in *Lusardi v. Dep't of the Army*, EEOC Appeal No. 0120133395, 2015 WL 1607756 (Mar. 27, 2015), the EEOC held that:

  o denying an employee equal access to a common restroom corresponding to the employee's gender identity is sex discrimination;

  o an employer cannot condition this right on the employee undergoing or providing proof of surgery or any other medical procedure; and,

  o an employer cannot avoid the requirement to provide equal access to a common restroom by restricting a transgender employee to a single-user restroom instead (though the employer can make a single-user restroom available to all employees who might choose to use it).

FIGURE 3.2   Bathroom/Facility Access and Transgender Employees

References

Abrams, M. (2019, December 20). 64 terms that define gender identity and expression. Healthline. https://www.healthline.com/health/different-genders

Bostock v. Clayton County, Georgia and *Altitude Express, Inc. v. Zarda*, 590 U.S. ___ (2020). https://supreme.justia.com/cases/federal/us/590/17-1618/

Butterer, K. (2015, March 18). Transgender employees in the workplace: What are an employer's rights and responsibilities? Foster Swift Employment, Labor & Benefits E-News. http://www.fosterswift.com/communications-Transgender-Employees-Employers-Rights-Responsibilities.html

Clark, D. (2015, February 5). What to do when your colleague comes out as transgender. *Harvard Business Review*. https://hbr.org/2015/02/what-to-do-when-your-colleague-comes-out-as-transgender

Guerin, L. (2017). Discrimination based on gender identity. Nolo Press. http://www.nolo.com/legal-encyclopedia/discrimination-based-gender-identity.html

Human Rights Campaign Foundation. (2017). Navigating gender inclusion in gendered spaces: Best practices for employers. http://hrc-assets.s3-website-us-east-1.amazonaws.com//files/images/general/Module_3_Navigating_Gender_Inclusion.pdf

Human Rights Campaign Foundation. (2017). Restroom access for transgender employees. http://www.hrc.org/resources/restroom-access-for-transgender-employees

Liptak, A. (2020, June 16). Civil rights law protects gay and transgender workers, Supreme Court rules. *New York Times*. https://www.nytimes.com/2020/06/15/us/gay-transgender-workers-supreme-court.html

Macy v. Holder, ATF-2011-00751 (EEOC, 2011). https://www.eeoc.gov/sites/default/files/migrated_files/decisions/0120120821%20Macy%20v%20DOJ%20ATF.txt

Princeton University. (2017). Principles for use of preferred name. https://registrar.princeton.edu/student-services/preferred-name-policy/

Safety & Health Assessment and Research for Prevention (SHARP) Program. (2011, April). Workplace bullying and disruptive behavior: What everyone needs to know. Washington State Department of Labor & Industries. http://www.lni.wa.gov/Safety/Research/Files/Bullying.pdf

U.S. Department of Labor. (2015). Best practices. A guide to restroom access for transgender employees. https://www.dol.gov/asp/policy-development/TransgenderBathroomAccessBestPractices.pdf

U.S. Equal Opportunity Commission. (2021). https://www.eeoc.gov/

U.S. Equal Opportunity Commission. (2021). Processing complaints of discrimination by lesbian, gay, bisexual, and transgender (LGBT) federal employees. https://www.eeoc.gov/federal-sector/management-directive/processing-complaints-discrimination-lesbian-gay-bisexual-and

U.S. Equal Opportunity Commission. (2021). Preventing employment discrimination against lesbian, gay, bisexual or transgender workers [Brochure]. https://www.eeoc.gov/laws/guidance/preventing-employment-discrimination-against-lesbian-gay-bisexual-or-transgender

U.S. Office of Personnel Management (OPM). (2015, June). Addressing sexual orientation and gender identity discrimination in federal civilian employment. A guide to employment rights, protections, and responsibilities. https://www.opm.gov/policy-data-oversight/diversity-and-inclusion/reference-materials/addressing-sexual-orientation-and-gender-identity-discrimination-in-federal-civilian-employment.pdf

Western Michigan University. (2017). Preferred name. Human Resources. http://www.wmich.edu/hr/preferredname

Figure Credit

Fig. 3.2: Source: https://www.eeoc.gov/eeoc/publications/fs-bathroom-access-transgender.cfm.

Work and Family

Berner, Flector, and Shein

Overview

This case focuses on an accountant, Caitie Orlov, who is a successful CPA at Berner, Flector, and Shein (BFS), a regional accounting firm. Caitie has been employed at BFS for over 6 years. She is a single woman who adopts a child and manages her new and exciting personal life while continuing to meet and exceed her job goals. Until one day. ...

Scenario

Caitie Orlov works at the Berner, Flector, and Shein accounting firm in Triangle Corners, Wyoming. She started as an accountant, became a nonequity[1] partner after 6 years, and planned to become an equity partner and shareholder in the firm. She had hoped this would happen by the end of this year. Caitie worked long days and

___
1   An equity partner has a financial ownership in the company and often must financially contribute to that ownership. This is different from a non-equity partner who participates only in management decisions.

Objectives

- Explain the importance of strong organizational skills and their relation to career success.
- Summarize the benefits and steps to effective delegation and time management.
- Describe how a direct report, peer, or supervisor can enhance or sabotage a career.
- Discuss whether employees are treated differently based on marital and child status and how employer work expectations may differ based on an employee's personal life choices.
- Analyze the federal Family and Medical Leave Act (FMLA) and what benefits it offers to new parents.

Key Words and Concepts

career planning, child status, delegation, Family and Medical Leave Act, marital status, organizational skills, time management many overnights to accomplish all the requirements to earn the promotion. She knew she had to sacrifice her personal life for this goal.

For the last 6 years, Caitie's typical workday followed a set routine. It minimized anxiety because she knew what to expect. Her "exemplary organization planner" had almost the same tasks listed for each day. It was simple because her life focused on work. Period. She was single, did not have a significant other, nor did she have children. On the weekends, Caitie often visited the office to catch up on projects needing attention. As a result, her week always started on Monday, without stress, at 6 a.m.

Even though her career professionally fulfilled her, Caitie wanted to have a family. As a single woman, she decided adoption was the best choice for her, and she pursued an international adoption from the Philippines. When her daughter Jasmine arrived, Caitie's schedule changed, but she made detailed arrangements for Jasmine's care, so she could continue to be as productive at her job as she had in the past.

Caitie felt the adoption was personal, and she did not share her daughter's arrival with those in the office. However, her administrative assistant, Sally, knew about the baby. One day, the social worker from the adoption agency had called her office in error (rather than her cellphone) to confirm a scheduled home visit.

Within 3 months of starting this remarkable chapter in her life, Caitlin's boss, Mr. Flector, approached her in the lunchroom and mentioned that he hadn't seen her as much in the office. Caitie was caught off guard and asked him to clarify. She shared that she was here every day, her client accounts were current, and her revenues were up this year by 29%. Mr. Flector commented again that he just wanted her to increase her visibility in the office. It was true that she was in the office less at night, yet she still arrived early every day, worked complete days, and even ate lunch at her desk rather than leaving the office. She had reworked her schedule to arrive even earlier in the morning to compensate for not working into the night.

The following week, she was given three new projects that would require long hours and evening work. Caitie was extremely nervous because she would need to adjust her home schedule. Professionally, she did not feel the due date was realistic, and she was not confident she could complete the projects within the compressed timeframe. That afternoon, Monday, Caitie called her mother and asked her to stay with Jasmine, because she knew she would not be home until after 11 p.m.

On Tuesday morning, Caitie looked at her planner and began to panic. Each project had several steps and deliverables. She had to think quickly. Not finishing the projects was NOT an option, and she had to present the results on Friday. She always met deadlines, even if it meant sacrificing her personal life. However, it was different now. She had a baby and didn't have the same personal flexibility as before. Fortunately, she did have a giving and thoughtful mother!

Caitie managed by delegating to a few associates and dividing the work assignments so no one would be expected to work all three nights (Tuesday, Wednesday, and Thursday). She also located a sitter. This would allow her to be in the office every evening and not depend on her mom's generosity. At first, it was very time consuming explaining each project in detail to the group. Then Caitie was surprised at how much more she could accomplish by splitting up and delegating the tasks. The associates were happy to take on new responsibilities because they learned different skills and grew professionally.

On Friday, Caitie presented the summaries of the three projects to Messrs. Berner, Flector, and Shein, and they seemed pleased with the results. She also gave credit to the individuals who worked extended hours to meet the end of week deadline.

In particular, she recognized Adam Spade's efforts, a tax associate, who long ago had expressed an interest to take on additional work and contribute more to the team. Adam had aspirations to also become a partner, and just like Caitie he had put in grinding hours to make it happen. He appreciated Caitie's acknowledgment. Her praise showcased his ability to generate results under challenging conditions. They both knew that being endorsed by others was vital in the process for "making equity partner."

A few weeks later, Mr. Flector again gave Caitie a last-minute project to complete. This time Caitie asked one of the other partners if a few associates in his group could help. She felt she couldn't ask her same staff to work extra hours. The partner refused and said he and his team were unable to assist. He told Caitie she needed to take responsibility and determine how to "make it work." Caitie then went to another partner and received the same response. Knowing that she and her team could not meet the deadline, she asked her boss, Mr. Flector, for an extension that he denied. He said she needed to manage herself and her associates better to complete projects in a timely manner. She was "made a non-equity partner because she had been dependable, but now he and the other equity partners had lost confidence in her." Caitie was dismayed. Within 8 months, she went from being on a solid career path toward an equity partner and now, "no confidence" with no explanation!

Before long, Mr. Flector asked her to leave the firm. He said that he wasn't satisfied with her performance and didn't see the skill set to reach full partner status. Mr. Flector said he wanted to be honest with her and allow her to pursue employment at another firm, where she might have a better chance of career mobility.

It was clear; her dream was not going to happen. She offered to resign. Mr. Flector gave her an exit package and mentioned that it's probably a good time for a change since she was a new mother. He told her she should be "focused on her baby and staying home." Emotionally, she was crushed. Physically, she was drained.

As she left the office that day, she overheard applause from the boardroom for Adam Spade. He had been fast-tracked and named to equity partner, bypassing the step of nonequity partner. Mr. Flector said, "My boy, you stepped up, and you stood out. All those extra hours paid off, and there is no one we would rather have as a partner than you!"

Discussion Questions

1. Caitie delegates the additional work to her team. What other ways could she have been successful in getting the extra tasks completed?

2. Caitie is competent in her job. Do you think someone at the organization sabotaged Caitie's career? Why or why not?

3. The author of this case intentionally refers to Caitie by her first name and not as Ms. Orlov. However, Mr. Flector is always addressed formally as Mr. Flector. Why the difference in formality?

4. Do employers treat employees differently based on their marital and child status (i.e., their personal life choices)? Discuss if and how workload is imbalanced using the broadly defined groups below:

   a. single, divorced, widowed, married

   b. single, divorced, widowed vs. married with child(ren)

5. The federal Family and Medical Leave Act (FMLA) (see Figure 4.1) allows employees to take 12 weeks of work leave in a 12-month period to support the birth or adoption of a child. Why did Caitie not take advantage of the leave time?

FAMILY AND MEDICAL LEAVE ACT

Overview

The FMLA entitles eligible employees of covered employers to take unpaid, job-protected leave for specified family and medical reasons with continuation of group health insurance coverage under the same terms and conditions as if the employee had not taken leave. Eligible employees are entitled to:

- Twelve workweeks of leave in a 12-month period for:
  - the birth of a child and to care for the newborn child within 1 year of birth;
  - the placement with the employee of a child for adoption or foster care and to care for the newly placed child within 1 year of placement;
  - to care for the employee's spouse, child, or parent who has a serious health condition;
  - a serious health condition that makes the employee unable to perform the essential functions of his or her job;
  - any qualifying exigency arising out of the fact that the employee's spouse, son, daughter, or parent is a covered military member on "covered active duty;" **or**
- Twenty-six workweeks of leave during a single 12-month period to care for a covered servicemember with a serious injury or illness if the eligible employee is the servicemember's spouse, son, daughter, parent, or next of kin (military caregiver leave).

FIGURE 4.1   Family and Medical Leave Act

6. If Caitie had taken time off under the FMLA, do you think she would have been in a better position of "strength" if Mr. Flector subsequently asked her to leave the company? If there was public knowledge of her daughter's adoption, would Caitie have had more leverage in the discussion? Discuss.

7. How did Mr. Flector know that Caitie had adopted a baby? Was there a moral or ethical breach of confidentiality in the office?

8. Caitie delivered results, was organized, and prioritized tasks appropriately. Why was she asked to leave?

Assignments

1. Locate several templates for time management online. Start with "Stephen Covey's Grid" that evaluates tasks by urgency and important. (Mueller, 2020). If a person is considered most effective, in which quadrant do most tasks fall?

2. Create a grid for your personal life with a list of 10 random tasks that need to be completed in the next week (see example in Table 4.1).

   a. Assign them to the correct quadrant. Based on the location of your tasks, what are your personal conclusions?

   b. Evaluate and determine if you will be able to complete all the tasks next week, and explain why or why not. If you can't, what's the next step? If this happens within the workplace and you can't complete all the tasks, what's the next step?

TABLE 4.1   TIME MANAGEMENT GRID

	Urgent	Not Urgent
Important	• Taxes due today (April 15th) • Get gas (on empty) • Complete business plan for boss (due yesterday) • Book flight for out-of-town meeting for tomorrow	• Organize client files • Pay dog sitter for last month • Pay charge card bill
Not important	• Stock up on munchies for out-of-town guests coming in tonight	• Clean coffee stains off desktop at office

3. Caitie used an online planner to minimize stress which led to being organized. (See https://www.thebalanc-esmb.com/best-planner-apps-4174743.) Identify the action items that you can implement in your personal life starting today to help improve the productivity of your days.

4. Read the article, "How to Delegate More Effectively in Your Business" (https://www.forbes.com/sites/mar-tinzwilling/2013/10/02/how-to-delegate-more-effectively-in-your-business/#6ad4bd369bc6). Explain what makes delegation an effective management tool. What made it a useful tool for Caitie?

5. Many companies are offering adoption benefits to their employees. The Dave Thomas Foundation for Adoption regularly publishes a list of adoption-friendly employers. Locate the most recent list and review the adoption benefits for three companies on that list. What are the similarities between companies?

6. The federal government provides adoption subsidies to those adopting children with special needs. What do these benefits include? See https://www.benefits.gov/benefits/benefit-details/822.

References

Ayana, B. (2013, June 18). The single girl's second shift. *Marie Claire.* http://www.marieclaire.com/career-advice/tips/a7755/single-girls-second-shift/

Bacon, Wilson. (2013, January 30). When single employees are "discriminated" against. Employment Law Bits. http://bwlaw.blogs.com/employment_law_bits/2013/01/when-single-employees-are-discriminated-against.html

Balderrama, A. (2009, February 23). Are single workers treated differently? CNN online. http://www.cnn.com/2009/LIVING/worklife/02/23/cb.single.workers/

Benefits.gov. (n.d.). Adoption assistance. https://www.benefits.gov/benefit/822

Carroll, L. (2015, November 7). The brutal truth about being childless at work. *Fortune.* http://fortune.com/2015/11/07/truth-about-childless-at-work/

Cautero, R. (2021, January 7). The 9 best planner apps of 2021. The Balance Small Business. https://www.thebalancesmb.com/best-planner-apps-4174743

Dave Thomas Foundation for Adoption. (2017). Best 2016 adoption friendly workplace signature program. https://davethomasfoundation.org/2016-adoption-friendly-workplaces

Duggan, T. (n.d.). How to improve organizational skills through the use of graphic organizers. Chron. http://smallbusiness.chron.com/improve-organizational-skills-through-use-graphic-organizers-279.html

Family and Medical Leave Act of 1993, 29 U.S.C. § 2601–2654 (2006).

Georgia Virtual Technical Connection. (n.d.). Organizational skills. Technical College System of Georgia. http://www.gvtc.org/Contents/Organization.pdf

Johnson, W. (n.d.). What is the difference between having good organizational skills and being able to prioritize task? Chron. http://smallbusiness.chron.com/difference-between-having-good-organizational-skills-being-able-prioritize-tasks-35433.html

Linn, A. (2013, November 6). Office smackdown: Parents vs. childless workers. CNBC. http://www.cnbc.com/2013/11/06/s.html

Mueller, S. (2020, February 9). Stephen Covey's time management matrix explained. Planet of Success. http://www.planetofsuccess.com/blog/2015/stephen-coveys-time-management-matrix-explained/

Society for Human Resource Management. (2013, September 5). More employees providing adoption-friendly benefits. https://www.shrm.org/ResourcesAndTools/hr-topics/benefits/Pages/Adoption-Benefits.aspx

U.S. Department of Labor. (n.d.). Family and Medical Leave Act. https://www.dol.gov/whd/fmla/

Weydt, A. (2010). Developing delegation skills. *Online Journal in Issues in Nursing, 15*(2). http://nursingworld.org/MainMenuCategories/ANAMarketplace/ANAPeriodicals/OJIN/TableofContents/Vol152010/No2May2010/Delegation-Skills.html

Zwilling, M. (2013, October 2). How to delegate more effectively in your business. *Forbes.* https://www.forbes.com/sites/martinzwilling/2013/10/02/how-to-delegate-more-effectively-in-your-business/#51fb394669bc

Figure Credit

Fig. 4.1: Source: https://www.dol.gov/agencies/whd/fmla.

Driving to Be the Best!

Overview

Family businesses are among the oldest types of business organizations (*Inc.*, n.d., para. 1). They offer a unique set of personal and business dynamics that consists of people connected by birth or marriage. BusZipp is one of those companies. It is a 24/7 boutique transportation company that operates several fleets of vehicles. It provides bus services, airport transportation, and local delivery of packages. Józef Kotwicki is the founder of the company, and his four sons work in the business. In "Driving to Be the Best," Kami, a successful businesswoman, leaves her corporate job and becomes a key player through marriage. She takes the business through a transition that brings family conflict, yet significant profits.

Objectives

- Explain the unique stressors that affect members of a family-owned business.
- Describe the challenges experienced by having an "outsider" join a family business.
- Recognize the significance of being a change agent of an established business.

Key Concepts and Words

business planning, change agent, family-owned business, operational plans, succession planning

Background

THE KOTWICKI FAMILY MEMBERS
Kami Zale is married to Lorenz Kotwicki. They have been married for over 10 years. Kami had 10 years of corporate business experience before coming to BusZipp. She earned a graduate degree in product development from a Big Ten university. Kami had strong project management skills. On a personal level, she was the firstborn daughter of a family of three girls. Her mother was a college professor, and her father was a production supervisor.
Lorenz Kotwicki was president and CEO of BusZipp and the oldest of the four Kotwicki boys. As president, his crucial role was to increase sales. Lorenz single-handedly expanded its services from airport transportation vans to a business that included a fleet of trained, uniformed, on-demand private sedan drivers and a package delivery service. Lorenz was an excellent verbal communicator and salesperson, but he was not a strong writer not a detailed person. Landscape architecture was Lorenz's major in college. His mother was a homemaker.
Róbert Kotwicki was the second-oldest son in the family. He was responsible for the dispatch of drivers, vehicles, and the coordination of passengers. Róbert was a hard worker, and he had an excellent memory. His people skills and ability to work with the public were marginal. Róbert barely graduated from high school.
Eryk Kotwicki was the third son in the family. Eryk was a loner and liked to do things "his way." He was not a strong team player and took little direction. He wanted to own and drive an airport van with no responsibility for anything or anyone else. Eryk worked when he wanted and when he had bills to pay. He skipped class half the time while in high school. Eryk married his wife Antonia 2 years ago. The family believed Antonia only married Eryk because she though he had money as she "spent it as fast as her husband made it." She was responsible for the accounts payable and receivables for the company. Antonia had limited work experience in accounting, and she was more interested in socializing with other employees instead of working. She also had a drinking problem. Antonia earned a general education degree (GED) soon after marrying Eryk.
Luiz Kotwicki was the youngest child in the family. He was responsible for all aspects of fleet maintenance and purchasing. Luiz was a hands-on learner and had no formal training in fleet repair. Similar to Lorenz, he had excellent customer service skills. He had a high school degree and was very analytical. Luiz had the potential to replace Lorenz as CEO; however, his lack of education held him back.
Józef Kotwicki was the father of Lorenz, Róbert, Eryk, and Luiz and patriarch of the family. Mr. Kotwicki, a widower, started the company in 1990 with the purchase of one vehicle. In 2009, he retired and transferred the business over to his children. Józef felt the company should keep him on the payroll for life and that his sons should keep him in the lifestyle to "which he had been accustomed." At the time of his retirement, the company had $1 million in annual sales, and services were limited to airport transportation services.

Scenario

Kami was employed as a regional manager for a Fortune 100 Company called Data4X2 whose main product was electronic publishing. She operated a sales and instructional team of 20 people who worked in 13 states. Last year the revenue target for the group was over $50 million. The position was demanding, and extensive travel was a vital component of the job.

Kami enjoyed the job responsibilities and income. However, the travel was exhausting, and she was the mother of two children under the age of 10. Her husband Lorenz was the primary caregiver for the children, because he owned BusZipp, a local transportation company with his brothers. Having his own company gave him the flexibility to leave work when needed to parent their children.

Although exciting and engaging, the travel took its toll on Kami. After 6 years and 6 different bosses, Kami was ready for a change. Her husband was supportive of her job efforts, and he suggested looking for a position at the company headquarters. Kami liked the idea and applied for and was offered a promotion at the main office. This required the family to move to a new state about 500 miles from home. Kami's husband agreed to forsake his company and relocate with Kami and the children. The family looked at schools for the children and even put an offer on a new house.

However, something did not seem right. Kami was tired, both physically and emotionally. She knew she had excellent management skills from her experience at Data4X2, but uprooting the family bothered her. Kami had verbally accepted the position, but on the day she was to sign her offer letter, she called Human Resources notifying them she would not be taking the new position. That same day, she also submitted her resignation letter giving 2 weeks' notice.

Her brother-in-law Luiz was excited to hear Kami was leaving Data4X2 and he looked at this as an opportunity to bring her into their company, BusZipp. Lorenz and Luiz owned the business with their brother, Róbert. Luiz knew Kami had strong business skills, and he also knew the limitations he and his brothers had as entrepreneurs (Steiner, n.d.). Luiz asked Kami to join the company. She hadn't been directly involved with BusZipp in the past, but she accepted with little thought. After all, she had been married to Lorenz for over 10 years. Her goal was a simple one for this family-owned entrepreneurial business—grow revenues.

Lorenz and Luiz were supportive of Kami becoming involved with the company. Róbert said little about it. The brothers had worked all their adult lives in the family business and were proud of what they had built. Besides the brothers, there were nine full-time employees and over 20 contractors. Unlike the employees, the contractors would establish their own work hours and use their personal vehicles for client services. Brother Eryk was a contract driver for BusZipp, and he had no company ownership. The remaining three owner-brothers performed a specific job function in the company.

Day One

On her first day working at BusZipp, Kami walked around the company offices, introducing herself to the employees. Immediately, she was horrified at the antiquated technology and lack of efficiency. Drivers used handheld mobile radios to contact dispatch. There were no cell phones. The company had little web presence, and customer orders could be placed only by phone. In dispatch operations, the company did not have a multiline telephone system. Instead, there were eight different physical phones, each associated with their own phone line. Kami made updating technology her first task and immediately purchased an integrated network system that handled all company operations.

Before her first day at work, Kami had never visited the company offices or reviewed its financials. Everything she knew about the company was based on what her husband had told her. At the end of the first day, she realized there was a large disconnect between what she had observed and how her husband viewed the operation.

Day Two

Kami had a meeting with the three owner-brothers to develop a company business plan. To her surprise, Eryk was also in attendance. She started the discussion by asking her brothers-in-law what their long-term goals were for the company. There was silence in the room. She asked them what their short-term goals were for the company. There was no answer. She asked them what their gross revenues were for the previous year. Eryk asked her what gross revenues were. No one in the room had a clue what she was speaking about. Kami quickly learned that none of the brothers knew the importance of a balance sheet, profit and loss statement, or cash flow statement. Also, no one could read or interpret a financial report (Lester, 2016). The only items they mentioned were on the list below.

BUSINESS PLAN TO-DO LIST

- Look for a 20-passenger van.
- Add a soda machine to the break room.
- Order the orange flags to put on the cars for passenger pickup.
- Buy a new chair for Róbert. (Don't forget he wants it to recline.)
- Find someone to do the taxes for the company.

Day Three

Kami had been told the company was owned only by three of the four brothers (Lorenz, Róbert, and Luiz) and that Eryk had no financial interest in the company. However, on Day Three, Eryk approached Kami and asked if the company could purchase his interest in BusZipp. Kami was confused. Upon further discussion, she learned Eryk *thought* he owned 25% of the company. She was told his name was not in the corporate records as a shareholder because he didn't want his ownership documented.

Eryk was such a "free spirit" that he never paid income taxes. He would also give discounts to customers who would pay him cash. Kami was furious when she learned about his special client deals and his irresponsible financial behavior. To make matters worse Lorenz, Luiz, and Róbert confirmed Eryk had a hidden interest in the company, and Eryk had 25% ownership. This meant instead of Kami's husband owning 33% of BusZipp, he only owned one-quarter. Kami immediately hired an attorney to negotiate a settlement with Eryk. She also wondered how her husband could have kept this information secret from her. In her mind, an omission such as this was deceitful.

After learning about Eryk's ownership, things at home with Lorenz were becoming stressful. Kami was becoming distrustful of anything anyone in the company told her.

Day Four

Kami hired a certified public accountant (CPA) to review the company's books. No one in the organization could read a balance sheet to make any strategic decisions about its growth. This included simple analyses such as an income and expense evaluation. During this meeting, she learned her father-in-law was still receiving a substantial paycheck from BusZipp, although he had been retired for many years. She also discovered that vendors were not being paid on time, and there had been some payless weeks for the brothers. Her husband had again lied to her about the gaps in pay. The problem was caused by Antonia's group, who was slow in collecting monies from customers. Kami immediately procured a line of credit with BusZipp's bank, so employees and vendors were paid in a timely manner. She also changed the accounts receivable collection process. To force their payment, customers with unpaid bills after 90 days no longer received services.

Day Five

This day brought a serious verbal exchange between Kami and Luiz. He wanted to purchase a new luxury 20-passenger van for the fleet, but revenues could not support the expense. In the end, Luiz ignored Kami, bought the vehicle, and signed a contract that included an extensive loan at a ridiculous interest rate. To support the acquisition and keep the books fluid, Kami negotiated a more comprehensive credit line with a local bank to "fix" the financial mistake Luiz had made.

Day Six

Róbert decided he was taking a vacation from his dispatch management duties. He called Kami late in the day and said he would be gone for 2 weeks. There was no replacement on the schedule nor was anyone trained to handle his duties in his absence. Kami called a meeting with Lorenz, Róbert, Eryk, and Luiz to discuss BusZipp's employee and vacation policies. Róbert refused to attend the meeting, saying he was on vacation and didn't care what happened to the company while he was gone. Kami told him "family was family and business was business," and in no uncertain terms was he (1) taking a vacation when he felt like it and (2) using vacation time without coordinating the leave with his siblings and other employees. Kami told him she expected him back at work the following day. When Róbert failed to appear, she called him, and his phone went to voicemail. Kami left a voice message not to return to work and told him he was fired. Kami realized she needed to create an employee manual for BusZipp employees detailing all company policies.

Day Seven

A fleet maintenance employee, Michael, scheduled an appointment with Kami to discuss Antonia and her communications with him. He told Kami that Antonia regularly came to work with the smell of alcohol on her breath. Kami had already discovered several paycheck errors in her group. But, unknown to Kami, Antonia had also made unwanted sexual overtures toward Michael. In response, Kami called Antonia into the office and asked for an explanation. Antonia appeared confused by the accusation, and Kami told her to take a few days off with pay.

While Antonia was gone, Kami reviewed the accounting procedures for the company. To her dismay, she uncovered three missing checks from the check register. Upon further investigation, Kami determined that three checks, totaling $13,422.46, were cashed by Antonia. Upon Antonia's return to BusZipp, Kami confronted her about the checks. Antonia admitted embezzling the money. Eryk begged Kami to allow her to keep her job at BuzZipp. Reluctantly, Kami allowed her to repay the missing funds and transferred her to a different company position to handle customer service calls in the evening hours.

Day Eight

Kami questions her decision to quit her job and take over her husband's family company. She locates a new and bigger business problem at every turn, and she thinks she has taken on an impossible task. There is also a lack of trust in her marriage due to the lies about the business. She wonders if she made a significant career mistake. If you were Kami, what would you do?

Discussion Questions

1. Considering the unique characteristics of a family-owned business, what "due diligence" or tasks should Kami have completed before involving herself with her husband's family company?

2. Discuss the stressors for Kami, her husband, and her brothers-in-law. Are the stressors because she is part of the family and managing the business, or would these be the same regardless of the marriage relationship to Lorenz? Do you consider Kami part of the family, or is she an "outsider"?

3. What are the benefits of operating a business managed by family members?

4. In one part of the case, Kami states that "family is family and business is business." Is that the appropriate position to take with this type of company? What do you think she meant by this statement?

5. Was Kami's management of the following situations appropriate?

   a. Reaction to Luiz's bus purchase;

   b. Robert's unilaterally planned vacation and his firing; and

   c. The complaint against Antonia.

6. Kami made several assumptions about the business operation and had expected the brothers to have created a detailed and thought-out business plan. As you learned, a plan did not exist. Kami said her main objective was to grow revenues. If you were Kami, what would be your top three short-term goals (i.e., 6 months) for the organization?

7. It seems like Kami arrived at BusZipp and started making decisions and changes without conversing with her husband or others. Is there any evidence this is true, or do you think she and the owner-brothers made the decisions? If true, why would the brothers accept this type of management? Explain.

8. The family actually includes six children: four boys and two girls. Why do you think the girls were not included as a part of the business? Is there any evidence of stress in the company caused by Kami's gender, a female in charge of a family-owned male company?

9. After learning that her father-in-law was receiving a sizeable weekly paycheck after his retirement, which harmed the company's finances, is there anything Kami could have done to stop or lower the payments to her father-in-law?

Assignments

1. *Inc.* magazine has published an article on the successes of family-owned businesses. Review that article. Based on your reading of this commentary, what piece of management advice would you give to Kami to improve her management skills with the family's business? See https://www.entrepreneur.com/article/247077.

2. Literature defines family dynamics as "family alignments, hierarchies, roles, ascribed characteristics and patterns of interactions within a family" (Jesuit, 2009, para. 1). Assume after 1 year, Kami accomplished her goal to grow the revenues of the business by 15%. Based on your reading and study, what was the cost to the family dynamics even though business objectives were met?

3. Kami brought many changes to the business. Are changes easier or more complicated in family-owned businesses? Do you think this business survived? See https://www.entrepreneur.com/article/235447.

4. Many family businesses stop operating with the death or disability of a founder, so experts suggest that family businesses plan for the future with a succession plan. Read "The Key to Successful Succession Planning for Family Businesses" in the *Harvard Business Review* (https://hbr.org/2020/05/the-key-to-successful-succession-planning-for-family-businesses). What advice would you give the Kotwicki family on creating a succession plan for their business? Or should they plan on selling it at some point in the future?

References

Alcorn, S. (2015, June 15). 4 secrets to highly successful family-owned businesses. *Entrepreneur.* https://www.entrepreneur.com/article/247077

Baron, J., & Lachenauer, R. (2014, June 16). Working with your in-laws isn't always a terrible idea. *Harvard Business Review.* https://hbr.org/2014/06/working-with-your-in-laws-isnt-always-a-terrible-idea

Berry, T. (2012, June 12). How I raised a family of entrepreneurs. *Entrepreneur.* https://www.entrepreneur.com/article/223698

Entrepreneur. (2008, March 7). Starting a business. 8 mother-daughter businesses. https://www.entrepreneur.com/slideshow/178090

Entrepreneur. (2014, June 15). How a family-owned firm can beat the odds and pivot. https://www.entrepreneur.com/article/235447

Haqqi, T. (2020, November 30). 22 largest family-owned businesses in the world. Yahoo! Finance. https://finance.yahoo.com/news/22-largest-family-owned-businesses-115831691.html

Inc. (n.d.). Family-owned businesses. http://www.inc.com/encyclopedia/family-owned-businesses.html

Jesuit Social Services. (n.d.). Family dynamics. http://www.strongbonds.jss.org.au/workers/families/dynamics.html

Lester, P. (2014). Essential financial statements for your small business—Blogs: financing. https://www.sba.gov/blogs/3-essential-financial-statements-your-small-business

Steiner, D. (n.d.). Together forever—6 challenges every family-owned business faces. Business.com. https://www.business.com/articles/6-challenges-every-family-owned-business-faces/

Tabor, W., & Vardaman, J. (2020, May 15). The key to successful succession planning for family businesses. *Harvard Business Review.* https://hbr.org/2020/05/the-key-to-successful-succession-planning-for-family-businesses

The Family Business Consulting Group. (n.d.). In-laws or outlaws? Making siblings" spouses part of the team. https://www.thefbcg.com/in-laws-or-outlaws-making-siblings-spouses-part-of-the-team/

Real-*Life*-Estate Rita

Overview

Rita Smitts is a real estate agent selling residential homes and property. As a young teenager, she was diagnosed with attention deficit hyperactivity disorder (ADHD), and as an adult, she continues to be treated for this condition. As a single mother with two children, she is often under stress, especially since one son has a learning disorder (dyslexia), and the other has ADHD. Rita's career in real estate has been unstable, which causes tension in her life as well. This case showcases mental health challenges in the workplace and work-home conflicts through Rita's story.

Objectives

- Discuss the importance of making a career choice to maximize personal strengths.
- Describe how personal health issues can stalemate one's career.
- Define work-home conflict.
- Explain how work-home conflicts make it difficult for a person with ADHD to function.
- Articulate the professional impact of disclosing mental health diagnoses to an employer.

Key Concepts and Words

mental health, organizational skills, professional strengths, professional weaknesses, time management skills, work-home conflict

ADHD

"Attention-deficit/hyperactivity disorder (ADHD) is a brain disorder marked by an ongoing pattern of inattention and/or hyperactivity-impulsivity that interferes with functioning or development" (National Institute of Health, 2016, para. 1).

Scenario

Rita entered her psychiatrist's office at 10:30 a.m. like she always did on the first Tuesday of every month. She wanted to discuss the divorce settlement from her husband of 16 years. Rita was still distraught 9 months after the divorce was formalized, and she struggled to support her children and work full time. Financially, her income was unstable. She worked for a real estate company, and house sales were sporadic in the winter. Her life was not going well. Through her therapy sessions over time, her psychiatrist documented key events in Rita's life that helped develop a treatment plan.

Rita's mental health history began in the fourth grade at age 10. She had a difficult time in school. English and history made her anxious because reading books was "hard," and she had no curiosity about the past. In the fifth and sixth grades, Rita continued to struggle and failed two subjects. Her parents also recognized that she was disengaged but thought it was just a phase all kids go through in school. However, during teacher-parent conferences, it was suggested that she might have attention deficit hyperactivity disorder (ADHD) because Rita could not stay interested in a topic for any length of time. After several visits to a psychiatrist, the diagnosis was confirmed, and she began taking medication to help her focus.

The medication aided Rita's concentration, and her grades improved immediately. Nonetheless, she struggled with assignments that took a long time to complete. Like most children, Rita still had likes and dislikes at school, and homework was one of the "dislikes." She became more social and made more friends after she started therapy as well. As a sophomore in high school, she made the girls' varsity softball team. Her pitching skills were solid, and she eventually earned a scholarship to play college sports. She was never passionate about academics, and Rita was excited that her sports talent got her to college.

In college, she often arrived late for classes. This was a similar pattern she repeated from her high school days. Daydreaming was the norm during many lectures, and Rita found writing papers a "drain on her brain." She talked to her college counselor, who recommended that her medication be changed. He reminded her she was in a new situation, much older, and may need adjustments to her therapy. However, Rita was resentful and ignored her counselor's advice. With much difficulty, she graduated with a liberal arts degree and an uncertain career path.

Rita's best friend was Martha Brake, and her mother, Elenor, was a real estate agent. When Rita was younger, the girls would often join Mrs. Brake on Open House Sundays. It was fun running around the houses with potential buyers, and Rita thought she might like a career selling residential homes. She located an online realty licensing course that could be completed at her leisure. To Rita's surprise, the testing company allowed students to take pretests to help pass the final exam. These enabled her to succeed, and she eventually earned her real estate license.

Her sales career with Tulippe Real Estate in Holland, Michigan, started not long after receiving her license. It was a small employer with only five agents, and Rita would be the sixth. Once hired, she immediately visited houses for sale because she thought she could sell a home better if she viewed the house in person. Rita also watched videos online that showcased the homes, but she was confused navigating the sites. Completing the paperwork for her sales was difficult, and she didn't realize that a "closing" involved several pages of documents. It was tedious and repetitive work, with strict regulatory requirements. There was no room for error. Because she was frustrated and worried, she asked an administrative assistant, Jackie, to attend the closings with her and help complete the sales documents. Rita recognized her kindness with gift cards from the local department store.

The owner of Tulippe Real Estate, Gertrude Tulippe, was reasonably pleased with Rita's first-year sales as a new agent until she discovered that Rita was utilizing her administrative assistant at every closing. Gertrude immediately forbid Jackie to help Rita once this was revealed. This forced Rita to complete all her closings on her own, which caused considerable stress and anxiety. She had depended upon Jackie for many months and was unfamiliar with the closing paperwork. However, she mustered up her confidence as she had done at other times in her life and focused on succeeding.

But Jackie's removal was the beginning of a downward spiral in Rita's career. At her next closing, the seller and buyer missed signing several places on the documents. Rita had to reschedule the meeting with these clients, and rightfully so, they were angry. The closing took over 2 hours the first time, and it was challenging to coordinate another meeting. When they finally did, Rita met with Jackie ahead of time, so she was clear on how the clients completed the documents. Unfortunately, it happened again, and numerous signatures were missed. The buyers were so frustrated that they backed out of the sale. Gertrude was furious with Rita, who was secretly embarrassed. She knew the failure was likely due to her ADHD. There were so many details in the paperwork that she just got overwhelmed. When she saw her psychiatrist the following week, her medication was changed.

Rita then lost her confidence. Her new prescription seemed effective, but she was unsure since she was having difficulty with some of her job activities. She worked even harder and went back to earlier behaviors like viewing more houses live rather than on the computer. This took away time from finding new clients. Rita was still selling homes, but she loathed the closing meetings. There was no assistant, so she would spend hours the night before a closing, highlighting every area that required a signature.

Her sales were dropping, and the closings were taking much longer than before. Another real estate company that had listed a buyer's property complained to Gertrude. Rita was not paying close attention to the details of her listings, and it was frustrating when they needed to partner with her on a sale. Then, one last situation occurred that caused Gertrude to lose all patience.

Rita had a Sunday Open House for a seller. She hadn't planned well and failed to secure a babysitter for her children. Having no options, she brought her boys to the seller's home for the afternoon. She asked them to watch television or play on their tablets while showing the home to potential buyers. Unfortunately, the boys ran in and out of the house all day, rang the doorbell several times, and they disrupted potential buyers. They were challenging to keep under control, and when it was time to end the Open House, Rita was relieved. According to her normal routine, Rita checked that all lights were off and all doors locked. Unfortunately, the boys were mischievous and had turned on all the water faucets in every bathroom sink and the bathtubs. To the owner's dismay, he came home to a flooded second-floor bathroom and a leaking ceiling. The owner demanded full reimbursement from Tulippe Real Estate for the repairs, and he immediately canceled his listing.

Gertrude met with Rita. Rita revealed that she had ADHD all her life, and she overcame weaknesses by working harder and longer. In response, Gertrude stated that it would have been helpful to have known about Rita's challenges. Tulippe could have adjusted procedures to compensate for her ADHD. But, Gertrude also told Rita that her performance for the past year had been marginal. This did not surprise Rita. She knew as hard as she tried, being a sales agent required the management of many details and she continuously struggled. Gertrude had other bad news to deliver. Due to the destruction of the customer's home by her children, she was immediately terminated from her employment.

Rita's future career and direction were now very uncertain. She was angry at herself because she had never consistently or seriously addressed her ADHD. At the age of 33, she was unemployed and the mother of two young children, both who had medical issues. Knowing she had ADHD, Rita thought she had chosen the right career with Tulippe. Being a sales agent allowed her to be creative, set her own schedule, and do something SHE liked. Maybe, it was the wrong company or industry. She just wasn't sure.

Rita took a deep breath, stared into the sky, looked at the beautiful fluffy clouds, and promised herself things would get better. With a cup of coffee, she opened her computer and went to her favorite dating app to see what new matches she had. She was hoping for at least three new potential dating partners. Yes, tomorrow will be a better day.

Discussion Questions

1. What thought process did Rita follow to decide on a career? Did she make the right decision?

2. Share what you have done or are doing to determine your career path with the other college students in your discussion group.

3. What actions did Rita take to hide her ADHD while she was working at Tulippe Real Estate?

4. Did Rita have an obligation to disclose to her employer that she had ADHD? Explain.

5. Had Rita revealed to the owner that she had ADHD, do you think her employer would have instituted some changes in workplace procedures to help her succeed? What kinds of changes could be made? Explain how electronically signing documents could help Rita today.

6. Assume Rita's employer recognized her signs of ADHD. Would it be an appropriate discussion to have with an employee who had chosen to keep her medical condition private? Why or why not?

7. Rita brought her sons with her to work. Why did she do this and think it was acceptable?

8. Should Rita be able to keep her job? What changes must occur for her to succeed?

Assignments

1. Test your personality to learn more about your strengths and weaknesses by completing the Keirsey Temperament Sorter-II. Are you an artesian, guardian, idealist, or rational? How does your personality type apply to your career choice? See http://www.keirsey.com/sorter/register.aspx.

2. Employees rarely want to reveal to their employer they suffer from a medical and/or mental illness. Explore why. What does the research suggest?

3. How common is ADHD in the workplace? What does it take for someone with ADHD to succeed at work? See http://adhdatwork.add.org/success-in-the-workplace-for-adhders/.

4. Search https://www.ada.gov/ada_intro.htm and summarize the Americans With Disabilities Act. What obligations does an employer have to help those who suffer from a mental illness? Is there a difference between a medical illness or disability and a mental illness and disability?

INTRODUCTION TO THE ADA

"The Americans With Disabilities Act (ADA) was signed into law on July 26, 1990, by President George H.W. Bush. The ADA is one of America's most comprehensive pieces of civil rights legislation that prohibits discrimination and guarantees that people with disabilities have the same opportunities as everyone else to participate in the mainstream of American life—to enjoy employment opportunities, to purchase goods and services, and to participate in State and local government programs and services. Modeled after the Civil Rights Act of 1964, which prohibits discrimination on the basis of race, color, religion, sex, or national origin—and Section 504 of the Rehabilitation Act of 1973—the ADA is an "equal opportunity" law for people with disabilities." (ADA.gov, n.d. para. 1)

5. If you have access to Chapter 3 in the book, *Good to Great*, by Jim Collins (2001), the author uses the phrase "get the right people on the bus in the right seat." Summarize and explain what this means for an employee and employer.

6. After completing Assignments 1 and 5, locate three industries that interest you and identify careers where you could succeed. Use the U.S. Department of Labor, Bureau of Labor Statistics, *Occupational Outlook Handbook* to begin your research. See https://www.bls.gov/ooh/.

References

Anderson, A. (2013, February 27). Successful companies put the right people in the right jobs. *Forbes*. https://www.forbes.com/sites/amyanderson/2013/02/27/getting-the-right-people-into-the-right-seats-on-the-bus-is-essential-to-a-companys-success/#7a5658367dde

Attention Deficit Disorder Association Work Committee. (n.d.). http://adhdatwork.add.org/

Collins, J. (2001). *Good to great: Why some companies make the leap … and others don't*. HarperBusiness.

Collins. J. (2001, October). Good to great. *Fast Company*. http://www.jimcollins.com/article_topics/articles/good-to-great.html

Keirsey.com. (n.d.). Keirsey temperament sorter-*II*. http://www.keirsey.com/sorter/register.aspx

National Alliance on Mental Illness. (2017). http://www.nami.org/

National Institute of Mental Health. (2016). Definition: Attention deficit hyperactivity disorder. https://www.nimh.nih.gov/health/topics/attention-deficit-hyperactivity-disorder-adhd/index.shtml

U.S. Department of Health & Human Services. (n.d.). Health information privacy. Employers and health information in the workplace. https://www.hhs.gov/hipaa/for-individuals/employers-health-information-workplace/

U.S. Department of Justice and Civil Rights Division. (n.d.). Information and technical assistance on the Americans with Disabilities Act. ADA.gov. https://www.ada.gov/ada_intro.htm

U.S. Department of Labor. (2015, December 17). Occupational outlook handbook. https://www.bls.gov/ooh/

Walker, L. (2016, October 16). Success in the workplace for ADHDers. http://adhdatwork.add.org/success-in-the-workplace-for-adhders/

More Than a Nanny

By Katrina Bezak

Objectives

- Summarize the unique challenges of working as an in-home child-care worker.
- Explain the components of self-employment contract negotiation.
- Summarize the benefits and disadvantages of a confidentiality agreement.
- Discuss how to evaluate a problem and assess possible solutions.
- Describe the impact of rushing to judgment in a conflict situation.

Key Concepts and Words

child care, communication, confidentiality agreement, conflict, employment agreement, negotiation

Overview

Claudia Murphy is a self-employed nanny with over 15 years of experience in the child-rearing field. She specializes in sibling conflict resolution, interactive healthy dietary habits, and family adjustment for first-time parents. The Cho family has employed Claudia for the last 3 years. She started her initial employment with one child, and a second was born almost a year and a half later. Professional and personal conflicts began, and Claudia was terminated.

Scenario

Mrs. Claudia Murphy loved children. She had no children of her own, but the combination of a child's innocence and boundless energy invigorated her. When Claudia was 12, she started babysitting her next-door neighbors' 3-year-old, and she immediately knew this was the career for her. She attended a local community college and received an associate's degree in psychology. Claudia was very fortunate to live in a suburb of Baltimore, Maryland, as the need for nannies in the Washington, DC, area was never-ending.

Three years ago, Claudia connected with Mrs. Cho through a mutual friend, Sally Grendel. Claudia had worked for the Grendel family for 11 years, but after Mrs. Grendel's assignment ended at the South African Embassy, the Grendel family transferred back home to Cape Town. Claudia interviewed with Mr. and Mrs. Cho, and the relationship appeared to be a good match. Mrs. Cho was impressed that Claudia was fluent in English and Spanish, and she had "elementary"[1] knowledge of Mandarin. Mr. and Mrs. Cho were both bilingual and fluent in Mandarin and English. Mr. Cho was a physician's assistant, and Mrs. Cho was a foreign diplomat employed by the Embassy of the People's Republic of China.

Claudia started working for the family on a trial basis in October 2017. Initially, she was responsible for the care of one child, a boy (Sean), who was 4 years old. In January, Mrs. Murphy and Mrs. Cho formalized the working relationship with a negotiated employment contract. The terms of the contract were to be renegotiated each year. The first-year agreement signed in January 2018 included the following terms and conditions:

- her top priority must be the child(ren)'s safety:
- an hourly wage of $16.10;
- cash for services paid every Friday;
- an annual raise every year;
- responsibilities to include child drop-offs, pickups, playdates, socialization, and "nanny parenting" during educational activities;
- an option to transition to full-time once additional children were born; and
- full-time employment would include health benefits.

Things went well for the first year. Sean was a delightful, active toddler. As planned, Mrs. Cho became pregnant, and baby Mia was born in February 2019. Mr. and Mrs. Cho felt blessed since it had been almost 5 years since Sean was born, and they desperately wanted two children. When the contract was due for

---

1   This is a classification of languages on Interagency Language Roundtable (ILR) scale. This is the lowest level of language competency on this scale.

renewal in January 2019, Claudia negotiated a full-time position (because of the baby on the way) for 50 hours per week at an hourly rate of $16.25. She became a full-time employee of the Chos and received a regular paycheck with federal and state tax deductions. The Chos also paid the employer's portion of her federal Social Security. In hindsight, she realized she should have negotiated for more money. Caring for a newborn and a five-year-old was far more work than tending to one toddler.

After baby Mia was born, things started to get tense in the Cho home. There seemed to be a strain between the couple. Mr. Cho would complain to Claudia about Mrs. Cho and how she wasn't as pretty as when they were first married. In parallel, Mrs. Cho would criticize Mr. Cho that he was working too many late evenings. There was never-ending friction between the two of them. Sean was misbehaving, perhaps jealous from the attention his little sister was getting, and his crying and screaming were nonstop. Claudia mentioned Sean's irritability to Mrs. Cho. She instructed Claudia to take him to the playground as often as possible to tire him. The baby also became fussy and rocking with a pacifier no longer worked. Mrs. Cho told Claudia that the crying from both children in the evenings was becoming very annoying to her and her husband. She often lamented, "We need our sleep!"

Things came to a major blowup when Mia was 5 months old. Claudia discovered a significant water leak in the Chos' laundry room. She was bathing Sean and thought the floor was wet because he was throwing toys around. She was distracted because she noticed several bruises on his knees and his elbow. Then she realized water streaming from under the vanity. She quickly got Sean out of the tub and dried him off. While he stomped and splashed his feet in the water, Claudia took everything out from under the sink. The bottom of the cabinet was soaked, and she finally located the source of the water in the adjacent laundry room.

Claudia called Mrs. Cho on her cellular telephone, but she did not answer. Claudia then called the emergency telephone number at the embassy to speak with Mrs. Cho. Claudia told her a pipe was leaking water in the second-floor laundry room, and the floor was saturated in the bathroom too. It needed immediate repair from a plumber. Mrs. Cho told her she was in a meeting and "to call whomever fixes those things" and charge the repair to Mrs. Cho's credit card.

Claudia knew nothing about plumbing but was able to turn the water off by the washing machine. The water damage was extensive to the floors, walls, and even the first-floor ceiling. Mr. Cho returned home first that evening. When he heard about the leak and saw the damage, he was seething! He yelled and screamed at Claudia and called her several unflattering names in front of Sean and the baby. Even though it was time for Claudia to leave for the day, Mr. Cho demanded she remain at the townhouse until Mrs. Cho came home. Claudia had been at their home since 7:30 a.m. and it wasn't until 10 p.m. that Mrs. Cho returned. As soon as Mrs. Cho opened the front door, the couple began yelling and screaming at one another to the point that Claudia feared the Chos might be involved in a physical altercation.

Claudia took the children to the third floor of the townhouse away from the Chos. Mia seemed unfazed by the noise, but Sean was irritable. After a while, he fell asleep in her arms, and Claudia saw another bruise on his left elbow. All of a sudden, she had a horrible feeling. The Chos seemed to be going through a struggle in their relationship since the baby was born. Mrs. Cho had said how bothersome the crying had been with the children. Sean was acting different, and the Chos arguing was leading her to a terrible conclusion. Claudia's mind was racing. She was only at peace for the moment because she knew the two children were safe with her. After a while, she dozed off.

About an hour later, Claudia awoke to a quiet home. She wasn't sure if she should get up or just wait until one of the Chos came upstairs. Finally, Mrs. Cho found her in the study. She asked if Claudia would stay overnight since Sean was already peacefully sleeping with her on the couch. Claudia could tell Mrs. Cho had been crying, and it looked like she had a bruise on her lip.

The next month seemed rather calm. Then, unexpectedly, Mr. and Mrs. Cho told Claudia they were taking the children on a trip to Wuhan, China, to visit family. Mr. Cho's father was ill, and it was important for the children to spend time with their grandfather before his health declined further. He had long suffered from rheumatoid arthritis and was wheelchair bound due to deformity in his joints.

Claudia was happy about the break. Under her employment contract, she would receive 3 weeks off per year and be paid! But she was very concerned about Sean. He continued to "act up," and the day before, his shoulder looked swollen. Sean said it hurt badly and Claudia gave him some children's Tylenol. She wondered what would happen to him if he misbehaved on the long plane ride. What would happen if he cried and cried and wouldn't stop? While the family was gone, Claudia decided to research who to call to anonymously report abuse of children.

When the family returned to the United States, there seemed to be more tension again between the couple. Sean returned with new bruises. Claudia also noticed that some of the cuts Sean had before he left for China had not healed. She asked the Chos if Sean had gotten hurt while away. The Chos said he played and played with his cousins every day, had a great time, and learned how to play Chinese ball, a throwing game. (Activity Village, 2021). He was a bit young for this type of sport, but Sean loved soccer, football, and basketball. Mrs. Cho said that in China, he was a happy child who ran around and just wanted to have fun.

In January 2020, Claudia renegotiated her employment terms and conditions. She originally agreed to a salary increase of 50 cents more ($16.75/hour), but she really wanted $17.25. She was offered disability and healthcare but decided against accepting both benefits. Mrs. Cho explained to Claudia that "if she declined, she would pay her the $17.25/hour she wanted, and Claudia could buy insurance on her own." This seemed like a great option, and Claudia was very excited she won in the negotiation. She was now an official employee of the Chos, and she could apply for unemployment if necessary.

However, at the end of the contract discussion and signing, Mrs. Cho caught Claudia by surprise. She asked if Claudia had made purchases for the holiday on her credit card. She noticed some unusual charges. Having given the credit card to Claudia last year for the water repair, she told her if she had wanted something from Lululemon she should have asked her! Claudia wore that brand of leggings daily, but she was miffed that Mrs. Cho would even consider she had used her American Express card—let alone suggest she stole from her. At this point, Claudia became angry. If she was accusing her, now seemed the perfect time to further inquire about Sean's bruises. They had a loud exchange over this, and Claudia left that day exasperated. Mrs. Cho said she was not concerned about Sean because he was a 6-year-old boy, and young boys fight and fall and bump into walls! Mrs. Cho also told Claudia that she had no right to speak to her in that manner as her employer.

Claudia returned the next day, and Mrs. Cho had already left for work. Mr. Cho was awfully cold to her when she arrived and departed quickly to his medical office. Before doing so, he mentioned that he had met her sister, Amber, at the office the previous day. He had treated her for a nasty female infection. If Claudia spoke to her sister Amber, she should remind her not to take the antibiotic with antacids because the efficacy of the medication would be reduced. Claudia called her sister and mentioned the conversation. Amber felt ashamed, cried, and called her doctor's office to complain about Mr. Cho. Amber couldn't understand how he could violate her privacy. Mr. Cho was reprimanded by the supervising physician for this indiscretion. Then, Claudia shared with Amber what was happening in the Cho residence. After that morning, Mr. Cho rarely acknowledged Claudia when she arrived or left for the day.

Soon, the calendar turned to March 2020, and COVID-19 began wreaking havoc in the United States. Many employers, including Mrs. Cho's, decreased their onsite staff, and Mrs. Cho started working from home. Quickly, conflicts arose between Claudia and Mrs. Cho's parenting styles. One morning, Sean started screaming that he wanted ice cream for breakfast. Claudia explained they were having oatmeal with milk and berries. Sean started having a temper tantrum with screaming and kicking. His voice reverberated throughout the townhouse. Mrs. Cho came down from her office and demanded that Claudia give Sean the ice cream. This created a precedent, and Sean learned to repeat his tantrums with Claudia to get his way.

His bruises continued to appear, and little Sean again complained of pain in his knees and frequently pointed to his "boo-boos." Because it was still winter in Washington, DC, he played inside, kicked the soccer ball, amused himself with Disney games, and did nothing strenuous to cause the bruises. Claudia decided it was time to report the Chos to the Child and Family Services Agency (CFSA). She also told Mrs. Cho that Sean needed a pediatric physical for his vaccinations. This was true, but she really wanted a doctor to evaluate him for child abuse.

Based on Claudia's anonymous report, Child and Family Services made an unannounced visit to the Cho residence. Mr. and Mrs. Cho demanded to know who reported them. They were told it was an anonymous complaint and explained, without assigning guilt, the Department's process is to make an unscheduled visit to check on the child(ren) and evaluate the situation. Both parents were embarrassed, angry, and distraught, because this lie could get back to the embassy and force their return to China immediately.

When the CFSA worker arrived, Claudia was not there, because it happened on Sunday when she was off for the weekend. On Monday, she arrived at 7:30 a.m. and had no idea that CFSA had been to the home the day before. The Chos were furious and asked her if she had reported them. She denied it for fear of her own safety. Claudia wasn't sure who was abusing Sean. It had been happening for months, and even if it were only one of them, both were guilty in her mind. Fortunately, Sean's appointment for his physical was at 8:15 a.m. that morning. Claudia left quickly with the baby and Sean.

Claudia's motive for the visit was to get the pediatrician to see the bruises on Sean and support her claim to the Child and Family Services Agency. Notably, the doctor was equally concerned by what she saw. Dr. Tang asked many questions about the Chos and Sean's behaviors. She took photos and ordered a complete blood panel, which included an analysis of his platelets because he had so many bruises.

That evening, Mrs. Cho came home with a "confidentiality agreement" for Claudia to sign. Many things had occurred since Claudia had been employed. Mrs. Cho wanted to be sure that none of what had transpired (the violation of Mr. Cho speaking about Claudia's sister and the CFSA complaint) would be shared outside of their family. She said she had her reputation to protect. Claudia was appalled with this request as she thought Mrs. Cho should be protecting her children instead of talking about confidentiality in her home! But, since Claudia had seen Mrs. Cho's lip swollen after the fight with her husband, she had an inkling that he might be the abuser. Regardless, she had already provided a detailed report to CFSA about the Cho household, the turmoil in the Chos marriage, and Sean's relationship with his parents. Therefore, she signed the agreement.

Within a week, Sean's lab work was back, and the doctor called. She asked for Mr. and Mrs. Cho to make an appointment without Claudia to discuss their son's results. Claudia was afraid that Dr. Tang would reveal why she had brought their son for the physical. Perhaps Mr. Cho even knew Dr. Tang professionally. This entire situation was getting scarier, but Claudia was consoled that she was protecting Sean and Mia. In fact, her employment agreement stated her priority was to keep the children safe. She never envisioned that clause meant from their parents.

The Chos returned from their visit with Dr. Tang, and they looked shaken. Claudia was waiting for the "hammer to fall" and be fired. Instead, Mr. Cho sat down at the kitchen island and started scanning through a stack of articles on hemophilia A. Mrs. Cho went up to her bedroom without a word. Claudia was feeding the children and built up the courage to ask what had happened at the doctor's appointment.

Mr. Cho revealed that Sean had been diagnosed with a rare blood-clotting disorder and that his swollen joints, bruising, and the delay in healing cuts were due to the genetic condition. The incidence is rare and only found in 7% of Asians and, therefore, uncommon. Immediately, Claudia felt faint and caught herself before falling to the ground. She thought, what have I done?

Claudia continued to care for the children for 3 more weeks, and then her employment was terminated. Mrs. Cho said that it was in the best interests of their family. Claudia filed for unemployment but found that there was no record of her nanny services with the District of Columbia (DC) Department of Employment Services Unemployment Compensation Program. This meant the Chos had NOT registered as an employer and did NOT make payments into the unemployment system.

Claudia still didn't understand how this was possible. She had a contract from Mrs. Cho that guaranteed she could file for unemployment. Claudia called the emergency number at the embassy to reach Mrs. Cho. She was told that Claudia's name was on the "blocked" list and no messages would be forwarded. Claudia felt helpless. She realized at that point, she had been deceived. She wrote down all the "red flags" that had occurred over the last 3 years and posted it on her refrigerator. She wanted to learn from her mistakes. The next time she negotiated a full-time nanny job, she would be smarter!

Discussion Questions

1. Look at the terms of the employment agreement between Claudia and the Chos. Who seemed the stronger negotiator: Claudia or Mrs. Cho? Why?

2. Why would Claudia want a written contract for her child-care duties? Why would Mrs. Cho want one?

3. Based on the terms of the renewed contract (January 2019), Claudia didn't get the salary she expected. Why do you think she conceded to making less money than she thought she deserved?

4. Mrs. Cho accused Claudia of credit card purchases and rushed to judgment. Describe a better approach Mrs. Cho could have followed.

5. Similarly, did Claudia rush to judgment in making an anonymous call to the Child and Family Services Agency? How would you have approached the situation?

6. On termination, Mrs. Cho said, "It's in the best interest of the family." Discuss what she meant by that statement.

7. Claudia's passion is child-care, so she will likely pursue another opportunity to be a nanny for a family.

   a. What was her greatest challenge?

   b. What three things do you think she learned from her employment with the Chos?

8. At the end of the case, Claudia states she felt deceived by the Chos. Is it possible the Chos didn't understand all the financial implications of the employer/employee relationship?

Assignments

1. Many people choose to be self-employed after they have been company employed during the early years of their career. Research why. Summarize the advantages and disadvantages of self-employment.

2. Share with your peers if you have an example of a time that you accepted a job for less money than you wanted or conceded in some way. Explain why you made the decision.

3. Explain a time you made a conclusion about a person or event and found out later, your assumption was incorrect. Share the consequence of the conclusion. In hindsight, was your conclusion justified, and would you or would you not have done something different to determine the truth or accuracy?

4. Research what kinds of employers have confidentiality agreements. Identify three and summarize the reasons for the privacy. Explain the benefits to both the employer and the employee. If you find the confidentiality agreement advantages or favors the employer, why would an employee agree to sign?

5. The U.S. Nanny Association is a professional organization whose members must abide by a written code of ethics and professional conduct. Go to the organization's website at https://www.usnanny.org/about. What parts of the code did Claudia follow regarding reporting child abuse?

Additional Learning

- To learn about the signs, symptoms, and treatments of hemophilia A, research the World Federation of Hemophilia (WFH) at https://www.wfh.org/en/page.aspx.

References

ActivityVillage.UK.com. (2021). Chinese ball. https://www.activityvillage.co.uk/chinese-ball

Centers for Disease Control and Prevention. (2021). COVID-19. https://www.cdc.gov/coronavirus/2019-ncov/index.html

Child and Family Services Agency. (2021). Report child abuse and neglect. https://cfsa.dc.gov/service/report-child-abuse-and-neglect

Gerson, E. S. (2020). How to successfully negotiate your pay rate for a caregiving job. Care.com. https://www.care.com/c/stories/2634/negotiate-pay-rate-for-caregiving-job/

International Nanny Association. (2021). https://nanny.org/

Pupulidy, I. (2018, August 28). Rush to judgment. Safety Differently. https://safetydifferently.com/rush-to-judgment/

U.S. Nanny Association. (2021). Code of ethics. https://www.usnanny.org/about

World Federation of Hemophilia. (2021). Our vision and mission. https://www.wfh.org/en/page.aspx

Women and Leadership

5

Domnick's Printing

Overview

An unexpected visit from the company owner and CEO for a digital printing business reveals that Veronica Fathey, the director of sales and marketing, consistently arrives late to work. Veronica, a young rising star, is a salaried employee who justifies her tardiness by working extended days and is thought to be in a relationship with an employee she supervises. Another colleague, who was asked to investigate the allegations, discovers certain documentation inaccuracies and thwarts Veronica's expected promotion.

Background

7:45 a.m. on Wednesday—A conversation is overheard from the conference room.

"Mr. Peters. What a nice surprise to see you this morning. What are all the balloons for?" asks Suzette, his administrative assistant.

"Suzette, gather up the team!" he says. Behind Mr. Peters is a catering company, which sets up a full breakfast buffet in the conference room. "Mr. Peters, this is amazing. The bacon smells so good and smoked

Objectives

- Explain how an employee's career can be hindered by perpetual tardiness.
- Discuss the effect of a manager's perpetual tardiness on workplace morale and the efficiency of a team.
- Describe the value of honesty and integrity in a work environment.
- Defend an employee choosing to keep their marital status private from their employer.

Key Concepts and Words

company culture, employee handbook, honesty, integrity, marital status, perpetual tardiness salmon, Krispy Kreme donuts, and a full Starbucks coffee bar ... what a treat!" Suzette was beyond impressed. Not only was this a surprise for the other employees, but it was for her too. She is usually informed of everything, and she had nothing to do with ordering the food. "You really must have major news for the team."

"Suzette, you have known me too long. Yes, I am starting a new chapter for our company, but I wanted to share it with everyone. Everyone, together. I bought Domnick's Printing over 23 years ago, and I never thought we would be so successful, surviving the online office supply chains."

"This team has made me proud," he continued. "My father used to say, take care of your employees, and they'll return the goodwill sevenfold. Our business has grown far more than that, and now is the time to celebrate."

8:00 a.m. on Wednesday—Mr. Peters thinks to himself.

"Where are all my employees? Why is Veronica not here?"

Scenario

John Peters, CEO of Domnick's Printing, has made a surprise visit to his company. He asked that all directors and managers meet in the boardroom in 15 minutes. He planned to make an important announcement about a change in company leadership. Noticeably absent was Veronica Fathey, his director of marketing and sales, as well as Nolan Manning, a manager in Veronica's business unit. Peters asked where they might be, and he learns from Steven Pension, an employee in the room, that they are always late and not to expect them until at least 8:30 a.m.

Mr. Peters, who is rarely at the office, is visibly upset that two of his leadership team are late, and in particular, Veronica, who had not even arrived. He had made it clear in company communications that all leadership was to arrive at work at least 30 minutes before the day started at 8 a.m. This allowed management to post daily goals for the employees and review leadership tasks for the day.

Fathey had been on the "fast track" at Domnick's Printing, and Mr. Peters had been incredibly proud of her. She was a hard worker, committed, and he could depend upon her to "get things done." He saw a bit of himself in her. He respected that she had focused on learning all aspects of the printing and graphics business beyond her direct management responsibilities. Veronica consistently copied him on emails (often sent after regular work hours), which kept him abreast of company achievements and significant issues.

The announcement or "the major news" was that Veronica would be promoted to vice president of commercial operations. All directors would be reporting to her instead of Mr. Peters. Veronica knew about the promotion, and they agreed it would occur the next quarter. Since the position had not existed previously, Veronica created her own job description. Peters and Fathey had also discussed salary, and Veronica anticipated the new role and responsibilities with excitement.

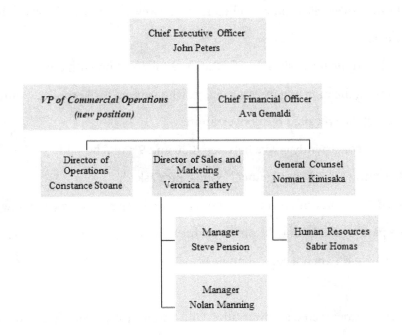

FIGURE 5.1   Current Organizational Chart for Domnick's Printing

Once it turned 8:35 a.m. on that Wednesday, Mr. Peters chose to get started. Veronica and Nolan were not in the office yet; he had no idea when they would arrive. It forced him to delay his planned announcement. Instead, Peters recognized all the employees for their excellent first-quarter earnings. To everyone's amazement, each individual would be receiving a $900 bonus. Since Veronica's department was responsible for 80% of the profit, her bonus would be significantly more money.

After the meeting, Mr. Peters asked his director of operations, Constance Stoane, to explore Veronica and Nolan's absence. Constance suggested Human Resources might do a better job, but Mr. Peters said he trusted her. Later that morning, Constance saw Veronica and Nolan in the coffee room. When she walked in, they were talking about Mr. Peter's generous bonus to all employees. Both said they couldn't believe they missed Mr. Peters's announcement and were extremely disappointed. They were caught in traffic.

Veronica told Constance that she went to Peters's office immediately after she arrived and was told by Suzette that he had left for other appointments. Veronica also sent a text apologizing for missing his visit and hoped he would reply. In the past, Peters typically responded quickly to her, but had not replied by early afternoon. It caused Veronica some mild concern; however, she knew he was busy and had other obligations for the day.

Constance investigated the tardy situation further and followed up with Steve Pension, the manager who mentioned it during the morning meeting. Steve, who worked for Veronica, commented that "they were always late." Constance recalled the conversation:

"Veronica and Nolan consistently arrive between 8:30 and 9 a.m.," he said.

"Are you sure they always show up together?" Constance asked.

"Yes," Steve replied, "and they often come in the same car. I can see out my window, and it is usually Veronica's car in the parking lot. I think they meet for breakfast or something. Not sure. It's a bit annoying because I get here early, and I am not sure what the priorities are for the day, but I always have something to do."

Ironically, Constance remembered a conversation with Veronica about Steve's tardiness nearly 5 months ago. Veronica had reached out to Human Resources regarding a plan for him. Since Constance and Veronica were peers, she wanted her advice on handling the situation professionally as well.

The conflicting information was perplexing. She asked herself, "If Veronica and Nolan are always late, then how does Veronica know Steve is late?" Veronica stated she had verbally addressed the tardiness with Steve on numerous occasions. She had also told Constance that Steve's late behavior was written in his previous year-end review, and it stressed the importance of being on time. Constance asked Human

Resources for a copy of Steve's and Nolan's annual evaluations. She uncovered that there was no documentation of any kind in Nolan's personnel file regarding his work tardiness, but only in Steve's.

Constance became flustered and wasn't sure who was telling the truth. She met with Mr. Peters and proposed a plan to document employees' daily arrival and departure times. The following week, Constance completed office "walk-arounds" at three designated times in the morning: 7:30 a.m., 8 a.m., and 8:30 a.m. She uncovered that Veronica and Nolan arrived about 8:30 to 8:45 a.m. daily. She also noted that Steve was an "early bird." He would wait patiently for the office doors to open at 7:30 a.m. and had walked in with her on several mornings. Perhaps he arrived late in the past, but he certainly was at the office on time now.

For 7 business days following, Constance had continental breakfast delivered to Veronica's group, compliments of Mr. Peters for their recent contributions. It seemed like an innocent way to observe arrivals while she had a bagel and chatted with others about the day's priorities. At the end of the day, she observed that Veronica and Nolan left together about 6 p.m., later than almost everyone in the office.

When she reported her findings to Mr. Peters, he quickly concluded that Veronica had broken his trust by arriving late and that she had disrespected him. He felt the expectation was clear; all leadership was to arrive at Domnick's Printing early in the morning! Peters was disillusioned and angry with Veronica. He met with his Human Resources director and decreased the monetary bonus that Veronica would receive for her first-quarter earnings success. The CEO also decided that her betrayal warranted a consequence beyond her bonus reduction, so he forfeited her promotion. The following day, the decisions were communicated to Veronica when she arrived at work through an email from Human Resources.

Veronica sat stunned at her computer screen. The email mentioned tardiness and "impropriety" with an employee. She couldn't believe that her arrival time was a performance issue and she frequently stayed late to finish projects. She reflected and thought about her recent marriage, too. Yes, she and Nolan came and left work together. But, there was no affair or inappropriate behavior with him or anyone else! The couple had married 7 months ago and thought there was no reason to share the news with Mr. Peters or her team. Their relationship was a private matter.

She was angry and distraught and asked for the day off to mull over her next steps.

Discussion Questions

1. With such important news to share regarding a change in leadership, was it appropriate for Mr. Peters to show up unexpectedly? Did he need a reason to appear without notice?

2. Veronica showed up late, worked later than others, and put in longer hours than most employees. Yet, Mr. Peters focused on her tardiness. Why did her dedication, talent, skills, abilities, and performance not drive his decisions?

3. Mr. Peters rescinded his offer to promote Veronica and lowered her bonus within 24 hours. Do you think these consequences are commensurate with her behavior? Do you think it was fair?

4. The term "hot button" describes an idea, thought, or issue that a person deems important to them.

   a. Was tardiness a "hot button" for the CEO or something else?

   b. How important is it to uncover your boss's "hot buttons" and accept them as an employee?

   c. Share your "hot button." Explain why it is so important to you.

5. Do you believe Veronica falsified Steve's tardiness at his year-end review? If yes, explain why and what she had to gain.

6. Veronica is told through an email about her bonus change and that her promotion would not occur. Is it appropriate to communicate disciplinary information by this method? Explain.

7. Assume Nolan does not report to Veronica. If Nolan did not directly report to Veronica, did she have any obligation to share her marital status with her employer? Does your answer to the question change if Nolan now reports to his wife?

8. It is common practice for an employer to ban married couples from working in the same department. From the employer's perspective, what would be some reasons to institute this policy?

9. Discuss what Veronica's next steps should be with Human Resources, Constance, or Mr. Peters.

Assignments

1. Explain why Mr. Peters and the Human Resource Department addressed Veronica's tardiness through an email instead of a verbal discussion or reprimand letter (https://www.thebalancecareers.com/

written-reprimand-sample-1917916). Do you believe she should have had an opportunity to explain her behavior before suffering the consequences of lost bonus and promotion?

2. Chronic tardiness can have significant financial implications for an employer. Assume a business employed 15,000 full-time workers at $12.50 per hour. Suppose half of the employees showed up to work 10 minutes late each day, yet the company paid them for the entire hour. What is the negative financial consequence for the employer annually? Explain other impact that an employer could experience.

3. Locate two company policies (typically found in an employee handbook) that discuss the reporting structure and supervision of family members working in the same organization. Compare and contrast the language in each policy, explaining how they are similar and how they differ. Consider, for example, how the term "family member" is defined.

References

Green, A. (2015, May 12). Is it worth making an issue over an employee's lateness? Fast Company. https://www.fastcompany.com/3045917/is-it-worth-making-an-issue-over-an-employees-lateness

Heathfield, S. (2019, November 25). Written reprimand sample. The Balance Careers.https://www.thebalancecareers.com/written-reprimand-sample-1917916

Hess, A. (2017, November 3). Interviewers still ask illegal questions but fewer want to know, "Are you married?" CNBC.com. https://www.cnbc.com/2017/11/02/interviewers-still-ask-illegal-questions-study-shows.html

Hogan, M. (n.d.). The effects of tardiness on employee morale. Chron. http://smallbusiness.chron.com/effects-tardiness-staff-morale-1891.html

Investopedia. (2013, July 10). The costs and causes of absenteeism in the workplace. *Forbes*. https://www.forbes.com/sites/investopedia/2013/07/10/the-causes-and-costs-of-absenteeism-in-the-workplace/#551eebd13eb6

Lewis, K. R. (2011, June 9). When your spouse is also your coworker. *Fortune*. http://fortune.com/2011/06/09/when-your-spouse-is-also-your-coworker/

Spors, K. (2019, August 27). What to do when an employee always shows up late. The Hartford. Small Biz Ahead. https://sba.thehartford.com/managing-employees/employee-always-late/

Young Amanda

Objectives

- Describe and list the most significant challenges for a new manager.
- Identify the top mistakes a new manager can make and actions that can be taken to avoid them.
- Evaluate how a new manager should handle a traumatic work event.
- Explain the management challenges a woman faces in a traditionally male industry.

Key Concepts and Words

communication, crisis management, female-intensive occupation, gender stereotypes, leader, leadership style, leadership traits, male-intensive occupation, manager, people-centric leadership, professional goals, task-oriented leadership, team building

Overview

Amanda Grace is a professional civil engineer. She has just received an outstanding alum award from the Georgia Institute of Technology (GIT) in Atlanta, Georgia, where she earned her master's degree in civil engineering. After graduation from GIT, Amanda moved to Virginia and worked for 3 years for a large municipal water department. She is currently manager of a municipal stormwater unit, overseeing 150 workers who enforce stormwater pollution ordinances by making necessary repairs to the infrastructure and water delivery systems. In an interview for the *GIT Alumni Magazine*, Amanda provides an overview of her background, challenges, and reasons for her success.[1]

---

1   This interview is fictional and was created for the purposes of this book.

Scenario

AMANDA'S GUIDING PRINCIPLES

✓ Be Yourself

✓ Learn the Culture

✓ Communicate

✓ Be Positive

✓ Teamwork!!!

✓ Everyone Has Value

✓ Open My Door

✓ Celebrate Success

Interviewer: Congratulations on receiving the Outstanding Alum Award from the Georgia Institute of Technology. The university here only chooses the best and brightest. Your family must be very proud of your accomplishments.

Amanda: Yes, they are, George, and I appreciate the compliment. It is my pleasure to return to Georgia. This state has always been a favorite of mine.

Interviewer: One of the reasons you received the award was your meteoric rise in the water department at Fairway Beach, Virginia. What would you say contributed to your success?

Amanda: As a new manager, I remember a quote from my grandfather that the "road to success is always under construction."[2] He was a tool and die worker, and I remember hearing this quote when I was a young child. So, just like building a new home, you need blueprints and plans to help you meet your goals.

---

2   The author of this quote is late golfer Arnold Palmer.

MANAGERS AND LEADERS: ARE THEY DIFFERENT?

"Managerial work involves performing a number of regular duties, including ritual and ceremony, negotiations and processing of soft information that links the organization with its environment" (Mintzberg, 2020, p. 3).

... emphasizes rationality and control. Whether his or her energies are directed toward goals, resources, organization structure or people, a manager is a problem solver. The manager asks, What problems have to be solved, and what are the best ways to achieve results so that people will continue to contribute ..." (Zaleznik, 2020, p. 16).

Interviewer: So, how did you design your blueprint to successfully manage?

Amanda: It is a step-by-step process, with the ultimate goal of finding personal and professional satisfaction.

Interviewer: So, what steps did you take?

Amanda: I would say first, be yourself. In other words, be true and genuine. Second, learn and embrace the culture. You have to fit into the culture to earn people's respect. You can do this by observing and listening to those around you, so you can gauge what is important to the organization and the team. Your employees will realize you understand the job they are doing, the resources they need, and their pinch points. You need their trust, and this will establish that confidence with them.

Interviewer: So how do you establish that trust?

Amanda: As you know, I manage a team of 150 all-male water maintenance and water service technicians. Most of them are older than me and have been with the city for several years. I knew I had to establish my knowledge and presence in a field capacity. So, on my first day of work, I put on my steel-toed boots, jeans, hard hat, and safety vest to meet my team at the yard. I decided it was important to introduce myself where they spent their day to demonstrate how important they were to the city. I also told them I would be active in the field and advocate for them when they needed something. No skirts or suits for me!

Interviewer: How did that first day go?

Amanda: It went well. The team thought I was professional, but they didn't think I had the field and construction experience that I would need to be successful. When I first met them, it was at 6 a.m., which is their typical starting time. I introduced myself and laid out my principles for the group. I told them we are a team and we will do good work together. I emphasized that my main job is to be their resource and make their job easier. And I encouraged everyone, even the entry-level employees, not to hesitate to come to me with any issues. I also welcomed everyone to stop by my office and introduce themselves during the next few months. This established my open-door policy, and my employees knew I was sincere in making the offer.

Interviewer: How did the team respond?

Amanda: They said I was intimidating, but not in a negative way. Instead, it was more of "Wow, she caught my attention. She is different and unique."

Interviewer: So, you had initially mentioned the importance of learning the culture. Can you give me an example?

Amanda: When I speak to the crew, I talk to them in very straight "down-to-earth" ter-minology. Occasionally, I do swear. On the first day, I thanked them all for their excellent work, and told them to enjoy the rest of their workday and "kick some ***!" My comments might be inappropriate in another field, but it worked well in this environment because my crew recognizes I am different, I am unique, and I mean business. My choice of words certainly did catch their attention, but I use this type of language very strategically. It is not a part of my everyday style, and I do it with discretion.

Interviewer: Did anyone take you up on your offer to drop in and visit you in your office?

Amanda: Actually, many did. I purchased t-shirts for everyone on my staff that said, "WATER is the LIFE of our City." I told them they could pick up their shirt at my office to encourage them to come by and introduce themselves. When they did, I gave them their t-shirt and handed them two blank Post-it Notes: one green and one yellow. On the first, I asked them to write down what they liked about their job. On the second one, I asked them to write what they thought we did well. I wanted them to think about the positive aspects of their job that would also give me the opportunity to learn what was important to them.

After meeting with everyone in the crew, I made a collage of the "what I like about my job" notes and hung that on my wall. Then, I placed the other group (i.e., what we do well) and put those on our conference room board to remind everyone of our strengths. This was my way of telling the team that everyone's input is valued and appreciated.

Interviewer: What was your motivation for the Post-it Note activity? Was it successful?

Amanda: Yes, it was very successful. I had done this management exercise to set a positive tone with the group and emphasize we were a team. In general, my management techniques have worked very well. I have had many entry-level workers (i.e., laborers) talk to me asking for small things like a new nozzle that would make their job easier. When a team member asks for a new purchase, I always respond, "Tell me about it!" or "Let's just get it!" This makes us more efficient and more productive. But I have also had employees come to me with personal problems. When that happens, I try to be supportive and helpful, but deep down inside, I am thinking, "I am not your therapist. Isn't there some other place you can go besides my office to talk about this, that, and the other?" My mother says that is a good thing. They trust you!

Interviewer: You have had many successes. How did you learn to manage so well? Where did you learn all this?

Amanda: By having a kick *** mother. I learned from having strong, empowered women in my life who don't act like women but who act more like men and that women can do anything and everything.

WHAT IS A MANAGEMENT STYLE?

"… can be described as a particular way managers go about achieving their objectives. It's about how they make decisions, how they prioritize and organize their work, and how they exercise authority in the workplace" (Meganinterview, n.d., para. 3).

Interviewer: I notice a ring on your left finger. Are you married?

Amanda: Actually no. But I wear it for a purpose. There are always misperceptions about women and leadership, and for me, appearing to be in a long-term relationship has added to my credibility.

Interviewer: I know that you moved up very quickly in the water system. How did you handle issues that you weren't familiar with, but were expected to know simply because of your position and title?

Amanda: I learned early on that being thrown into a position of power and decision-making forced me to think on my feet. If I did not show dominance, I would have been "eaten alive."

I needed to set the tone on the construction site from the moment I set foot there. Otherwise, the group would have walked all over me. I would have never gained their respect.

Second, when I was in college, I had a summer internship where I was sent to a construction site without knowing anything about the project. I was maybe 19 or 20 years old at the time. My philosophy was "fake it until you make it." I was always a confident young woman, and I had enough knowledge to act like I knew what I was doing. No one ever questioned me, but it made me realize that your outer image and mannerisms are important keys to success.

Interviewer: Does your budget allow you to give any "perks" to your team, such as coffee and donuts in the morning? Does your team appreciate these types of efforts from you?

Amanda: Because the crew is often spread across the city on new construction and job repairs, the coffee and donuts idea isn't convenient. It would be a small gesture and a nice one, but I like to think in terms of what is important to my employees. Their working conditions, vacation, and pay are their top three concerns. I am very fortunate to have a supplemental vacation bank where I can award an employee paid time off to recognize them for a job well done. So, a couple of times each month, I give an employee a commendation letter for their employee file with 4 hours of "free" vacation time. Not everyone can have a time bank as I do, but my employees appreciate this small perk. And, it lets me celebrate their success.

Interviewer: Amanda, I am curious. Why did you want this job?

Amanda: I wanted the job because I like being connected to activities on the ground and seeing the measurable impact of what we do every day. The things we do add to the growth and progress of the residents and the city.

Interviewer: No job is perfect. What has been your greatest challenge?

Amanda: This is a complicated question. I … well … um, it is actually difficult to talk about this.

It happened on a Friday afternoon about 3 months ago. I had one of my best crews working on a water erosion project. The project was located very close to an intersection of Main and Seventh on a two-way side street in the city. My crew had their city water truck parked in the right lane of Seventh Street. They parked their truck as far off the road as they could without obstructing the sidewalk. Orange caution cones were placed around the city vehicle to alert the public of the work.

While my technicians were working on the project, they heard someone frantically yelling from Main Street, "Stop, STOP!" As they looked up, my guys saw a skateboarder about 75 feet from the truck. He had his head down, no helmet and was speed tucking to go as fast as he could. He came racing around a slight bend in the road and was unaware of the parked truck. When he finally looked up, he had a panicked expression on his face, and it was too late for him to stop. The young skateboarder collided with the back of the city truck. He was seriously injured. 911 was immediately contacted, and the police and EMS arrived quickly.

I was the second call the crew made. I immediately drove to the accident site. I wanted my own eyes and ears on the scene and wanted to have a single message disseminated about the accident. The local media was already there when I arrived, and I talked to them and the police. I also needed to report back about the skateboarder's injury to the city attorney and our risk management department, as well as to the mayor's office.

The most difficult part in dealing with the accident was supporting my four team members, all of whom were men. Seeing a 50-year-old grown man cry was never something I expected to experience in my life. My team saw the accident happen and were distraught. The scene was visually disturbing, and the skateboarder's friend was crying hysterically. There was more, but enough said.

Interviewer: This had to be awful. It sounds like you were very strong emotionally during this crisis, and you did a great job leading that day. You demonstrated leadership, professionalism, and calm in a complicated situation. What did you do when it was all over?

Amanda: I got back in my car and drove back to the yard. After making a few phone calls, I went home and slept the entire weekend. In a crisis like this, you must have poise and composure. The result is you demonstrate solid leadership. But from a personal perspective, I was very, very tired. I was physically and emotionally drained. There was nothing left in me to give. The sleep allowed me to recharge.

Interviewer: Do you have any final thoughts you would like to share with me?

Amanda: After the accident, one of the city's newspapers recognized me and my four employees for the support we provided to the skateboarder and his family that day. Although we were not found responsible for any wrongdoing leading to the accident, my employees started a fund to help pay for the injured boy's surgeries and his rehabilitation. He may never walk again or ever achieve his dreams, and I still feel guilty about the accident. I constantly review our safety precautions for my team and for the safety and well-being of the public.

The situation caused me to look at my life, my career goals, and my blessings. My learning is that no person should wait for a dramatic event or New Year's Day to pause and take stock of the life they lead. One should pause frequently to check in with themselves and confirm they are on the path they desire, both personally and professionally.

Interviewer: Oh, one more question. By the way, do you have a favorite quote?

Amanda: Yes, I do. It is from Elon Musk. "Communication should travel via the shortest path necessary to get the job done, not through the chain of command. Any manager who attempts to enforce chain of command communication will soon find themselves working elsewhere" (Reisinger, 2002, para. 2).

Discussion Questions

1. Amanda has created a list of personal "Guiding Principles" she uses professionally.

   a. What benefit, if any, does the list provide to her and her direct reports?

   b. Which traits reflect those of a manager?

2. Amanda's story is very positive and demonstrates tremendous success.

   a. Describe Amanda's management style.

   b. What might be a weak link in her style?

   c. Was her style effective with her team?

3. Describe the value Amanda places in communication with her team.

4. Amanda mimics her crew by dressing and "talking" like them and at times "strategically swears."

   a. Why does she do this?

   b. Is there a downside of mirroring the behaviors of one's employees?

   c. Is swearing at work appropriate? Why or why not?

5. The case study demonstrates certain gender stereotypes. Please provide three examples.

6. The injury of the skateboarder was clearly a turning point in Amanda's career. Would you have handled the situation any differently? Describe.

7. Amanda's favorite quote is from Elon Musk. Discuss how Amanda incorporates Musk's philosophy in her management style.

Assignments

1. How do young managers learn to manage? How do they learn to lead? Research these two questions and share your ideas with the class.

2. Amanda found herself in a very difficult situation with the skateboarder accident. Managers and leaders often find themselves in challenges where they must guide a team during a significant negative work event. Research the topic "crisis management," and prepare a short paper on a person who has been successful during a crisis and one who has failed.

References

Arnold Palmer Quotes. (n.d.). BrainyQuote.com. https://www.brainyquote.com/quotes/arnold_palmer_465530

Belanger, L. (2017, January 25). Single ladies are more likely to downplay career goals, study finds. *Entrepreneur.* https://www.entrepreneur.com/article/288316

Bursztyn, L., Fujiwara, T., & Pallais, A. (2017, May 8). The ambition-marriage trade-off too many single women face. *Harvard Business Review.* https://hbr.org/2017/05/the-ambition-marriage-trade-off-too-many-single-women-face

Bursztyn, L., Fujiwara, T., & Pallais, A. (2017, May). Acting wife: Marriage market incentives and labor market investments. Scholars at Harvard. https://scholar.harvard.edu/files/pallais/files/acting_wife.pdf

Ely, R. J., Stone, P., Ammerman, C. (2014, December). Rethink what you "know" about high-achieving women. *Harvard Business Review.* https://hbr.org/2014/12/rethink-what-you-know-about-high-achieving-women

FGK. (2019, April 28). Women: Managing leadership, marriage. *The Sunday Mail.* https://www.sundaymail.co.zw/women-managing-leadership-marriage

Meganinterview. (n.d.). Management interview questions and answers. https://megainterview.com/home/management-interview-questions-answers/

Meganinterview. (n.d.). How to answer: Describe your management style. https://www.megainterview.com/how-to-answer-describe-your-management-style/

Mintzberg, H. (2010). The manager's job. *Harvard Business Review.* https://hbr.org/2004/01/the-managers-job-folklore and-fact

Moore, S. (2016, July 7). Amy Cuddy TED Talk—Fake it till you make it [Video]. YouTube. https://www.youtube.com/watch?v=RVmMeMcGc0Y

Reisinger, D. (2020, July 18). Companies should learn Elon Musk's "chain of command" rule. *Inc.* https://www.inc.com/don-reisinger/companies-should-learn-elon-musks-chain-of-command-rule.html

Schleckser, J. (n.d.). What's your leadership style: task or people? More important, what should it be? *Inc.* https://www.inc.com/jim-schleckser/whats-your-leadership-style-task-or-people.html

U.S. Bureau of Labor Statistics. (2021). Fastest-growing occupations. *Occupational Outlook Handbook.* https://www.bls.gov/ooh/fastest-growing.htm

Webb, K. (2021). 5 traits every young leader needs to be successful. https://keithwebb.com/5-traits-every-young-leader-needs-to-be-successful/

Zaleznik, A. (2010). Managers and leaders, are they different? *Harvard Business Review.* https://hbr.org/2004/01/managers-and-leaders-are-they-different

Oxford Construction and Concrete

Overview

Amanda Grace is the CEO of a corporation listed in *Future's Greatest Companies*. She has been invited to participate in a webinar featuring the 100 Most Influential Female CEOs of the Decade. In the webinar transcript, she provides an overview of her background, challenges, and reasons for being successful as a CEO under 40 years old.

Scenario

(This is a transcript from a webinar interview.)

Interviewer: Congratulations on being listed as one of 100 Most Influential Female CEOs of the Decade. That is a fabulous accomplishment. Amanda, I know our viewers will want to first know, how did your interest in construction begin?

Amanda: As a child, I enjoyed building things. During our family summer vacations, I built spectacular

Objectives

- Explain how to establish a leadership presence in an organization.
- Debate whether CEOs are predisposed for success naturally.
- Describe the mistakes of a CEO and what could lead to their failure.
- Explain the benefits of selecting a CEO through an internal promotion versus externally hiring.

Key Concepts and Words

board of directors (BOD), chairman of board (COB), chief executive officer (CEO), corporate community involvement (CCI), leadership style, leadership traits, professional goals, promotion sandcastles on the beach and reinforced them with shell exteriors so the tide wouldn't wash them away. My goal was to have the castle survive at least 3 nights at high tide. That is my first recollection. Over time, I built a doghouse, a 90-square-foot treehouse, and a 6-foot-tall miniature southern mansion in my family backyard.

Interviewer: That's impressive! Where did you go to school?

Amanda: I earned my dual bachelor's degree in civil engineering and construction management from Virginia Tech and completed my graduate work and my PhD in construction management from the Georgia Institute of Technology in Atlanta, Georgia.

Interviewer: Did anyone inspire you from an early age?

Amanda: My mother, my younger sister (a Special Olympics athlete), and Michelle Obama. They are strong women for different reasons, and their work motivated me to follow my dream and cherish happiness.

THE SPECIAL OLYMPICS

"The mission of Special Olympics is to provide year-round sports training and athletic competition in a variety of Olympic-type sports for children and adults with intellectual disabilities, giving them continuing opportunities to develop physical fitness, demonstrate courage, experience joy and participate in a sharing of gifts, skills and friendship with their families, other Special Olympics athletes and the community.

The Special Olympics mission remains as vital today as it did when the movement was founded in 1968. Special Olympics strives to create a better world by fostering the acceptance and inclusion of all people.

Through the power of sports, people with intellectual disabilities discover new strengths and abilities, skills and success. Our athletes find joy, confidence, and fulfillment—on the playing field and in life. They also inspire people in their communities and elsewhere to open their hearts to a wider world of human talents and potential ...." (Special Olympics, 2021, para. 1)

Interviewer: Why did you choose to work at Oxford Construction and Concrete?

Amanda: I wanted to find a company that offered advancement, but more importantly, one that aligned with my personal values and had an established charitable footprint.

Giving back to the community is very important to me. At the beginning of college, I won a scholarship, entitled the "Inner City Community Development Scholar Award," which covered my undergraduate tuition. As part of the scholarship, I traveled two summers to several third world countries, promoting housing and freshwater supplies for the poor. Then, I volunteered at a high school vocational center, teaching high school students basic construction skills while completing my graduate degrees.

Post college, I located a job as a manager for the water department of a large municipality on the East Coast. On weekends and two paid volunteer workdays, I donated time to Habitat for Humanity, building and refurbishing homes for those in need. Three years later, I decided it was time to move my career forward. Identifying and selecting a company active with community support was a critical component to my decision.

While researching opportunities, I learned Oxford Construction and Concrete (OCC) might be a perfect match. They were a large company honored with a philanthropic award for building and donating houses in Indonesia after the 2004 tsunami, one of the worst disasters in recent history. The company sponsored and donated food and distilled water for 20,000 families while constructing safe water reservoirs. I also found that the U.S. government recognized OCC for rehabilitating homes in New Orleans after the levees broke in 2005 with Hurricane Katrina and 273,000 residents lost their homes (National Weather Service, n.d., para 2).

Based on this, Oxford Construction and Concrete was a company that used its resources to help those less fortunate. It was also listed as one of *Future's Greatest Companies.* Its vision and objectives were complementary to my goals. So, I was determined to join OCC, and ultimately that's what I did!

Interviewer: You have been at Oxford for 7 years and moved up quickly. How did your career begin?

Amanda: Instead of sending my resume, I created a strategy to get hired. This included making an appointment with the chairman of the board (COB), Theodore Oxford. My goal was to capitalize on my platform from my scholarship and propose how OCC and I could partner and be catalysts for supporting countries suffering from natural disasters. During this meeting, Mr. Oxford inquired about my background, and he was excited that my undergrad and graduate degrees were in construction.

Interviewer: What happened after that?

Amanda: I was invited back to meet with Mr. Oxford the following Wednesday to complete our conversation and determine the next steps. He had asked his administrative assistant to coordinate a meeting with several of the executives and myself to share my ideas. Unbeknownst to me, he was strategizing and wanted to find a place for me in the organization. By having several of his leadership team present, he achieved two goals. First, he hired me to be the spokesperson for OCC during the next natural disaster and, secondly, he identified a position for me within the corporation. His team was informally analyzing me, and ironically, I was doing the same without a traditional interview.

Interviewer: After you got hired, what was your first project?

Amanda: My team was asked to design a temporary fix for a hydroelectric dam. There were elements of my graduate thesis that I incorporated and referenced. The original concept was updated, modernized, and enhanced to be environmentally friendly. I led the project from design to selecting contractors, site preparation, material procurement, and construction.

Interviewer: When do you think the company recognized you were destined to become CEO?

Amanda: Mr. Oxford asked me to relocate to Arizona and establish a new office. It was a difficult geographic market because any construction had to consider the rock beds that were costly to demolish. The margins for profit were narrow, so managing the expenses was critical. There was also a federal government contract that Oxford had been awarded, and our board of directors had decided I was the best person to lead the project.

The project was to design a solution for a potentially dangerous situation that could occur in the future with the state's water supply. Arizona received a large amount of water from the Hoover Dam, and a fault line was discovered near it. The state was worried that an earthquake could threaten its access to water. It had contracted with OCC to analyze the situation and provide viable solutions without increasing taxes. I was proud that Mr. Oxford had trusted and believed in me, but frankly, I was a bit scared.

I was given an office address and asked to start the following week. The company would cover all housing expenses for the next 6 months because the request to move was urgent. I arrived on Monday at 8 a.m. and was met by the building supervisor with the keys and alarm code. To my surprise, I walked into 15,000 square feet of empty space. There were only six lights in the ceiling: no employees, no cubicles, no computers, no chairs, no phones, nothing! I thought this was a joke, but it really was an opportunity to build the business and solve a critical issue facing the government. The outcome of the project was one of my most significant accomplishments.

Interviewer: Congratulations! Moving on to a different line of questioning. You work with mostly men. How were you received when you first started at OCC versus now?

Amanda: It was challenging and can still be. I have been told that I am a tall, attractive woman and early on my physical appearance created a distraction. I found that my construction expertise was often dismissed, so I worked hard on establishing my credibility and leadership qualities. Intentionally, I lead most external meetings, so that it's clear, I am the decision-maker. The technique is often referred to as a "V formation," which describes how birds fly in a flock. Everyone follows me. But I have experienced other challenges as well.

Interviewer: Can you expand?

Amanda: There are several examples that I could share. Others may have experienced these similarly. These events have often driven my passion for change.

First, it has not been uncommon for colleagues and customers to ask me out. It's uncomfortable. One time, an influential client invited me to attend the Kentucky Derby for the weekend. He was very persistent. The invitation included travel to Louisville on his private airplane, accommodations at a five-star hotel, and an offer to accompany him to several VIP parties. I declined, and OCC lost future business. I am convinced that the loss in business was a direct result of my refusal.

Another time, Mr. Oxford and I arrived for a business meeting, and the receptionist introduced us as Mr. and Mrs. Oxford. I am still exasperated about that experience. What could the receptionist have been thinking?

And there are small things that have happened over time, like assuming I would take the minutes of our meetings when our administrative assistant wasn't in attendance. I can assure you, it was not because my penmanship was the best of the group.

Interviewer: What were some of your mistakes or regrets?

Amanda: A loaded question for sure! I am passionate about my work. In a meeting with several colleagues, my determination turned into emotion, and I walked out of a meeting. I couldn't believe the group was not aligned with my thinking and I was disgusted with myself in hindsight. It decreased my credibility instantly. After that, I learned to hold mini sessions before a large meeting with those I thought would be adversarial. I could forecast what obstacles I would face, plan, and build support for my ideas before the group discussion.

Another mistake involved hiring. There is a saying that "your first hire is your worst hire." It came true for me. My boss gave me the autonomy to fill an open position. I decided to recruit someone with a fresh perspective and new ideas externally rather than hire within the company. I used an outside recruiter and selected a candidate with impressive industry references who shined during interviews. I bypassed our process of reference checking. Shortly after the hire, Human Resources notified me that the individual did not work at one of the employers listed. We had to terminate the person immediately for falsification. My connection with the candidates' personality, hiring deadline, and "good feeling" clouded my judgment.

Interviewer: You have been promoted several times over the last 7 years and received board approval to become the CEO of Oxford Construction and Concrete. Why do you think you excelled so quickly?

WHAT LEADERS REALLY DO

"Good management brings a degree of order and consistency to key dimensions, like the quality and profitability of products" (Kotter, 1990, p. 26).

"... leading an organization to constructive change begins with setting a direction, developing a vision of the future ... aligning people instead of organizing people ... and motivating and inspiring ..." (Kotter, 1990, p. 26).

Amanda: I will start by saying it has nothing to do with being a woman. It's about my contributions, achievements, and strategic influence over time. I have a shared vision with our chairman and the board of directors on the company direction, short and long term. I also hired a team that complimented my strengths and who were individuals comfortable with sharing opposing ideas. My belief is that leadership must embrace others' thinking to "build a better mousetrap." I have never been intimidated by those smarter than me, and I have sought out the best employees who would challenge the status quo.

Interviewer: What is your advice for anyone on the trajectory to become CEO?

Amanda: Contribute fully. Be authentic. Push for improvement and take the company to a better place than it was before. Be a positive role model, and give credit where credit is due. Success is team-based, and I cannot thank others enough for the growth and expansion of Oxford Construction and Concrete.

Discussion Questions

1. Amanda excelled in her chosen field in school and her career. How did her childhood influence her success?

2. When Amanda made contacts at Oxford Construction and Concrete, there was no open position with the company, yet Amanda created a situation that resulted in a job opportunity. Have you or someone you know, taken a nontraditional way to go after something you wanted in life. How did it turn out? Explain.

3. Why do you think Amanda was hired to work at Oxford Construction and Concrete?

4. Amanda's high level of education suggests she is intelligent. Do you think all CEOs exhibit high IQ (intelligence quotient)? Is intelligence a pivotal factor to being successful as a CEO, or is it something else?

5. Amanda mentions her mother, younger sister (a Special Olympics athlete), and Michelle Obama as individuals who inspired her. How do you think each of these women influenced her in her life to achieve her goals?

6. Do you think being an attractive woman fostered or hindered Amanda's career path? Explain.

7. Is Amanda a manager, a leader, or both? Explain.

8. It is unusual for an employee to reach the CEO level in the short time that Amanda did.

   a. What traits do you think helped her achieve her position by 40 years old?

   b. How did she establish her leadership presence?

9. Could Amanda have been promoted to CEO without a strong relationship with the chairman of the board? Support your response.

10. Discuss Amanda's following traits.

    a. Would you define Amanda as being humble? Explain.

    b. Do you think Amanda values her employees? Why or why not?

    c. Is her success directly related to finding an employer that was philanthropic? Support your opinion.

Assignments

1. Analyze the Fortune 500 (https://fortune.com/fortune500/) companies in the most recent year available and identify those with CEOs under 40. Are there similarities among the group? Do they exhibit similar traits? What was responsible for their early success? Describe. See https://fortune.com/40-under-40/.

2. The 2020 list of Fortune 500 companies identifies only 37 women as CEOs. Explain why so few women led the highest revenue-generating companies in the United States that year.

3. Establishing leadership presence is different from one's physical appearance. Assume you are a professional coach for a CEO. Create an action plan to improve their leadership presence. Be sure to define what leadership presence means.

4. Leadership style refers to the way a leader directs and motivates people and approaches handling tasks. Leadership style can be influenced by work culture or circumstances. Effective leaders change their style depending on the situation. Using the six styles of leadership created by Daniel Goleman (2020) in his *Harvard Business Review* article "Leadership that Gets Results" (see http://smallbusiness.chron.com/5-different-types-leadership-styles-17584.html), locate two CEOs in the 2020 list of Fortune 500 companies, and compare and contrast their leadership styles.

5. Uncover why CEOs fail. Review and summarize the article located at https://hbr.org/2019/02/why-highly-efficient-leaders-fail.

6. Research whether companies prefer to promote their CEO from within or hire externally, often engaging an executive search firm. Are there any statistics to suggest that one type of hire is more successful than the other? Create a chart that compares the advantages and disadvantages of both practices for identifying candidates.

References

Bellstrom, K. (2016, March 24). Meet the world's greatest female leaders. *Fortune.* http://fortune.com/2016/03/24/greatest-female-leaders/

Career One Stop. (2017). Job description writer. https://www.careeronestop.org/businesscenter/jdw/gettingstarted.aspx

Dezso, C. (2017, October 7). How do you transition into a career you love? *HuffPost*. http://www.huffingtonpost.com/consuela-dezso/how-do-you-transition-int_b_12376032.html

Fortune. (2020). Fortune 100 best companies to work for. https://fortune.com/best-companies/

Fortune. (2020b). Fortune 40 under 40. https://fortune.com/40-under-40/

Fortune. (2020c). Fortune 500. https://fortune.com/fortune500/

Fortune. (2020d). Fortune most powerful women. https://fortune.com/most-powerful-women/

Ganesan, S. (2016, August 17). What do women leaders have in common? *The Atlantic*. https://www.theatlantic.com/business/archive/2016/08/what-do-women-leaders-have-in-common/492656/

Goleman, D. (2020). Leadership That Gets Results. *Harvard Business Review*. https://hbr.org/2000/03/leadership-that-gets-results

Habitat for Humanity. (2020). Learn about our work. https://www.habitat.org/about/what-we-do?keyword=brand-button

Hedges, K. (2011, August 3). The best interview questions you never ask. *Forbes*. https://www.forbes.com/sites/work-in-progress/2011/08/03/the-best-interview-questions-you-never-ask/#7b3d252b29ac

Hinchliffe, E. (2020, May 18). The number of female CEOs in the Fortune 500 hits an all-time record. *Fortune* https://fortune.com/2020/05/18/women-ceos-fortune-500-2020/

Institute for Women's Leadership. (n.d.). http://womensleadership.com/

Kotter, J. (1990). *A force for change: How leadership differs from management*. Free Press.

Leonard, K. (2019, January 28.). Six leadership styles. Chron. https://smallbusiness.chron.com/six-leadership-styles-54300.html

Llopis, G. (2014, February 3). The most undervalued leadership traits in women. *Forbes*. https://www.forbes.com/sites/glennllopis/2014/02/03/the-most-undervalued-leadership-traits-of-women/?sh=5338b32d38a1

McGregor, J. (2013, July 9). Women leaders and the Goldilocks syndrome: Not too harsh, not too soft. *Washington Post*. https://www.washingtonpost.com/news/on-leadership/wp/2013/07/09/women-leaders-and-the-goldilocks-syndrome-not-too-harsh-not-too-soft/

National Weather Service. (n.d.). Significant Louisiana floods. Hurricane Katrina August and September 2005. https://www.weather.gov/safety/flood-states-la

Special Olympics. (2021). Our mission. https://www.specialolympics.org/about/our-mission?locale=en

Sullivan, J. (2016, February 10). 7 rules for job interview questions that result in great hires. *Harvard Business Review*. https://hbr.org/2016/02/7-rules-for-job-interview-questions-that-result-in-great-hires

Zucker, R. (2019, February 12). Why highly efficient leaders fail. *Harvard Business Review*. https://hbr.org/2019/02/why-highly-efficient-leaders-fail

Enough Is Enough

Overview

Tamika Walker, age 37, works as a Hardware Design and Engineering Department supervisor for Heare Air Communications (HAC). She started her employment with HAC over a year ago when her previous employer sold her division. She has been with six different corporations over the last 11 years and has had a variety of work experiences. Her reputation with each employer is positive even though it appears she "jumped" from company to company. However, this is not unusual for one of the fastest-growing industries in the United States: telecommunications (Deloitte, 2021). Each time Tamika takes a new job, it is for additional responsibilities, a promotion, and increased salary.

In "Enough Is Enough," she is promoted into an international role in which she has had little exposure previously. At the time of her promotion her skill set consisted of project management, cross-functional collaboration, strategic thinking, critical thinking,

Objectives

- Describe the qualities and skills of a strong leader.
- Explain the importance and value of a company providing leadership training to its managers.
- Recognize the significance of cultural training for employees.
- Describe how to interconnect a globalized workforce to meet the business needs of a U.S.-based organization.
- Review when and how to accommodate cultural differences within a global workforce.

Key Concepts and Words

communication, cultural diversity, culture, global workforce, leadership, leadership and management training, management, personal skills, tradition flexibility, and relationship building. This case illuminates the challenges she faces as a leader working with a diverse team that includes several international direct reports.

MANAGEMENT QUOTES

"Management is efficiency in climbing the ladder of success; leadership determines whether the ladder is leaning against the right wall."

—Stephen Covey

"Leadership is hard to define and good leadership even harder. But if you can get people to follow you to the ends of the earth, you are a great leader."

—Indra Nooy

Scenario

Heare Air Communications (HAC) is an international mobile telephone communications company with major manufacturing facilities in San Francisco, California; Stockholm, Sweden; Bengaluru, India; Dubai, United Arab Emirates; Seoul, South Korea; and Melbourne, Australia. It also operates a few small, specialized facilities scattered in other countries across the world. As a privately owned organization, HAC acquired several low-producing but potentially profitable companies over the last 10 years. This past year HAC went "public" on the NASDAQ stock exchange (Chen, 2019) to raise additional capital for expanding. It had one of the most successful initial public offerings[1] (IPOs) in the industry.

HAC headquarters in San Francisco employs 11,020 individuals and includes three office buildings, a research and development facility, a test lab, and two factories. HAC employs another 20,943 globally, and international travel is prevalent with employees flying back and forth for projects. The Hardware Design and Engineering Department is one of the organization's largest units, responsible for identifying new creative technologies to market, ahead of the competition.

---

1   An IPO or initial public offering is when a company moves from a private to public status and offers its stock to the public for sale.

Tamika Walker is one of five managers in hardware design and engineering. She leads a team of 14 managers: Five work in the United States, and nine are abroad. An additional 161 hardware design engineers comprise the group. Walker's role is complicated because she interfaces with HAC's international offices in different time zones, and English is the second or third language for many of her associates and employees. This diversity has created a skilled and vibrant team.

This is a new job for Tamika. About 1 year ago, she started at HAC as a Hardware Design and Engineering Department supervisor and was recently promoted to this leadership position. Like most, Tamika was excited about the new opportunity, and the increase in salary and matching of employee retirement savings were very enticing. She also liked the company because its Human Resources department offered excellent internal classroom training for self-improvement and professional growth.

Tamika's promotion was to be effective in a month, and in anticipation of the new job, HR encouraged Tamika to sign up for its Leadership HAC course. It was a 1-week-long intensive session, and most new managers who enrolled in the class felt it was time well spent. Those who completed the course, received a Leadership HAC pin to wear. Others recognized it as a symbol of success in the organization. Last year Tamika asked about the training but was told it was only for new managers. So, she was excited to participate now.

On the first day of training, Tamika Walker was introduced to Lonnie Ollie, the Human Resources director. Tamika had heard good things about Lonnie but didn't know much about this person, except that Lonnie had been with HAC for over 25 years. Lonnie began the training session with an overview of the HAC's leadership philosophy and talked about the importance of corporate ethics, both in the United States and abroad. Lonnie's presentation ended with an overview of the week's schedule that focused on the classic management principle "doing things right," advocated by the late Peter Drucker. Topics focused on HAC hiring procedures, completing performance reviews, coaching problem employees, and managing your department budget. The sessions also involved brainstorming and networking activities. At the end of the week, Tamika was energized and ready to start working with her new team. She spent that weekend strategizing and making plans for her first few days and the coming week. Tamika wanted the first interactions to be perfect for herself and her team.

Walker knew an introductory meeting was necessary and a priority. It would serve to establish a baseline for goals and objectives and allow her to review the most critical projects in process and their due dates. There was a sense of urgency in scheduling this team meeting because several deadlines from their suppliers were approaching.

Tamika set up an initial conference call with the managers in major markets. She decided to prioritize and include only the managers who were her direct reports. A meeting later that month would occur with the entire team. The time zones varied drastically between 8 and 16 hours ahead of the United States, so Walker selected 7:30 p.m. Pacific Time to accommodate her direct reports in other parts of the world. This scheduling meant the manager in Stockholm would be on the call at 4:30 a.m. his local time, and at least two different countries would have start times between 11:30 a.m. and 12:30 p.m. the following day. Unfortunately, her team in the United States had to be on the video teleconference past the traditional 8 a.m. to 5 p.m. work hours.

TABLE 5.1   **TIME MAP**

Location	Day and Local Time
San Francisco, California	7:30 p.m. Tuesday
Stockholm, Sweden	4:30 a.m. Wednesday
Bengaluru, India	8:00 a.m. Wednesday
Dubai, United Arab Emirates	8:30 a.m. Wednesday
Seoul, South Korea	11:30 a.m. Wednesday
Melbourne, Australia	12:30 p.m. Wednesday

Tamika planned to have all the U.S. managers in a room together for the first call, yet the after-hours scheduled time did not allow for this dynamic. Therefore, they were participated from home. Also, she had one U.S. manager traveling to Australia.

Once she started the conference, Tamika uncovered that many of her managers in the United States and abroad used their Heare Airphones (a Heare product) instead of joining the video on their computer with sound connection. At first, this seemed to be no problem. Over time, it made it difficult to converse. Some connections were fuzzy and sporadic, and everyone wasn't using the video feature. Because of this, she wasn't able to establish a personal interaction with her managers. Walker was disappointed. She recognized she had to make the call interactive as possible through her facilitation and questions to encourage participation.

Walker began the meeting by taking a roll call. She could not pronounce many of her global managers' names, which embarrassed her. Tamika also realized she needed to speak more slowly and repeat herself several times. This was due to the poor phone connections as well as the international language barriers. She proceeded with introducing herself as Ms. Walker, started the agenda, and moved to the topic of business unit goals. When she asked about priorities, most managers were quiet. One manager replied but seemed offended by the question. After 30 minutes of limited feedback, she ended the call to the delight of some and irritation of others.

Tamika closed the conversation by stating, "I appreciate everyone's time, but it seems we are having some challenges with audio clarity. Please allow me to send you an email that will cover all topics. If you have questions, either send me a reply email or call me directly, and I will be happy to speak with you one on one."

Tamika was exasperated. Her agenda wasn't covered in its entirety, and her only option was to send the group a written summary with a list of items she needed from each of them. She programmed the email so the U.S team would receive it the next day at 8 a.m. Wednesday, and the global team would receive it at different times throughout their day (for example, Dubai at 5:30 p.m. and Seoul at 8:30 p.m.). She hit "send" on her email and then immediately regretted it. Walker quickly realized she didn't clearly define when she expected a reply or how the information was to be communicated to her. As suspected, emails, texts and calls came in over the next couple of days at all hours of the day and night.

Despite this debacle, the entire U.S. team was eager to meet with Tamika. One manager suggested a casual "meet and greet" in the cafeteria the following day. This time she introduced herself as Tamika, and the informal discussion gave her a boost of comfort and confidence. After that suggestion, she interacted with individual managers several times each day and provided immediate and ongoing support for their projects. Walker was in close contact if they needed her, and she felt she was doing a good job as their supervisor. But, with the global managers, she had a strong sense the team was disappointed with her management skills.

Fortunately, an exciting "intercontinental" project was already in progress, allowing Tamika to build and bridge her skills with a least one manager from abroad. The project was being led by Nathan Moore, a U.S. manager coordinating with his colleague, Jang Seong, the South Korean manager. Jang had been in the United States for the last 3 months and currently worked onsite in the San Francisco office. The project involved a futuristic three-dimensional (3D) concept, with Gen Z and Generation Alpha[2] as their target market.

Teenagers and young adults were the fastest-growing purchasing segment at the time, and those customers valued "choice and individuality." The idea was fun and interactive, where the consumer could design the shape of their cellular telephone. Nathan and Jang had negotiated with a 3D printer company, which allowed for this unique feature. The phone could be in the form of a dog, cat, an airplane, circle, flower, comic character, emoji, or football. Almost anything that could be imagined, could be created. It would be a costly mobile telephone, yet the market research supported its future.

Nathan and Jang presented the business plan and project milestones to Tamika, but she had significant concerns over the flexible screen required for successful execution and the phone's utility. The underworking plate still needed to be shaped square or rectangular, and there were no designs in place for the foundational hardware. Without this, the telephone would fail. Nathan was confident that HAC's supplier was set and ready to go along with several internal teams who had been working together for months to meet the rollout date. Jang agreed, but when manufacturing began on the various prototypes, the models' testing failed, and the project was scrapped.

Tamika caught Jang in the hallway and asked him for an impromptu debrief on the design disaster. Nathan was on vacation. After speaking with Jang, he revealed he knew the prototypes would fail, but he didn't want to go against Nathan because he led the project. Tamika was distraught that the co-leaders had not agreed, yet presented the project plan and updates as unified partners. She was determined to encourage openness and to challenge ideas, so the cancellation of a project like this could be avoided. The strength of individual ideas AND opinions was valued.

---

2   Gen Z is typically described as those born after 1996. Generation Alpha is those born between 2010 and 2024.

Over the next couple of months, several issues, patterns, and experiences occurred with both her global and U.S. teams that caused her angst.

- After reviewing expense reports, she uncovered some managers were submitting charges for alcohol tabs during their lunch hour and in the evening.
- Another overseas manager, who had a 2-week trip to the United States, had expensed double meals for breakfast and lunch. They were for his wife, which was not allowed.
- Tamika's emails noting "immediate response required" were ignored by several employees.
- One manager complained about a cubemate whose body odor was intolerable, and Walker was unsuccessful solving the problem with HR.
- Some of her team members worked 14-hour-long days and then took 4-day weekends, while some global workers enjoyed 2- to 3-hour-long lunches compared to those in the United States who only took 30 minutes.
- One employee hosted clients at adult entertainment bars late into the evening.
- Two managers, one female and one male, kept touching Tamika's shoulder and rubbing her back as they walked by her chair.
- Deadlines were ignored by employees, particularly the overseas team.
- Tamika wore skirted suits to work, and one manager commented that he "really, really, liked women who wore skirts," because he liked the "leggy look."
- One global manager complained of the constant swearing by another U.S. manager.
- Tamika terminated one employee for a drinking problem, only to learn 1 week later about the company's employee assistance program, which counsels employees for addiction issues without being punitive.

The list of items to address continued to grow day after day. Her frustrations multiplied several-fold, and the constant stress escalated until she was about to have a nervous breakdown. She needed some help. "I am talented. I am smart. But this is crazy! Enough is enough!"

Discussion Questions

1. Tamika had a long history of being promoted and leading successfully. Discuss the reasons that demonstrated she was prepared for her global management position.

2. Time zones created a problem from the beginning. Were there any other times Tamika could have selected to avoid inconveniencing the U.S. team, yet accomplishing her goal? Why do you think she chose an evening time for the U.S. group instead of an evening time for the Asian, European, or Middle Eastern managers?

3. When Tamika conducted her first global team conference call, she introduced herself formally as Ms. Walker. At the informal "meet and greet" with the U.S. managers only, she did the opposite and used her first name.

   a. Is there any significance to varying her introduction to the different managers?

   b. When would you suggest using a proper title (for example, Mr., Ms., Dr., Professor) or respectful address (such as Sir, Ma'am)?

   c. Discuss the importance of etiquette in the workplace.

4. Tamika refers to Nathan and Jang as co-leaders, yet Jang did not share his concerns about the pitfalls of the 3D idea. What actions could Tamika have taken for a better project result?

5. What are some examples that alert you that Tamika is struggling in her new role?

6. Most global companies hold all employees accountable to their corporate rules and guidelines as well as the business code of conduct and ethics. Several items are listed in the case could be social norms or customs in other countries, but not acceptable in the United States. Discuss how Tamika could ensure that all managers adhere to the corporate standards.

7. In its training session, HAC's leadership philosophy focused on corporate ethics. It did not provide teachings for building global teams. It failed to provide language and cultural training, nor did it encourage new managers or leaders to self-analyze how to succeed in a global position. Who was responsible for Tamika's failures? Was it Tamika, HAC, or both?

8. Frustration is a common theme throughout this case from the very beginning. Why do you think this occurred? What needed to be done to help Tamika be successful? Identify three to five topics that would have been helpful for Tamika's transition into her new role. Would one be cultural norms? How could that have helped?

9. This case is written from Tamika's perspective.

    a. Is there any evidence to suggest her global team was not accepting of her? Did her own insecurity play into her feelings of nonacceptance?

    b. Outside of her not having international experience, what could be other reasons the overseas management team was "disappointed in her" or not accepting her?

    c. Could gender or her U.S. background and residence be a reason?

    d. Do you think any managers were taking advantage of her "newness"?

Assignments

1. Read "What Makes a Leader?" (Goleman, 2020) available at https://www.businessandleadership.com/leadership/item/33518-what-makes-a-leader/. The author identifies three capabilities present in all leaders and focuses on competencies called emotional intelligence (EI). Explain why EI is critical to the success of all leaders and organizations.

2. Research how skills, traits, and behaviors differ between a manager and a leader. What is the difference? Can a person be both at the same time? Can you be a leader without being in a management role or position without direct reports? Summarize your findings.

3. Many companies limit the number of employees reporting to a supervisor/manager. Tamika had at least 14 managers, the majority living outside of the United States. Listen to the podcast or read the article at http://knowledge.wharton.upenn.edu/article/is-your-team-too-big-too-small-whats-the-right-number-2/. What are the advantages and disadvantages of a tall or flat organization?

4. Review the article "What Kind of Leader Are You?" located at http://www.businessnewsdaily.com/2704-leadership.html. What type of leader was Tamika? Was her leadership style the most effective for her international team? If not, what style should be her default management style?

5. Research how Asian business colleagues address "conflict" in the workplace. Explain why the U.S. 3D project failed due to a custom not shared by both the U.S. and South Korean managers. (See https://www.commisceo-global.com/resources/country-guides/south-korea-guide). Had Tamika known this social norm, do you think the project would have been successful?

References

Alderton, M. (2019, October 11). What your business can learn from Peter Drucker. Business.com. https://www.business.com/articles/management-theory-of-peter-drucker/

All Author. (2021). Leadership quotes. https://allauthor.com/quotes/35035/

Caramela, S. (2018, June 8). 4 ways to define leadership. *Business News Daily*. https://www.businessnewsdaily.com/3647-leadership-definition.html

Chen, J. (2020, December 3). NASDAQ. Investopedia. https://www.investopedia.com/terms/n/nasdaq.asp

Commisceo Global Consulting Ltd. (2021). 안녕하세요 (Hello) and welcome to our guide to South Korean culture, customs, business practices & etiquette. https://www.commisceo-global.com/resources/country-guides/south-korea-guide

Covey, S. (1989). *The seven habits of highly effective people,* (4th ed). Simon & Schuster

Deloitte. (2021). Telecommunications industry outlook 2021—Growth opportunities and challenges in a connected world. https://www2.deloitte.com/us/en/pages/technology-media-and-telecommunications/articles/telecommunications-industry-outlook.html

Fallon, N. F. (2016, June 27). Leadership language: Why your word choices matter. *Business News Daily*. http://www.businessnewsdaily.com/9186-leadership-language.html

Goleman, D. (2020, December 20). What makes a leader? Business & Leadership. https://www.businessandleadership.com/leadership/item/33518-what-makes-a-leader

Hahn, M., & Molinski, A. (2015). Managing vacations when your team is global. *Harvard Business Review*. https://hbr.org/2015/09/managing-vacations-when-your-team-is-global

Knowledge@Wharton. (2006, June 14). Is your team too big? Too small? What's the right number? [Audio blog post]. http://knowledge.wharton.upenn.edu/article/is-your-team-too-big-too-small-whats-the-right-number-2/

Martin, J., & Nakayama, T. (2018). *Intercultural communication in contexts* (7th ed.). McGraw Hill Higher Education. https://www.mheducation.com/highered/product/intercultural-communication-contexts-martin-nakayama/M9780073523934.html

Neck, C., Houghton, J., & Murray, E. (2015). *Organizational behavior: A critical-thinking approach*. Thousand Oaks, CA: SAGE.

Patel, D. (2017, March 22). 11 powerful traits of successful leaders. *Forbes*. https://www.forbes.com/sites/deeppatel/2017/03/22/11-powerful-traits-of-successful-leaders/?sh=36434873469f

Rampton, J. (2015, May 15). How to grow and manage international teams. *Forbes*. https://www.forbes.com/sites/johnrampton/2015/05/15/how-to-grow-and-manage-international-teams/#5c8133712c60

Sandberg, J. (2020, April 1). Best practices for managing remote and global teams. *International Educator*. https://www.nafsa.org/ie-magazine/2020/4/1/best-practices-managing-remote-and-global-teams

Schooley, S. (2019, September). What kind of leader are you? *Business News Daily*. https://www.businessnewsdaily.com/9789-leadership-types.html

SHRM Foundation. (2015). Engaging and integrating a global workforce. https://www.shrm.org/hr-today/news/hr-magazine/documents/3-15%20eiu%20theme%202%20report-final.pdf

Uzialko, A. (2018, April 4). 15 international business customs that could make or break the deal. *Business News Daily*. https://www.businessnewsdaily.com/5176-unusual-international-business-customs.html

Friend to Foe, Making Work "Work"

Objectives

- Summarize the management dilemmas supervising a team with a close friend.
- Describe how to transition from a friend and colleague to an effective manager.
- Identify the strategies a manager can use to establish boundaries in the workplace with personal friends.
- Explain the importance of providing feedback to direct reports.

Key Concepts and Words

consultative management style, employee friendship, management training, manager and friendship balance, peer-to-manager career path, power shift

Overview

Best friends, Tabitha and Christen are asked by mutual college acquaintances to join a start-up technology company shortly after graduation from the California Institute of Technology. One excels and becomes the other's manager, creating conflict for their friendship and professional relationship.

Scenario

Image 5.1

Hi, my name is Tabitha Gorheg! My friend Christen Bahar (she is on the right) and I have been best friends since sixth grade. We went to high school together and participated in most everything at the same time. She and I were interested in computers since we were kids. Our parents always bought us the latest version, which meant we were continually discovering. We frequently focused on solving tough math questions in calculus and those that our teachers said were unsolvable. Ha! We always could. We founded a technology club in high school to create "something," which included three other students in our class. What that "something" was ... was the question!

Christen and I specifically targeted the same college, California Institute of Technology (Caltech), and we both were accepted. While there, we attended a California Technology conference and met three guys from the University of California at Berkeley. They had just dropped out to start a company called 3G's Tech, which intrigued Christen and me. We were in our last year at Caltech and couldn't imagine dropping out, but it seemed exciting and a bit radical!

Back at school, we kept in contact with our 3G's friends, and they hinted that they might want us to come on board after graduation. Since it was our last year, we interviewed with several companies, and our employment options were numerous. Christen and I had been friends for so long; we thought it would be fun if we could get hired by the same company. So, we sent our resumes to the same employers with hopes we would both be called for interviews. We also considered joining the 3G's guys from Berkeley but Christen and I weren't sure a start-up was the way to go.

However, 1 month before graduation, Kevin, Mark, and Andrew—the guys from Berkeley—asked us to meet them one night for a beer to discuss an "opportunity." At first, we thought they might be suggesting a "date night" but quickly decided that didn't make sense. Then, we thought they might want us to collaborate on something or hire us, and they did! Since we had not decided which job offers to accept, this was perfect timing.

Mark laid out their business plan for the start-up. Kevin had an idea for an artificial intelligence (AI) software program that could read the thoughts in a user's brain and type them into a computer. This concept would increase the productivity of anyone who had to write documents. Literally, anyone in the world would no longer have to type or write physically. A user's thoughts would be sent to the computer, and the software would enter them grammatically correct into a word processor. The user could access the document by instructing the computer (through brain waves), or the writer could make changes by manually altering the document. Then, it could be printed or sent as a final document. For people who were paralyzed and could no longer write or suffered from an illness like multiple sclerosis (which can cause tremors and visual impairment), their lives could be more normal day to day because they could communicate in this familiar way. They coined it appropriately the "Brain Project"!

Both Christen and I were sold. The company had elements of excitement and of impossibility, just like our math equations in high school. We signed on with 3G's Tech and put our heads together to help take the AI concept to market. In the summer, we put in long days. Monday through Thursday, we hunkered down in the office and brainstormed early in the day to evening, so we could scam out on Fridays about 11 a.m. for weekend surfing. We did the same thing in winter but drove east to Mammoth Mountain for skiing and snowboarding. We loved our lives.

Christen and I had also set up a company called Gorbah Ventures to purchase rental real estate in California. The market had shifted, and rental properties were an investment with a strong return on one's money. It was one of our dreams to go into business together when we were in college. We couldn't believe how well our lives had turned out!

After our first year at 3G's, the company partnered with a small start-up called AIcog to assist with the "Brain Project" software. Kevin approached me and asked if I wanted to take lead of the collaboration. He explained I would manage the execution of the business plan, the timelines, communications both internally and externally, and supervise the work team developing the software. But there was one significant change with this promotion. Christen and I would no longer be peers. Instead, she would report to me with three other software engineers.

I was elated by the opportunity, agreed immediately, and searched out Christen to share the news. At first, I thought she felt the same excitement I did, but then I wasn't so sure. She congratulated me and said she had to get back to work and abruptly turned and headed down the hallway. Usually, we chatted for several minutes when we saw each other. I was bummed because I wanted to give her all the details.

She was my best friend and seemed happy for me, but I couldn't tell. I could always read her mind in the past, kind of like the "Brain Project," but not this time.

The following morning, the first thing I did was to meet with the three other employees reporting to me. Since I knew Christen like a sister, I didn't have to have a "meet and greet" with her. I knew everything about her already! I asked each of the engineers to give me a rundown of their expertise and their ideas for the "Brain Project."

In the afternoon, Christen and I continued with our regular, daily "whiteboard session." But this time, I had to invite and facilitate creative thinking with the entire workgroup. In the past, Christen and I held our own session (just the two of us), so this was different for us. She usually scribed, and I rattled off ideas as fast as they came to mind. Also, to be inclusive of the team, I asked another teammate, Jason, to write down the ideas. I thought Christen would appreciate just providing input, but I was wrong. In fact, she was always free with her ideas, but she was "quiet as a mouse" in this setting.

I was irritated because we needed her ideas. She was very creative and innovative, but she wasn't contributing. I knew she could almost solve any software glitch, so I finally asked Christen if she had any thoughts. She responded that "there were plenty of ideas from others on the team, and any of them would work." In one meeting and just 1 hour, I had seen a side of Christen I had never seen in our 13 years of friendship. Our lives had paralleled each other for so long; this was the first departure from us not being on the "same page."

At the end of that day, Christen left the office without me knowing. We had always departed together and shared an apartment, too. When I got home, her bedroom door was closed, so I didn't knock. I thought maybe she was sleeping, but I knew she was upset and awake.

Over the next several days, Christen barely spoke to me. Our interactions were very awkward, and she was really "moody." If I asked her a question at work, she was very "matter of fact." She responded and quickly left my office. One evening, she asked about going to look at condos at the end of the week, but I couldn't because I had to present to 3G's investors on the progress of the "Brain Project." She stormed back into her bedroom and mumbled something about not caring about our friendship and moving out.

In truth, I missed both her friendship and our partnership at work. In just a couple of months, we seemed to have gone from friends to enemies. I was sad, and so was she. It was affecting us personally and damaging our performance at work. I didn't want to lose her friendship over a job, and it was clear our relationship changed when I was promoted.

I asked Christen to meet me at our favorite hangout on Friday evening, but I wasn't sure she would show up. She did, and we had a tough conversation. I told her that being her boss did change things between us. We agreed that our lives had taken a different direction, and she revealed that she was jealous. She felt her ideas didn't matter anymore and that our bond of friendship was broken. She said she wanted to quit.

I wasn't sure if I should respond as a "manager or a friend." For the first time, I put on my corporate hat, and I started re-recruiting Christen. She was valuable to the "Brain Project," and she was a brilliant engineer. I wanted Christen to remain with 3G's, and hopefully, our friendship would endure.

Discussion Questions

1. It is not uncommon for a person to be promoted to manage a team of previous peers. What facts suggest this was a difficult transition for Tabitha and Christen?

2. Tabitha made a mistake during her initial meetings as a new manager. Had she handled interactions differently with her friend Christen, their professional relationship and friendship may have been impacted differently. What did she do, and what should she have done and why? (Hint: Management style)

3. Christen appears to be forcing Tabitha to choose between their friendship and her new opportunity with 3G's Tech and AIcog.

   a. How can they remain friends and colleagues?

   b. Should the women continue their real estate investment partnership? If so, would any changes be necessary for their business relationship to thrive? Discuss.

4. If Tabitha stepped down from her management position, do you think their friendship would revert to when the two women were employed in the same role? If Christen was transferred to another project, would their friendship survive? Explain.

5. If the women can remain friends and colleagues, provide three suggestions and/or steps to keep their professional life and personal friendship healthy.

6. Tabitha did not address Christen's behavior during the team meeting at the office. When they got together as friends, they discussed some of the work conflict.

   a. If they had no friendship outside of the office, do you think Tabitha would have discussed the situation with her direct report?

   b. How did having a friendship with Christen alter her management behavior?

   c. How important is providing timely feedback (recognition or improvement) at work? Why?

7. It does not appear that 3G's provided management training for new managers. Looking at this from a larger perspective, what topics would you want included in a workshop for new managers?

Assignments

1. Research and prepare a short (seven- to 10-slide) PowerPoint presentation on strategies a new manager should follow, who has been promoted and will be managing a friend or former peers. See http://www.beleaderly.com/manage-former-peers/ to start your research.

2. Locate three friends or colleagues who have worked with a friend. Have them share their story with you. Was it a positive or negative experience? Explain your findings.

3. Many former start-up technology companies such as Google, Twitter, and Facebook encourage a social and work culture that supports innovation and creativity. Many of the established cultural norms of "big business" are not followed in these companies. Research what these businesses do differently that makes them so successful.

References

Armour, S. (2007, August 2). Friendship and work: A good or bad partnership? *USA Today*. https://usatoday30.usatoday.com/money/workplace/2007-08-01-work-friends_N.htm

Caprino, K. (2018, February 18). Can bosses and employees be friends outside work? *Forbes*. https://www.forbes.com/sites/kathycaprino/2018/02/18/can-bosses-and-employees-be-friends-outside-of-work/?sh=40f9c51d4140

Grant, A. (2015, September 4). Friends at work. No so much. *New York Times*. https://www.nytimes.com/2015/09/06/opinion/sunday/adam-grant-friends-at-work-not-so-much.html

Hedges, K. (2015, March 31). New rules! How managers can be friends with employees. *Forbes*. https://www.forbes.com/sites/work-in-progress/2015/03/31/new-rules-how-managers-can-be-friends-with-employees/#69ecfc0e4c5b

Hill, L., & Lineback, K. (2011, January 18). Be the boss, not the friend. *Fortune*. http://fortune.com/2011/01/18/be-the-boss-not-a-friend/

Laker, B., Patel, C., Malik, A., & Budhwar, P. (2020, September 24). What to do when you become your friend's boss. *Harvard Business Review*. https://hbr.org/2020/09/what-to-do-when-you-become-your-friends-boss

Office Team. (2015, June 5). 5 tips for managing your relationships with work friends. Robert Half. https://www.roberthalf.com/officeteam/blog/5-tips-for-managing-your-relationships-with-work-friends

Salemi, V. (2014, June 14). How to manage a team of your former peers. *Newsweek*. http://money.usnews.com/money/blogs/outside-voices-careers/2014/06/10/how-to-manage-a-team-of-your-former-peers

Figure Credit

IMG 5.1: Copyright © 2019 Depositphotos/gsstockstudio.

International Dimensions

6

International Negotiations

By Mary Blair

Overview

This case study involves an American woman named Becca Massey, who is responsible for leading the supply chain function[1] for a global corporation. Her management duties include purchasing and negotiating contracts for raw materials needed for the manufacturing of products at its national and international facilities. Becca is the lead negotiator for their "strategic team." Her group has three business units located geographically in North America, Europe, and Asia. Becca is traveling to Taiwan to work with her company's Asian division, consisting of four men whose native countries are China, Malaysia, Taiwan, and Japan. Each is fluent in English as a second language.

Objectives

- Define the cultural training necessary for successful global business interactions.
- Describe the differences in the planning, structure, and execution of a meeting in the United States as contrasted with a foreign country.
- Explain the value of utilizing an interpreter's services when hosting a meeting in a non-English speaking country.

Key Concepts and Words

action plan, agenda, business strategy, facilitation, meeting logistics, planning, post-meeting feedback, task-oriented leadership, time management, vendor

---

[1] "The functions in a supply chain include product development, marketing, operations, distribution, finance, and customer service. Supply chain management results in lower costs and a faster production cycle" (Kenton, 2020, para. 1).

STRATEGY

"The difference between success and failure in business largely depends upon your ability to look at your company through the lens of strategic planning and make sure that everything you are doing is contributing to the achievement of your most important business goals." (Tracy, 2015, p. 113)

Scenario

Becca is a senior procurement manager for a publicly held North American automotive manufacturer named Gautten. She began her career as a buyer for the company. In that role, Becca was responsible for conducting regional contract negotiations with North American suppliers. Three years ago, she was promoted to senior procurement manager. Her geography grew and expanded to include South America and northern Europe. Her career growth has been consistent, and she credits a cultural training class years ago for helping her feel comfortable traveling abroad.

Gautten's future business model has its company increasing its footprint (or presence) in Asia to add more suppliers and at least two manufacturing facilities. The goal is to move 80% of manufacturing from North America to overseas.

Due to a reorganization, Becca now has responsibility for all global negotiations. Gautten's three contracting teams or units (North America, Europe and Asia) report directly to her, which is an enormous increase in responsibility and accountability. This month she has been assigned to negotiate a multimillion-dollar contract for Gautten with a Taiwanese supplier. Becca is well versed in negotiating tactics, aware of the contract objectives and requirements, and has always maintained high ethical standards in contract discussions. However, she has limited professional experience in Taiwanese business practices.

Since she is an expert in negotiating and closing "deals," she has a set routine in preparing for the initial conversation with a customer. Becca always has an agenda for the meeting and creates a list of the "must-haves," "negotiables," and "giveaways" to ensure all critical topics are covered.

AGENDA

Wednesday, December 19, 202x

9-10 a.m.

Location: Manaught Hotel, Taipei

Attending: Myself, Gautten Asian team, BestMetals team

Discussion Items: must-haves, negotiables, giveaways

Follow-up

For this contract discussion in Taiwan, Becca emailed the Asian strategic team to remind them that the meeting outputs must be consistent with Gautten's global goals (expand the Asian network, increase corporate revenues, and promote sustainable industrialization).

In the email, she also provided the details for the meeting location as well. It would take place at the Taipei Maryaught Hotel, a western-style hotel.[2] Normally, Becca would schedule a premeeting with the Gautten group before the customer discussions to go over each person's role. However, she felt the Asian team was familiar with this supplier and all would be fine. Her flight schedule was tight, and she wanted to have time alone at breakfast to review the contract terms and conditions. About 24 hours ago, Becca had emailed everyone before she started her travel to Taiwan and was confident that they would be prepared. She checked her email when she landed at 2:18 a.m. local time, just in case anyone had a question. That morning, she had a full breakfast buffet, read through the contract document, checked her notes on her iPad, and had three cups of coffee to keep her energized.

As the meeting time got closer, Becca became a bit nervous. It was her first negotiation with an Asian vendor—ever, in her career. Although she felt she and her team were ready to go, she personally had spent little time with her own new employees. Just like her previous teams, she was depending upon them to

---

2   A western-style hotel appeals to U.S. travelers and will offer amenities typically found in American hotels such as breakfast buffets, double beds, and rooms with snacks and drinks.

"jump in" if they encountered any "bumps along the road." In fact, she was relieved that three members of unit were fluent in Mandarin and English.

Becca took the elevator to the 23rd floor and found the conference room in the hotel that her administrative assistant had reserved. Her team would be meeting with several suppliers throughout the day. BestMetals was the first appointment and the most important supplier. It owns iron ore mines and other high-demand metal mines across the world. BestMetals also operates its own processing facilities in many locations in Asia, and it is internationally renowned for quality and efficiency. As Becca watched the clock, she and her colleagues waited patiently for the supplier to arrive. They passed time by chatting about the hotel accommodations.

The BestMetals attendees entered the room. Becca noted that all the representatives were male except for one young woman named Lijuan, their interpreter. They chose to seat themselves on one side of the conference room table, and Gautten's team sat on the opposite side except for Becca, who selected the chair at the head of the table.

Becca began the meeting in English by welcoming the BestMetals representatives. She opened up her iPad to have her notes handy. No one else had a laptop or computer open, except Lijuan.

Becca gave copies of the agenda to the nearest BestMetals associate and asked each person to take one. Xīnyí, her Chinese rep, stared at her and tried to get her attention. But Becca was so focused on handing out the agenda, she missed his eye gestures. Lijuan, the interpreter, quickly jumped from her seat, took the pages, and gave one to each individual from her company.

Becca noticed the BestMetals group appeared confused, so she slowed down her speech. She remembered this technique from her cultural training course. She learned that it helps others comprehend English when it is their second language. She continued and then introduced her team and allowed BestMetals to do the same.

Xīnyí tried again to get Becca's attention without success. Lijuan asked who was empowered to award the business and when the senior officer from Gautten would be arriving. Lijuan directed her question to one male associate on Gautten's team, Yu-Chen, who is Taiwanese. Becca responded she was the senior officer and directed everyone's attention back to the agenda for the meeting.

The men from BestMetals continued to talk among themselves. Lijuan again asked when others would be joining the negotiations. There was still a disconnect between the two sides of the table. Becca explained her role and was anxious to get the meeting going. She then sent a draft copy of a contract around the table written in English.

At this point, Lijuan politely requested tea for her associates and suggested that all take a moment to have a general open discussion. Becca was embarrassed. She realized she had proceeded immediately into the business discussion without allowing time for tea and hospitality customs. Becca did not mean to be rude and recalled her class covering the importance of relationship building with the Taiwanese. She knew she had started the meeting incorrectly and quickly tried to reestablish the negotiation's proper setting.

Becca poured herself a cup of tea and sat directly across from the highest-ranking BestMetals associate who introduced himself as Mr. Hsu. A couple times he called on Lijuan to interpret, but overall the conversation seemed to flow well. Becca did not discuss business and instead talked about her flight to their country. She asked about the supplier teams' experiences traveling to the United States and her desire to visit the National Palace Museum in Taiwan.

As the BestMetals associates relaxed, Becca and her team could see the change in body language. For the next 2 hours, the group drank tea. The negotiations began during the informal discussions, and it had been initiated by BestMetals. While discussing U.S. current events, Becca positioned the supply negotiation as an opportunity for the United States and Taiwan to partner. She detailed the benefits for both companies. However, she remembered the goals for Gautten and made sure the contract would achieve those for the company. Becca encouraged her team to participate, but overall, they were very quiet during the discussion. Although the interaction was pleasant, BestMetals did not agree to a deal with Gautten.

When Becca returned to the States, she scheduled a virtual conference call with her direct reports in both Asia and the United States. Its purpose was to review the meeting's objectives and outcome. She was upset they were not able to convince BestMetals or any Taiwanese supplier to contract with Gautten. Becca needed to hear their perspective on why they failed. She could not understand why no one stepped up to facilitate the conversations. She mentioned how helpful Lijuan was from BestMetals and told her team they let her down.

She continued, "This cannot happen again." Next month, they had visits planned to India and Thailand and they needed to make changes to have a positive result. All eyes were on them to build the supplier network and secure the growth of Gautten in Asia. She sat back, stared at her team, and then blurted out, "If we can't figure it out, none of us will have jobs. So, what is the plan?"

Discussion Questions

1. How prepared was Becca to lead the meeting in Taiwan? Should she have asked one of her direct reports, like Xīnyí or Yu-Chen, to plan it and facilitate? Explain.

2. What did Becca do correctly in planning and handling the BestMetals meeting? What steps could Becca have completed with her team before the negotiation that could have improved the outcome with a signed contract?

3. An agenda was created for the supplier meeting.

    a. What is the purpose of an agenda?

    b. Who does the agenda benefit?

    c. What is the benefit of creating an agenda with all attendees ahead of the meeting?

    d. What are your recommendations when the agenda topics are not being covered as planned?

4. English is often described as the most understood language in the world. The negotiations with BestMetals were completed in English. The agenda and contract were in English. Is it important to agree to the language to be used when attending a meeting outside of the United States? Why?

5. Becca attended a cultural workshop sometime in the past. She says she felt comfortable traveling abroad. What do you think she meant by the word "comfortable"? Did it help her with the BestMetals meeting? Describe.

6. There was much confusion between the associates of BestMetals and Becca and her team. What was the confusion about? Why was the confusion occurring?

7. BestMetals brought an interpreter to the meeting, yet Gautten did not. Why do you think they did not have a translator for their team?

8. What was the purpose of the review meeting after her return to the United States? Did Becca handle the meeting correctly? Why or why not? How would you feel if your boss told you that you might not have a job after a failed customer intereaction?

9. After the meeting, what follow-up steps might Becca take so she and her team are better prepared for these types of meetings in the future?

10. Becca tells her team, they let her down. Perhaps she let them down. What do you think? Support your answer with facts from the case.

Assignments

1. Research the types of training courses for business professionals to successfully engage in other parts of the world. Compare the topics covered in at least two training programs. Provide a summary of which ones you would prioritize and why the training is important.

2. Suppose you were Becca and you were preparing for the initial meeting with your Asian team and a potential vendor. Prepare an agenda for this meeting and include all details as necessary. Feel free to research the standard elements that are included in an agenda for a business meeting.

3. Business articles often address effective processes for handling business meetings. One in particular is titled "7 Habits of Highly Effective Meetings." Look at the "habits" the author describes and think about meetings you have managed or attended. Based on your reading, how do you think these meetings could have been improved? See https://www.linkedin.com/pulse/7-habits-highly-effective-meetings-bruce-harpham/.

References

Chang, L. (2006). A comparison of Taiwanese and Chinese business negotiations and conflict resolution. *The Journal of Global Business Management 2*(2), 293–298. https://doi.org/10.5897/AJBM11.1563

Dezin Shira & Associates. (2010, November 1). Negotiations Chinese style. *China Business Review*. https://www.chinabusinessreview.com/negotiations-chinese-style/

Harpham, B. (2021). 7 habits of highly effective managers. Linkedin https://www.linkedin.com/pulse/7-habits-highly-effective-meetings-bruce-harpham/

Hodge, S. (n.d.). Success strategies for women in international business. Hodge International Advisors. http://www.hodge-ia.com/Articles_SS.php

Katz, R. (2010). Negotiating international business—Taiwan. https://instruction2.mtsac.edu/rjagodka/BUSM_51_Project/ Negotiating/Taiwan.pdf

Kenton, B. (2020, July 7). What is a supply chain? Investopedia. https://www.investopedia.com/terms/s/supplychain.asp

McNamara, C. (n.d.). Guidelines to conducting effective meetings. Free Management Library. https://managementhelp.org/misc/ meeting-management.htm

Pon Staff. (2020, September 17). Negotiation examples: The importance of relationship building in China. Harvard Law School Program on Negotiation Daily Blog. https://www.pon.harvard.edu/daily/international-negotiation-daily/negotiation-in-china-the-importance-of-guanxi/

Santandertrade. (n.d.). Business practices in Taiwan. https://santandertrade.com/en/portal/establish-overseas/taiwan/ business-practices

Shonk, K. (2015, April 13). Team building negotiation example: Chinese women face a "sticky floor." Harvard Law School Program on Negotiation Daily Blog. http://www.pon.harvard.edu/daily/business-negotiations/team-building-negotiation-example-chinese-women-face-a-sticky-floor/

Tracy, B. (2015). *Business strategy.* AMACOM.

Indi in India[1]

Overview

India Collins is a 30-year-old woman with a career-driven personality. She grew up in Virginia and would never miss an opportunity to move forward in her career. With American parents (her mother is of Asian Indian ancestry) (U.S. Census, n.d., para. 8), India has been exposed to multiple cultures and traditions. She embraces her religious beliefs and family traditions, and she is centered by living authentically.

As a child, India (her friends call her Indi) would close her eyes and dream of her future career and what she wanted to achieve in life. She was homeschooled until eighth grade and while in high school was dual-enrolled at the local university. When she graduated from high school, she had enough credits to start her junior year. However, academic excellence did not prepare her for the next chapter in her life.

Objectives

- Explain how religion can influence international business decisions.
- Explore the reasons a business relationship can succeed or fail.
- Discuss the importance of establishing a business confidant.

Key Concepts and Words

board of directors (BOD), communication, culture, decision influencer, decision-maker, fiscal year, interpersonal dynamics, religion, strategy

---

1 Many thanks to Professor Kustron's graduate assistants, Naveena Priya Darshini Pitta and Hema Vansarla, for their assistance in reviewing this case for cultural and social accuracy and to Hema Vansarla for permission for the use of her personal photographs to be included in this case.

Scenario

About 4 years ago, Indi and her friends started a company named Amicor IT to provide electronic healthcare solutions to medical facilities. Amicor developed analytics and software solutions to enable health systems to deliver top quality care with incomparable satisfaction. One of the friends involved in the business was an investor by the name of Skylar Gibson. Recently, Indi became engaged to Skylar, her life's love, and they planned to get married. Skylar was not involved in the operations of the business and preferred to travel and blog over working a traditional 9 to 5 job.

During the first 2 years of operation, Amicor grew quickly, and new business challenges arose beyond their expertise. The shareholders voted to create a financially aggressive and business savvy board of directors (BOD). Neither Indi nor any of her friends held seats on the board. They relied on the board's advice for critical strategic decisions such as joint ventures. Recently, the BOD suggested pursuing an international business relationship in Asia. In the past 6 months, Amicor had attracted some large clients and was searching for a company to outsource their information management and call center services.

Through various leads, Indi identified a company called Kalki Solutions that had over 15 years' experience in the IT industry. The company was located in Kolkata (part of northeastern India), and had aggressive expansion plans. Their management was interested in collaborating with foreign clients, and in particular, businesses in the United States. The United States had favorable laws that would support a strong partnership. This would be Kalki Solutions' first association with a U.S.-owned technology business. Last year, Kalki collaborated with a company in Qatar, and it was hoping that this relationship with Amicor would be equally successful.

Indi desperately wanted to "crack this deal" (TechnoITworld, 2020) in India. The reason was both personal and professional. On a personal level she had a strong need to fulfill a promise she made to her grandfather. He passed away earlier in the year and asked for his ashes to be spread in India's River Ganga. Indi was close to her grandfather, and he influenced her life greatly. He came to the United States from New Delhi in the late 1950s, fell in love, and married her grandmother (an American). Her grandfather was the inspiration for her passionate work ethic. The work trip to Kolkata, India, made it possible to coordinate a weekend trip to the Ganga. Indi added on a few days at her own expense, but it was worth it to have peace about her grandfather's final resting place. Professionally, the deal with Kalki Solutions would be a business milestone for Amicor.

Indi had been invited to visit Kalki Solutions headquarters to observe the company's operations and meet its employees and management. The visit was to ensure the two companies were strategically aligned before the agreement was signed. It was important to Indi that she had the opportunity to evaluate the operations and the corporate culture for an integrated and positive collaboration.

One week after the invitation, Indi flew out of Dulles Airport in Washington, DC, and landed in Kolkata (also called Salt Lake City by locals). It was the only metropolitan city in India's eastern part of the country and one of the major hubs for the IT industry. Upon arrival, Indi was greeted by a young man named Sachin, one of two individuals hosting her for the business visit. He had been given the responsibility to take care of her arrival and accommodations. He and another colleague, Sita, were her Kalki liaisons and provided her support while she visited.

On the way to her temporary home, Indi was amazed at the beauty of the country. It was the festive season of Durga pooja (Indian Goddess), and she was awestruck observing the celebrations and joy of the people in the streets. She remembered the stories about the culture and festivals from her grandfather. Even though it was her first time meeting Sachin, he invited her to the pooja (offerings and prayers to the goddess Durga) with family and friends at his house. He told her that Mr. Kalki, who owns Kalki Solutions, was also a guest. However, she declined and said she needed rest after traveling more than an entire day (28 hours) from the United States. She could see he was disappointed, but Indi could barely function because she was so tired.

After resting for a day, Indi was excited to begin work on Monday. She was up early and walked across the street to a nearby hotel to get transportation to the office. She wanted to create a positive first impression and provide a continental breakfast for her new colleagues. Indi bought sweet treats, coffee, and assorted teas from the bakery, conveniently located next door to the Kalki Solutions building. She pointed to the items she wanted in the glass case. The baker smiled and gathered a variety of pastries. The total bill was 2127.34 rupees (Murphy, 2020). Indi only had U.S. dollars in her wallet, and she did not know how to convert them to India's currency. Fortunately, she was able to pay with a credit card.

FIGURE 6.1   Durga Pooja, Prayers, Offerings, and Celebrations by Traditional Dance to the Goddess Idol

When Indi arrived at Kalki Solutions, the office door was locked, and she couldn't find any employees mulling around the entrance. She thought she had written down the wrong address and called Sachin. He explained since it was the festival, which lasted 5 days, she should not expect the office to open until Wednesday. She asked if it were possible for someone to open the office so she could get organized. Sachin reminded her that the holiday was a religious one, and business would not be conducted. Durga pooja was respected similar to other religions like Orthodox Judaism, which requires strict observance of the Sabbath (BBC, 2009).

Indi was so disappointed the office was closed, so she decided to get a ride home. She thought she could just "hail a cab" like in New York City or Chicago. But that was not the case. She ended up walking back to the house, and it took her almost 35 minutes. Even though it was still early morning, the sun was shining brightly, and the temperature outside was 92 degrees, warmer than usual in October.

On Wednesday, when the festive season was over, Indi returned to the office. At 9 a.m., she met her future team. A group of several staff members showed her the office space layout and the rest of the building.

Sachin invited her to join the team for lunch, too. During the meal, everybody offered her Indian food to sample. Some had leftovers of bhog (*Times of India*, 2019), a traditional food served during Durga pooja. It wasn't her favorite. She took only a couple of bites before clumsily throwing out her plate, hoping no one would notice. However, she felt very welcomed, and she was amazed at how everyone shared and ate together. Sita, the other manager working with Indi, asked about her family back in the United States. She told Sita about her parents, her grandfather, and that she was single. Then there was an awkward silence among the others, which she didn't understand. Later, Sita nicely explained that it's common for women in India to get married and have children by the age of 29.

At the end of the workday, Sachin offered to drop Indi at her home. Based on her prior experience on Monday, she was not confident using public transportation, and it was too busy to get an Uber. While she was in the car, she noticed the mixed transit. Most people were traveling on bikes, taking crowded buses, or riding in rikshaws (a three-wheeled automobile). She thought it would be terrifying to drive on these streets and decided she should not attempt it ... ever. Indi asked Sachin if she could carpool with him every day.

Overall, Indi thought her first day went well. Skylar would be happy to hear about her experience so far and how she enjoyed the Durga holiday. She sent a message to her Amicor colleagues. "First day, great day!"

The next day, Indi had her first formal meeting with the Kalki Solutions group. As the meeting progressed, Indi asked questions about the Kalki management team and services workflow. She recognized that the senior project manager (PM) was surprised by her inquiry. Later, Sachin mentioned that the senior PM had been working for the company since its founding. He was also the brother of the owner. Sachin explained that her direct

FIGURE 6.2   Three-wheeled rikshaw. The driver sits in the front and passengers in the back.

questioning of the PM in front of the whole team was inappropriate. He was much older than she, and it was a sign of disrespect. Sachin told Indi that, in the future, it would be best if any concerns or questions be discussed privately with the PM.

After that experience, Indi made sure she did not offend the company's employees or disrespect their customs in any way. However, it was very hard. India asked Sita to give her feedback and make her aware of things that she might be doing wrong. During the next conference, Indi asked the team to be open and share their ideas. She would gladly consider their advice. Everyone smiled, nodded but remained quiet.

Indi felt relieved that her "sins" had been forgiven, and she was on the path to correcting her wrongs. Over the next several days, she reviewed the financials, observed and conversed with all the IT managers, and shadowed six customer service call representatives. All of them were fluent in the English language, which was critical for Amicor's U.S. customers. Indi's colleagues (i.e., her friends back home) were getting updates from her every few days through email with the "thumbs up" emoticon. All of them were expecting to close the business agreement before the December holiday season began. Indi sent a message to the board of directors as well. They wanted the contract signed before the fiscal year ended on December 31. She told them she was confident it would happen. There were no obstacles so far.

Indi, Sita, and Sachin became close colleagues quickly. Sita and Sachin were passionate about their work just like Indi, and every day their professional relationship deepened. During a drive home after one long day, Indi revealed to Sachin that she was still struggling to learn about the company, the Indian lifestyle and the different religious beliefs. Sachin apologized and said that he didn't know she needed help. Indi said she was studying it on the internet. He suggested that he would be the best source of knowledge since he grew up in India and was Indian! She told him that she was happy she was learning more about her heritage. She thought to herself, "Dada[2] (Whelan, 2020) would be proud that I am respecting the religious beliefs and the cultural traditions."

---

2   Dada refers to grandfather.

FIGURE 6.3   Diwali

DIWALI

Diwali (for Goddess Lakshmi—Goddess of wealth and prosperity) is a 5-day Festival of Lights (BBC, 2020), celebrated by millions of Hindus, Sikhs, and Jains across the world. Diwali, which also coincides with harvest and new year celebrations, "is a festival of new beginnings and the triumph of good over evil, and light over darkness." (BBC, 2020)

A few weeks later, in early November, the festive season of Diwali began. Indi greeted everyone at the office on the first day, which was the only workday during the holiday. The business was closed again for the remaining days and celebrations. The staff decorated the office space and performed a "puja" dance for the Goddess over lunch. Indi felt lucky she found Kalki Solutions and this wonderful group of people.

Sachin approached her with a gift for the festival, and she was overtaken by emotion. She hugged him and felt that the two companies shared a common caring culture. However, those around them looked quickly away. Although she noticed this briefly, everyone was busy cleaning up the breakroom. The employees wanted to leave the office early to start their family celebrations. She sent a quick text to Amicor. "I am ready to approve the partnership. Everything is in order, and I am confident the managers will collaborate well."

Sadly, Sita briefly joined her at her desk and told Indi that it was inappropriate for her to embrace Sachin in the presence of senior management. Disheartened again by her ignorance, she suddenly realized that Kalki Solutions might back out of the partnership because of her actions. Even though the office was closed for the holiday, Indi told Sachin and Sita she would work those days. There was a deadline for a draft of the contract due in 2 days. She thought that she might make up for her improper gesture by completing the document, so they could relax and enjoy the holiday.

That evening, there was a knock at the door. Indi wasn't expecting anyone. It was Skylar! She had never been so happy to see her. Indi shared that she admired the people at Kalki Solutions and how kind they had been to her. Then, with a tone of embarrassment, Indi admitted she had made a few decorum mistakes at Kalki. Skylar gave her words of encouragement, and they spent the evening walking the streets and experiencing Diwali, the Hindu New Year, in all its splendor.

In the morning, Sita called and invited Indi to her home later that day to celebrate Diwali with her family and friends. Some of their work colleagues would also be there, as well as Mr. Kalki, his wife, and grandchildren. It would be an opportunity for Indi to finally meet him.

Indi mentioned that Skylar surprised her yesterday evening and that she was in India! She graciously declined the invitation. However, she immediately regretted it and remembered she also declined the invite from Sachin when she first arrived in Kolkata. Sita told her it wouldn't be a problem, and she could bring Skylar with her. As Indi hung up her cell, she recalled her error at the office yesterday. She felt lucky that she had the support of Sita and her friendship. The invitation was another example of her forgiveness and compassion.

Sita's home was beautiful, with decorative lights and lamps everywhere. Sita introduced Indi to Mr. Kalki and the conversation progressed about the New Year. He spoke about his traditions with his wife and family and honoring the God and Goddess, Ram and Lakshman. Indi remarked about the fireworks, the dancing, and that the food was "just like Fourth of July." Mr. Kalki disagreed. He said, "Diwali means far more than that American holiday to my family and me." He excused himself politely.

When everyone returned to work, Indi noticed the environment was a bit different. It seemed like Sachin and Sita were preoccupied. Unlike other days, they did not invite her for lunch. She also got a message from a U.S. colleague that Mr. Kalki wanted to have a call with the CEO of Amicor. He was not sure the two companies were a good match for a business investment. Indi panicked when she heard the news and called Skylar.

As an Amicor investor, Skylar was frustrated and remembered the "mistakes" that Indi had made. She told Indi to ask Sita and Sachin for a meeting to determine the reason for Mr. Kalki's request. The next day Indi, Sachin, and Sita had their discussion behind closed doors. Indi started by saying that she felt something was "off" and asked if they knew about the phone call to the United States.

It was an uncomfortable conversation for Sita and Sachin. After all, they had only known Indi for a short time, and they were excited about the potential partnership. They revealed that Mr. Kalki felt Indi had a poor understanding of the significance of their employees' religious customs. They continued that Mr. Kalki felt it was essential that the companies respect each other's beliefs if they were going to embark on a long-term relationship.

Indi knew that she was not educated about all the religious traditions and beliefs people practiced in India. She never intended to offend anyone. They listed some examples, such as declining invitations, her "disdain" for their traditional foods, and suggesting Diwali and the 4th of July were similar holidays. Although her intentions were good, offering to work or expecting the office to be open during these events was offensive to Mr. Kalki. In fact, as the owner of the business, it's his decision to open or close his office and direct his employees to work.

Indi was almost sick to her stomach but thankful that Sachin and Sita had been so honest. She asked for their advice. They said they would support her if they were asked about the quality of her work. Sachin recommended she ask for a brief meeting with Mr. Kalki. "Be prepared to apologize for your ignorance and discuss the synergies between Amicor and Kalki Solutions and how they align in values." Contrary to her attentiveness to not offend others, it seemed she had repeated it again and again, but this time with the company's owner.

Neither Sita nor Indi were aware that Sachin was a nephew of Mr. Kalki. He had been giving his uncle updates about Indi and their progress on the partnership arrangements. Sachin believed in the strategy all three of them had created together. The plan was clear and concise, and it was in the best interest of Kalki to progress with the contract. To smooth things over, he sent his uncle an email and suggested that the business agreement be finalized.

The contract was signed on December 23. It was important to Mr. Kalki that Amicor employees had a wonderful holiday season and enjoyed the final week of the year with their family and friends.

While the lights on her Christmas tree twinkled, Indi's eyes watered as memories of her grandfather came to mind. Indi and Skylar were fortunate to have made the trip to Ganga to spread his ashes. "It is believed that a Hindu's salvation (nirvana) is achieved when their ashes are immersed in the river Ganges" (Urns Northwest, 2019, para. 6). Now, she will have two happy reasons to return to India.

Discussion Questions

1. Indi created discomfort interacting with Kalki employees. Discuss several examples.

2. Describe the work environment at Kalki.

   a. What actions did Indi take to create a positive relationship with the staff?

   b. What actions did they take?

3. If Indi had researched the religious customs in India prior to her trip, how would it have helped her connect with the Kalki Solutions' employees?

4. Mr. Kalki was the decision-maker regarding the partnership between Amicor and Kalki Solutions. Indi missed her first opportunity to be introduced when she arrived in Kolkata at Sachin's home. Do you think Mr. Kalki decided not to partner with Amicor at that time because she declined to meet him? Explain.

5. Why do you think Mr. Kalki decided to continue and close the deal with Amicor? If you were he, would you have signed the deal? Why or why not?

6. There are thousands of things that can influence a business decision. Examples could include an employee's personal lifestyle (i.e., hobbies), alma mater, skill set (such as technical competency), and physical attributes. How does one determine what is most important to the decision-makers?

7. Discuss the importance of Sachin's and Sita's professional and personal relationship with Indi in relation to the collaboration between the two companies. Consider how it helped or hurt.

8. Indi communicated with her U.S. team that the Kolkata, India, visit was going well. Why did she not share with her colleagues that her mistakes might cost them the contract? Consider the benefits or downsides of communicating her blunders. What do you think would have happened if she had told them?

Assignments

1. In the United States, religion is protected under the First Amendment of the U.S. Constitution. In addition, under Title VII of the Civil Rights Act, employers are restricted "from discriminating against individuals on the basis of their religion." In many countries, religion is intertwined with business practices. Locate three countries where religious practices impact businesses and the economy, and provide a summary demonstrating their influence on economic growth, stagnancy, or deterioration.

2. Suppose U.S. Company XYZ needs to send an executive overseas to meet with a new client. The country is very traditional in its gender and cultural practices. As CEO of Company XYZ, do you send the best qualified executive who may be a woman and/or not familiar with the cultural practices of the country, or do you send the person overseas who is the best match culturally, regardless of gender, ethnicity, race or religion? Feel free to research the question. Is the answer to this simply a business decision, or are there possible discrimination issues facing the employer with this choice?

3. Let's flip Question 2. Assume Indian Company ABC has to send an executive to the United States to meet with a new client. As CEO of Company ABC, do you send the best qualified executive, or do you send the person to the U.S. who is the best match culturally? Is your answer to the Question 3 different from your response to Question 2? Explain your response.

References

BBC. (2009, July 15). Religions—Sabbath. https://www.bbc.co.uk/religion/religions/judaism/holydays/sabbath.shtml/

BBC—Newsround. (2020, October 21). Diwali—What is it? https://www.bbc.co.uk/newsround/15451833

Das, A. (2020, September 13). Does India need a new law that revises the age at which women are married? The Wire. https://thewire.in/women/india-new-law-age-at-marriage-women

Expat Arrivals. (n.d.). Working in India. https://www.expatarrivals.com/asia-pacific/india/working-india

Expat Network. (2021). Living and working in India. https://www.expatnetwork.com/living-and-working-in-india/

Just Landed. (2021). Working conditions in India: Working customs, hours, salaries. https://www.justlanded.com/english/India/India-Guide/Jobs/Working-conditions-in-India

Mackey, J., & Bose, S. (2020, December 18). 14 Hindu wedding ceremony traditions you need to know. *Brides*. https://www.brides.com/hindu-wedding-ceremony-rituals-traditions-4795869

Murphy, C. (2020, November 19). Indian rupee (INR). Investopedia. https://www.investopedia.com/terms/i/inr.asp

Rautray, S. (2021, February 25). Same sex marriages cannot be given legal sanction: Government. *The Economic Times*. https://economictimes.indiatimes.com/news/politics-and-nation/same-sex-partners-not-comparable-with-indian-concept-government/articleshow/81209328.cms?from=mdr

Sen, S. (2017, May 17). Working effectively with Indians: 12 things you need to know. https://www.linkedin.com/pulse/working-indians-12-things-you-need-know-sondra-sen/

TechnoITworld. (2020, May 6). How to crack your first professional deal. https://technoitworld.com/how-to-crack-your-first-professional-deal/

Times of India. (2019, October 5). What does traditional Durga Puja bhog consist(s) of. *The Times of India*. https://timesofindia.indiatimes.com/life-style/food-news/what-does-a-traditional-durga-puja-bhog-consists-of/articleshow/71441861.cms

Urns Northwest. (2019, May 16). Symbolism & significance: What does scattering ashes mean? https://urnsnw.com/news/symbolism-significance-what-does-scattering-ashes-mean/

U.S. Census. (n.d.) Race. https://www.census.gov/quickfacts/fact/note/US/RHI625219

U.S. Equal Employment Opportunity Commission. (2021). Title VII of the Civil Rights Act of 1964. https://www.eeoc.gov/statutes/title-vii-civil-rights-act-1964

Whelan, C. (2020, August 20). How to say grandma and grandpa in different parts of the world. *Readers Digest*. https://www.rd.com/list/grandma-grandpa-different-languages/

World Atlas. (2020). Major religions in India. https://www.worldatlas.com/articles/major-religions-in-modern-india.html

Figure Credits

Shanghai Cheri—Expat (Part 1)

A special thanks to Heng (Helen) Zhang, a graduate student at Eastern Michigan University, for her review of this case for cultural accuracy.

Overview

This case study consists of two parts. Part 1 introduces a young professional couple, Cheri and James Harlan, who are both employed by a manufacturing company located in the midwestern United States. As the company expands operations overseas, the Harlans are given an opportunity to live and work abroad for their employer; however, there is a disconnect between their expectations and their new life's reality.

In Part 2, and after relocating to Shanghai, China, with her husband, Cheri is unable to locate popular American products in Chinese retail stores, and she forges a business to purchase everyday household items and market them to expats living overseas. This becomes the foundation for a second career in the United States as an entrepreneur, and it takes advantage of her cross-functional skill set and strengths.

Objectives

- Identify the challenges dual-career couples face when relocating abroad for professional purposes.
- Explain how an expat working abroad can survive and flourish when language and cultural barriers exist in the workplace.
- Summarize the personal and professional challenges parents with children face when working abroad.
- Describe the value and pitfalls of geographic mobility in career development and progression.

Key Concepts and Words

business protocol, communication, dual-career couple, expatriate (expat), networking, overseas assignment, professional pathway, relocation, spousal job transfer, trailing spouse

Scenario

Cheri was a quality control supervisor for Corley Lawn Mower's manufacturing company based in a suburb outside Duluth, Minnesota. Corley specialized in small push lawn mowers that are gas-powered but eco-friendly. Cheri began her career at Corley immediately after high school by working on the assembly line. Her first role was organizing the lawn mower parts for shipping and ensuring every part was included and boxed before sealing. Like many employees, Cheri moved from area to area in the plant, and she was eventually promoted to the Quality Control Unit.

The Quality employees were responsible for warranty testing. They examined mower engines for safety and "guaranteed operational performance" to function at 100% for four separate lawn cutting seasons. The testing protocol required the team to start and stop a mower's engine 10,000 times without fault. They tested the mowers on rocks, branches, thick grass, and other objects that a lawnmower would scrape when cutting grass or lawns. Cheri enjoyed what she did and was satisfied with the job. Her career path had been slow but steady, and she continuously learned something new each day.

While in the Quality Control Unit, Cheri focused on networking and making extensive contacts in the organization because she had career aspirations outside of that department. Cheri was very opportunistic. Recently, Corley's sales and marketing brochures focused on her department and their marketing efforts that emphasized the rigorous quality initiatives of their machines.

One of the Corley vice presidents, James Harlan, was impressed by Cheri's high energy, and they started dating. He was fascinated by her creative marketing ideas and often set up extra meeting time to understand the reasoning behind her marketing suggestions. After a year and a half of courtship, Cheri and James married in Las Vegas in a small but lavish wedding with several Corley senior executives in attendance.

Not long after, James was offered and accepted a position in Shanghai, China, as a senior vice president for a 3-year assignment. It was a difficult decision because Cheri was 2 months pregnant when James received the job offer. This meant the family had to choose: Either Cheri had to stay back in the United States for prenatal care and delivery or move and have their baby in China. She was apprehensive about her medical care in China, only because she had an established obstetrician in Minnesota. Cheri was familiar with the local hospital and knew what to expect during the delivery of the baby. After much soul-searching, the couple decided that they wanted to be together. Fortunately, both Cheri and James had jobs in China (Corley had offered Cheri a position), and each garnered a salary with potential performance bonus incentives. They would also be expatriates, and the overseas experience would position them well for future positions.

EXPAT

"There are often advantages of being asked or assigned to work in another country and every company's benefits vary. An expatriate (expat) is the term given to an employee sent abroad. However, every company supports the employee with a generous 'move package' which covers moving expenses, finding a place to live (rent or purchase) and a specific number of complimentary visits back and forth to the United States." (InterNations, n.d., para. 6)

Because Cheri was also pregnant, Corley paid for all health care costs, a full-time live-in nanny, and private educational costs (up to $15,000 annually) for their child once they turned 3 years old. The relocation assistance included a "double move package." Because Cheri and James were both employees of the company, they received a moving allowance for two employees instead of one. The second relocation payment, worth several thousand dollars, was a surprise and was put aside for their child's college education fund. Although there was no job opening for a quality controller at the Shanghai plant, Corley Lawn Mower Company created a position specifically for Cheri as a quality control reviewer.

Cheri had never lived in Shanghai, so she was worried about creating a support network. Fortunately, she befriended a neighbor at the local coffee and tea shop, and they became confidants. She learned that Padama, an engineer and expat from India, lived with her family on the same street as Cheri and her family. She also discovered that they lived in a neighborhood that included only expatriates from different English-speaking countries. All children from kindergarten through high school attended the same private school. Padama reassured Cheri she would assimilate quickly into the new culture and make friends.

In China, Cheri and James had different work schedules, and they were driven to the factory at separate times by a professional car service. This allowed Cheri to get ready in the morning leisurely. As Cheri approached her first day of work, she set aside the same clothing she would wear back home, namely a short skirt and tight-fitting top. Many might consider her choice inappropriate for a manufacturing facility, but those who knew Cheri would not have been surprised by her choice.

At the Shanghai Corley factory, the workers wore company-provided uniforms (coveralls) with flat shoes, including all middle management. Cheri barely noticed this, but her husband was very aware of her difference in work attire. He mentioned to Cheri how unusual it was that the employees in China wear the Corley uniform and that the company also paid for laundering. When arriving at work each morning, every employee changed into the coveralls and then changed out of them at the end of the workday. However, Cheri was oblivious to her husband's gentle suggestions and continued to wear her personal clothing to the factory. Gossip was frowned upon in the workplace, but Cheri's clothes seem disrespectful to many employees, and they were unsure how to behave around her.

Cheri often came in late and had a short workday because the job created for her was considerably basic and could be completed very quickly. She reviewed quality results twice weekly and recommended changes. Since the Corley Company focused on quality as the foundation for its success, it was rare that Cheri needed to provide a recommendation. After 4 weeks (which was only 8 working days), Cheri recognized she had much free time. Most of the expatriate wives on her street did not work, so when Cheri was invited to attend a lunch or a book club "get together," she left the factory early and enjoyed a relaxing time with her expat friends.

While overseas, Cheri and James took advantage of their open weekends and visited other parts of China. James also traveled to other countries in Asia, and because he was a senior vice president, he was allowed to invite his wife to accompany him. This meant that Cheri would miss work, but she already knew her reports could be finished easily and rarely took more than a few hours. She assumed missing work would not be an issue because she was an efficient employee.

On these "business" trips, Cheri enjoyed shopping and visiting many historical and tourist landmarks. Even though she had not yet delivered her baby, their nanny Chenguang traveled with them and acted as a translator. The nanny also provided assistance with anything related to Cheri's pregnancy and essentially ran the household. Chenguang was told by Corley management to respond to any of Cheri's special requests. They wanted no distractions for James while he worked abroad. Chenguang cleaned, cooked, did the shopping, and helped with entertaining (although this only happened one time).

In anticipation of her child's birth, Cheri's neighbor Padama planned a baby shower for her. To Cheri's surprise, the decorations followed an American nursery rhyme theme. The special foods and cupcake dessert (made from a boxed baking mix and canned frosting) were all from the United States. Cheri was overwhelmed by Padama's thoughtfulness.

Finding familiar products from the United States in China was difficult, but Padama secured a way. Cheri soon learned about this common practice. Padama coordinated with another friend, an expatriate's wife visiting California, and the items traveled back with her. Some of the items were used to coordinate the baby's new nursery, which couldn't have made Cheri any happier! It was like being home in the United States. Cheri delivered her baby 1 week later, and the couple was thrilled with their new daughter, Anita.

Life was pleasant in China, and James thrived in his position at the Chinese Corley plant. Cheri couldn't believe that they had been in China for over 2 years now. She continued to work 2 days a week, and their new baby kept her busy while James traveled. Chenguang was a tremendous help to Cheri, and she depended on her not only as the baby's caregiver but as the translator at Anita's regular doctor's visits.

At 22 months old, Anita became very ill and developed unusual swelling of her cheeks and neck. Cheri was very worried about Anita because she was crying constantly and not eating. She and the nanny took Anita to the pediatrician, who referred her to an oncologist. Tests were performed, and the conclusion was that Anita suffered from a rare form of mouth cancer. Cheri was obviously devastated, and Corley immediately arranged for her to return home. She was granted a family leave of absence from work and quickly flew back to the United States.

Once home, Cheri was referred to a pediatric oncologist at Mayo Hospital in Rochester, Minnesota. Thankfully, Anita received an expedited appointment to see the doctor that week. Cheri provided the diagnostic paperwork that had been translated into English. After reading the documents and evaluating the blood test results, the doctor was surprised that the lab values contradicted a cancer diagnosis.

On further physical examination, the oncologist determined the young girl had infected gums and an abscessed baby tooth—not cancer. The overseas diagnosis was incorrect. It had caused Cheri emotional turmoil and lost workdays. Although relieved with the positive health outlook, Cheri told Corley she wanted to immediately leave her position in Shanghai.

Corley Lawn Mower Company, however, wanted her to return to China. They had invested in both Cheri and her husband, and the factory was exceeding its production target for the year. Cheri conceded, and after spending a month in the United States, arrived back in Shanghai. After the trauma of her daughter's illness, she did not want to return to work at the factory and leave her daughter with the nanny.

Fortunately, Corley allowed her husband to bring the quality reports home to Cheri, and he would return the documents the following day to Cheri's supervisor, Shao Fen. Shao did not have any Chinese employees working from home and was angered that she was given permission to handle her work in this manner. Mr. Fen was exasperated because Cheri rarely came to the factory before the baby was born, and now without his permission, she was working completely from home. He was also frustrated because he did not speak English, and Cheri did not speak Chinese. To communicate, they required the assistance of an interpreter. Cheri seemed happy with this arrangement, but clearly her supervisor was not!

So, what happens next to Cheri? Read Part 2 as the story continues.

Discussion Questions

1. Corley was a multinational company that transferred both Cheri and James overseas and created a special job for Cheri. Is it possible that Cheri was a "pawn" to ensure her husband's acceptance of the job abroad? Explain.

2. What challenges did the couple face as dual-career professionals when relocating to China for business purposes?

3. Cheri seemed to come and go to work as she pleased. For more than 2 years, she did not advance within the company, and her job status remained static. Is there any evidence she preferred or negotiated this freedom and independence? Or do you think Corley tolerated her behavior to encourage her husband to continue to work in China?

4. Cheri ignored the required work uniform (coveralls) provided by Corley Lawn Mower Company. Do you believe she made a conscious decision to wear her personal clothes to work, or was she simply ignorant of the custom?

5. If Cheri wanted her career in China to grow as it did in the United States, what actions or behaviors should she have exhibited to help her succeed? What would have been the advantages of immersing herself with her Chinese colleagues and their culture?

6. An enormous obstacle for expats is communication. Beyond having a nanny as a translator, how could Cheri have improved her communication skills at work? And, vice versa, how could Mr. Fen have improved his communication with Cheri?

7. At the end the case, Cheri's supervisor reveals his anger toward Cheri. Do you think it was warranted? Support your decision by reviewing facts in the case.

8. Was Cheri more interested in being a mother to her daughter than working for Corley in China? If Cheri and her husband returned to the States, do you think she would stay with Corley or leave the organization?

9. Would it be inappropriate for a company to refuse to transfer a female overseas because the country found it culturally unacceptable for a woman to be in a high-level management position? Why or why not? If a woman was the best qualified for the overseas job, what should an employer do?

Assignments

1. Research the workplace customs for China, Saudi Arabia, Germany, and India and the support provided by businesses and the government for working mothers. What did you learn? Were there any surprises?

2. Creating a career path to become an expat is challenging. When chosen, there are overwhelming benefits provided to those employees and families who agree to this change in their professional careers. However, many moves are not successful. Research the statistics and reasons that transfers fail outside of the United States. What percent of transfers are unsuccessful, and why? Summarize.

3. Building on Question 2, discuss any gender differences in statistics. Specifically, how could a company improve the success of an overseas transfer for a female employee with a family?

References

Black, S., & Gregersen, H. (March–April 1999). The right way to manage expats. *Harvard Business Review.* https://hbr.org/1999/03/the-right-way-to-manage-Expats

DeZube, D. (n.d.) What's inside an international compensation package? Monster.com. https://www.monster.com/career-advice/article/international-compensation

InterNations. (n.d.). What's an expat anyway? *Expat Magazine.* https://www.internations.org/guide/global/what-s-an-expat-anyway-15272

Laird, M. (2015, October 12). The pros and cons of hiring expats. HR Exchange Network. https://www.hrexchangenetwork.com/hr-talent-management/articles/the-pros-and-cons-of-hiring-Expats

Molinsky, A., & Hahn, M. (2016, March 16). 5 tips for managing successful overseas assignments. *Harvard Business Review.* https://hbr.org/2016/03/5-tips-for-managing-successful-overseas-assignments

Society for Human Resource Management. (2015, July 23). Developing employee career paths and ladders. https://www.shrm.org/ResourcesAndTools/tools-and-samples/toolkits/Pages/developingemployeecareerpathsandladders.aspx

Vorhauser-Smith, G. (2013, October 31). Global mobility: A win-win for you and your employer. *Forbes.* https://www.forbes.com/sites/sylviavorhausersmith/2013/10/31/global-mobility-a-win-win-for-you-and-your-employer/

Shanghai Cheri—Back Home (Part 2)

Overview

At the end of Part 1, Cheri Harlan, a skilled Quality Controller for the Corley Lawn Mower Company, was reexamining both her personal and professional lives. Her daughter had experienced a health scare, she felt unproductive in her job, and she was having difficulty adjusting to life as an expat. One reason for Cheri's unhappiness and frustration stemmed from her inability to find U.S.-made products in China. In Part 2, Cheri takes matters into her own hands by creating a business opportunity for herself and her family. She also solves a need for the large expat community in China.

Objectives

- Summarize the importance of change and innovation in one's life.
- Explain the significance of developing a business plan before embarking on a start-up.
- Describe the phrase "risk vs. reward" as it relates to the success of a new business.
- Illustrate the value of professional and personal relationships.

Key Concepts and Words

business plan, creativity, entrepreneur, innovation, networking, personal goals, risk vs. reward

Scenario

Hi, my name is Anita and I am 7 and ½ years old! My mom is the best and I love her alot! She is smart and funny and makes lots of money. I have lived in China, Germany, China (two times), and in Minnesota where its very cold because she has to work. She travels too much, and I miss her a lot. But she gets to meet cool people and always brings me back presents of all the stuff she learns about. She wears bright colors and is on TV. My friends think she is movie star because she is on TV and has long blond curly hare. I think you will like her and think she is really nice too!

Luv, Anita

Cheri enjoyed living in the United States. She loved the personal freedom, baseball and hot dogs, and going to the beach on hot, summer days. Cheri preferred not to live overseas, but she knew sometimes you make decisions that will make life better for you and your family.

On this particular day, Cheri was in a blue mood. She looked out the window and missed seeing the fall tree colors from her native Minnesota. For a moment, Cheri became teary-eyed. She composed herself and then started talking with her nanny Chenguang, about the limited selection of U.S. nonperishable food in China.

Cheri wanted to find a place to purchase specific products in China, but her search was going nowhere except back to the United States. She was tired of having "to compromise." If Cheri wanted anything American made such as a name-brand cereal, potato chips, or soda pop, she would have to wait until she traveled to the United States. Or she could collaborate with another U.S. expat to bring the items to China upon their return.

There were a few items she particularly missed. First, she could never find her husband's favorite southwestern spices and seasonings to make enchiladas and tacos. Second, her daughter, Anita, was a fussy eater and loved Smucker's grape jelly. Cheri, too, thought it made the best peanut butter and jelly sandwiches, but she couldn't purchase it anywhere. Last was her branded facial moisturizer that absorbed quickly into the skin and didn't leave an oily feeling. However, she did find a Chinese product that she substituted after trying several products. The cream was made from pearls and oysters, which sounded quite exotic to Cheri. It was harvested in Asia and claimed that it minimized wrinkles and rejuvenated skin cells. The facial cream was expensive, but it was advertised heavily and sold in China only at high-end department stores in Shanghai.

In frustration, Cheri sent a flier through the subdivision where they lived in Shanghai and asked her neighbors to identify products they wished they had in China. She specifically asked about their need for southwest cooking spices and grape jam. She was convinced there had to be a better way to purchase these products than waiting for someone to fly to the United States and return with a suitcase full of jelly!

To her delight, Donna, an expat from Dallas, Texas, responded quickly with a list of over 11 items. Before she knew it, five more neighbors replied with their "wish lists." She had no idea what to do next, so she asked Chenguang if she knew anyone who worked at a shipping or mailing company, similar to the U.S. Postal Service or a national shipping service. Her nanny knew of no one. She offered to be her translator, though, once she found one, to help with the business conversation.[1]

Cheri thought about the lists from her friends and felt confident she had a successful idea for a business. She took the next step and created a business plan for herself. (See guide below). She mapped her goals and her marketing projections, but she hit a roadblock in computing her financial projections.

TABLE 6.1   BUSINESS PLAN GUIDE

Market analysis	Before launching your business, it is essential for you to research your business industry, market, and competitors.
Organization & management	Every business is structured differently. Find out the best organization and management structure for your business.
Service or product line	What do you sell? How does it benefit your customers? What is the product lifecycle? Get tips on how to tell the story about your product or service.
Marketing & sales	How do you plan to market your business? What is your sales strategy? Read more about how to include this information in your plan.
Funding request	If you are seeking funding for your business, find out about the necessary information you should include in your plan.
Financial projections	If you need funding, providing financial projections to back up your request is critical. Find out what information you need to include in your financial projections for your small business.
Appendix	An appendix is optional, but a useful place to include information such as resumes, permits, and leases. Find additional information you should include in your appendix.

(Small Business Administration, 2021)

---

1   During this time, the Internet was not as advanced, and there was no shopping network like Amazon.com that shipped quickly and economically overseas, and particularly to China.

Specifically missing in her plan was the cost of shipping, but she had an idea. Cheri looked at the professional contacts on her phone. Since she initially worked in shipping at Corley in the United States, she called an old colleague Patrick, based in Minnesota. He provided Cheri with the name of a person who worked in Shanghai in the distribution field. He helped her identify a regional shipper who could estimate shipping charges. Now, she only needed to purchase the items from the United States. Finding a shopper was easy. Cheri had a best friend in Minnesota who was a stay-at-home mom with older children in school.

Cheri calculated the costs. She could charge a premium on the desired products, divide the shipping costs among those who ordered, and charge a coordination fee to support her friend. Any remaining money would be hers. The best part was being able to get the products she wanted for herself and her family consistently. This seemed like a win-win for everyone.

Just when Cheri was coordinating the first shipment to leave the United States, she encountered an obstacle. Cheri and her husband received word they would be transferred back to Minnesota. Excited yet disappointed, Cheri's focus shifted to relocating back to the states. It was difficult leaving Chenguang who developed a special bond with Anita, but Cheri missed seeing her siblings and parents back home, too.

Cheri and her husband wanted their nanny to join them in the United States. But she too had a family and couldn't move. Cheri realized her nanny would be without a job and suffer financially until she could find another employer. Cheri wanted to support her and wrote Chenguang a check for 6 months of services.

Shortly after getting settled in the United States, Cheri received emails from her expat friends in Shanghai inquiring when their shipment of items would arrive. At first, Cheri sent back a reply saying that she was no longer available to continue with the project. But then, she had an "aha" moment! "Why couldn't she be the shopper and the shipper?"

Cheri went to a discount container store to locate a box that was colorful and sturdy and purchased several spices in bulk from a wholesale store. She repackaged the southwestern spices (chorizo, fajita, hot chili, garlic, bean, triple pepper, onion, and tamale) into airtight envelopes in a serving size for two people. It was economical and convenient since the portion sizes were small. There was little to be wasted. If someone was cooking for a larger group, they would just use more packets, which were easy to store too.

Cheri had another thought. The spices could be autoclaved and made into small squares or discs, like chicken bouillon cubes. After that, she evolved the packaging into a lightweight blister pack. Shipping was the most expensive part of the project, so anything that could lighten weight or shrink size was beneficial.

At this point, Cheri had to decide if it was more economical to use a professional shipping company or mail the packages to her expat friends on her own. Since the spices were produced and packaged in multiples of six, she determined she could ship without an intermediary. The blister packs could be sent in a padded envelope at almost the same cost as mailing a letter. However, the padded envelopes were expensive, and she needed to cut costs to make a profit. Shipping in boxes was not feasible either.

Luckily, she received an email from her former nanny, who asked about the family. A "lightbulb" went off in her head. Chenguang could be her contact and business partner in Shanghai. Cheri could ship the blister packs in bulk by freight, and they could be mailed locally to customers. It was a solution to the shipping dilemma, and her nanny would earn an income. Her partner would be someone she trusted too! With this issue resolved, the business took off, and she made a profit immediately. Chenguang introduced the spices to several of her local friends, and by "word of mouth," demand increased. She hired a few employees to help with mailing and delivery and located a small shop interested in offering the spice packs for sale.

The business was progressing well and, a few months later, an expat friend, Caroline, called. She worked for a Chinese television station in Shanghai and asked if Cheri was interested in being featured in a segment about "Entrepreneurs from Abroad." She was ecstatic. It had to be prerecorded, so the Asian station coordinated with a "sister" network located in Chicago. It was easy for Cheri to drive to the city. The broadcast aired and it created an instant consumer market in China. Chenguang had no interest in being on television, but Cheri gave her partner credit for helping her solve the shipping hurdle.

Before she knew it, Cheri had orders for over 759 southwestern spice packs in 1 week. She immediately needed a website with an ordering page. At the same time, a popular Chinese actress taped a video for a social networking site showcasing a recipe for southwestern noodles! It went viral and within two weeks, it had 438,000 viewers! Cheri couldn't keep up with the demand, and she quickly hired four employees to help fill the orders in the United States. Her business venture took off.

Shortly after, the Chicago television station called again to record a follow-up piece recognizing her achievement and the positive relationship between Chinese and U.S. citizens. This time, Chenguang agreed to be interviewed and the segment featured Cheri and her together. Their trusted friendship became a loyal business relationship, "one to be duplicated," according to the newscaster. It aired in Shanghai and in the Chicago metropolitan area.

The story was picked up by the local television station in Minnesota, which led to an invitation from a women's business association. Cheri was honored at its national conference for her successful business venture. She was also in a feature article about establishing a business based on a true demand or need. For her, it was Cheri's need to experience authentic southwestern and Mexican flavor that helped her "feel" at home while living abroad in Shanghai.

Over time, Cheri continued to grow her business and built a larger company to export many U.S. food favorites to almost 22 countries around the world. She focused on countries with a high population of expat from the United States as her original target. After 5 years of tremendous success and growth, Cheri sold her business to a nationally known distribution company. With Cheri being Cheri, she already had an idea for her next new business!

Discussion Questions

1. The position at Shanghai Corley didn't provide professional growth for Cheri. If it had, do you think she would have been challenged and happy? Why didn't Cheri ask to do something different so her career would advance?

2. Cheri created a business because she had a need. How often are businesses created through a personal need or want? Can you provide an example?

3. The health issues with Cheri's daughter were a turning point in her personal life. How often do people make compromises in their career for their family? How does a person decide when their heart tells them one thing, and intellectually they are drawn to a different decision?

4. Cheri quickly thought through the obstacles of sending products to China, the first being frequency and the second being cost of shipping or mailing. Yet, her creativity drove her to success. How important are innovation and creativity to the success of an entrepreneur venture?

5. Networking assisted Cheri in locating a shipper. Do you think she could have found a partner in Shanghai without a contact through someone she knew?

6. Cheri was consistently faced with stumbling blocks. How did she overcome them?

Assignments

1. Do you have an idea for a business? Think of something you or someone you know needs but doesn't exist. Explain what it is, its purpose, and why you think it's important and/or beneficial to others. If you are further along in bringing your idea (product or service) to market, try filling out the business plan template listed in the case.

2. In some countries, it is easier to start a business than in the United States. Research and identify the top three countries where business startups are investment friendly. Explain why.

3. Often a business is thriving, and the goal is to expand. However, expanding too quickly has its advantages and disadvantages. Explore and create a chart to summarize both.

4. Research the difficulty of expanding a U.S. business internationally and into non-native English-speaking countries. What types of roadblocks must a company overcome to establish a global business?

References

Day, D., & Evans, M. (2015, May 4). 10 key steps to expanding your business globally. *Forbes*. https://www.forbes.com/sites/allbusines s/2015/03/04/10-key-steps-to-expanding-your-business-globally/#4315fd433803

Dizik, A. (2013, April 13). 10 questions to ask before expanding overseas. *Entrepreneur*. https://www.entrepreneur.com/article/226517

Parmar, N. (2013, September 13). You have a great idea. Now what do you do? *Wall Street Journal*. https://www.wsj.com/articles/SB1 0001424127887323623304579054622258666900

Ronick, D. (2011, May 25). 10 steps from idea to business. *Fortune*. https://www.inc.com/articles/201105/10-steps-from-idea-to-business.html

Tugend, A. (2013, August 23). Taking an invention from idea to store shelf. *New York Times.* http://www.nytimes.com/2013/08/24/

your-money/taking-an-invention-from-idea-to-the-store-shelf.html

U.S. Postal Service. (2017). Pay, print & ship internationally. https://www.usps.com/international/international-how-to.htm

U.S. Small Business Administration. (n.d.). Starting and managing: Write your own business plan. https://www.sba.gov/starting-business/

write-your-business-plan

The Female Entrepreneur

7

Too Big to Succeed

Overview

"Too Big to Succeed" is a story about a PhD student with aspirations and a sense of urgency to improve the world of medical devices. The student is energetic and naturally charismatic. Before she completes her dissertation, she drops out the program and decides to create and build a business to validate her ideas. She gathers financial support from investors to develop a medical device that eventually fails to meet expectations and never makes it to market.

Scenario

Charlotte Watson was a bright Ivy League bioengineering PhD student who enjoyed collaborating with her peers. While performing research as a university fellow, she invented and secured her own patent for a medical delivery system (her first device) that administered antibacterial drugs into the human body. She was excited about the patent, because it would allow her to apply for federal grants offered by the U.S. Department of Health and Human Services and the National Institutes of Health. In the past, the university had several

Objectives

- Explain the steps in the business cycle for a new start-up.
- Determine what influences investors and venture capitalists to fund an idea or product.
- Describe the obligations of an inventor/entrepreneur to investors.
- Analyze the reasons for the success or failure of a new start-up.

Key Concepts and Words

business cycle, business plan, entrepreneur, Federal Drug Administration (FDA), inventor, investor, research and development (R&D), Securities and Exchange Commission (SEC), startup business, STEM (science, technology, engineering, and math), venture capitalist students who had obtained patents based on their research, and it enjoyed the public relations benefits from the notoriety and success of its alumni.

Charlotte was always full of ideas and energy. That is what made Charlotte, Charlotte. She envisioned a modification to her patent (her second device) with more ambitious technology that could revolutionize how medicine was delivered to patients. This idea was so unique that many of her professors deemed it impossible to create. She believed the technology could significantly impact the medical community, both in the developed and developing worlds. She was determined and almost obsessive about the innovation.

As a result, at age 23, she dropped out of her PhD program. Charlotte used a $50,000 inheritance from her grandparents to start her own company and pursued the concept. She named her business, Medical-Device Design or Med-deS. Charlotte imagined becoming a multimillionaire before the age of 30. This device would make it happen! She already had her eyes on a rare, limited edition Ferrari, one of only 104 ever made. The roar of the engine was unmistakable!

Charlotte had a brilliant and entrepreneurial mind. Many compared her to a female Bill Gates or Mark Zuckerberg. She was smart, focused, charismatic, and very competitive. She was persistent in the face of the impossible. Charlotte set up a development lab in the technology start-up center of Silicon Valley, California. There, she sought funding from individual investors to pursue her ideas. She sold them on the prototype of the second medical device and its remarkable health outcomes. Her sales pitch was mesmerizing and almost every investor was as enthusiastic as she. The funds poured in.

Within a year, she had raised over $8 million in funding and immediately began extensive research and development (R&D). In the following 2 years, she raised another $100 million, valuing the company at over $1 billion. Although Charlotte and her team quietly struggled to finalize the new device and technology, she was able to keep its doors open.

During its early years, Med-deS worked much like other technology start-up companies (in stealth mode[1]), which drew criticism from the medical and scientific communities. Fortunately, in its third year,

---

1   Stealth mode means secretive.

Charlotte and her R&D team achieved mild success in developing the technology and gained Federal Drug Administration (FDA) approval for investigational use of the device and system.

The media found out about Charlotte's device when they attended a massive STEM conference in Las Vegas during that year. Charlotte was a featured speaker on innovation, and her company won the prestigious Medical Device Company of the Year award from the conference sponsors. This catapulted her into the limelight, and she loved it.

The media lauded Med-deS because it had been built and led by a noticeably attractive young female. Multiple news outlets picked up the story and aired segments about Charlotte and her life. With the visibility, the company raised another $500 million and secured large partnerships, one with a device manufacturer, which increased the company valuation to over $10 billion. Med-deS grew quickly and employed over 800 employees in just the 6 years of its early business cycle.

Lurking in the background with all the excitement was an enormous challenge. The functionality of the device in its entirety was never consistent. For this technology to be truly revolutionary and the company achieve its valuation, the device had to work without fault. Charlotte hired an engineering consultant, Cathie Hadid, who specialized in Six Sigma. This is a process improvement methodology that Med-DeS needed to implement for the production of a flawless device and make the system free of defects. It took Cathie 4 and a half months to complete her review and analysis. On the day Charlotte was to receive the report, she had an ominous feeling.

It was, in fact, terrible news. The lab would need to be completely reconfigured and the testing processes rewritten. The company would need to complete its internal quality assessment (which could take several months) before the other phases of change could occur. Cathie estimated it would take between 30 to 36 months for all the corrections to be made at the cost of millions and millions of dollars. However, Charlotte reacted calmly, asked only a few questions, and ended the meeting shortly after Hadid finished the presentation. Charlotte thanked her for her evaluation and said, "I'll give you a call about executing a plan to implement the changes and redesign." The call was never made.

Because many eyes focused on Charlotte's company and billions were riding on this specific device, the truth about its lack of functionality could not be hidden after 9 years. Charlotte appeared, several times on national television and emphatically defended the device, the system, and herself. The doubt, however, could not be undone.

Med-deS couldn't secure the final FDA approval or keep any of the promises to its investors. Things crumbled quickly. Within a few weeks, the big partners severed their ties to Med-deS, and investors asked for their investment to be returned. The valuation of Med-deS went from $10 billion to just $1 billion (the amount owed to investors) nearly overnight and bottomed out at $127 million, or 1% of its highest value.

Charlotte, who was once seen as a golden child of device innovation, was the center of a growing controversy. The Security and Exchange Commission (SEC) launched an investigation, and several investors filed lawsuits. Cathie Hadid, the consultant, was called as a witness for the prosecution to explain her analysis. And, finally, creditors came from everywhere demanding payment for capital equipment, which Med-deS could not fulfill.

Where is the company now? Med-deS and Charlotte are regarded as massive failures. The company survived but downsized its employees by nearly 90%. It changed its focus from perfecting an impossible device to refining three others. Charlotte does not own the company.

She is rumored to be working with one of the professors from her PhD program, attempting to take to market the patented medical delivery device and system she developed as a university fellow. Once she dropped out, the innovative concept was given no attention and gathered dust. Only time will tell if Charlotte will ever regain her credibility in the medical research community and surface again.

SURVEY OF BUSINESS OWNERS FACTS
Women-Owned Businesses in the United States

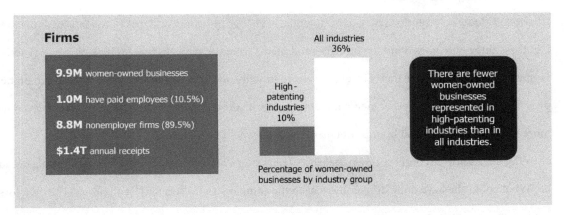

Firms

9.9M women-owned businesses

1.0M have paid employees (10.5%)

8.8M nonemployer firms (89.5%)

$1.4T annual receipts

All industries
36%

High-
patenting
industries
10%

Percentage of women-owned
businesses by industry group

There are fewer
women-owned
businesses
represented in
high-patenting
industries than in
all industries.

Employment

**Share of employment at
women-owned firms by firm size**

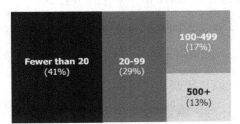

8.4M employees at women-owned businesses

7.3M at small firms with fewer than 500
employees (87.1%)

5.9M at firms with fewer than 100 employees
(70.4%)

Fewer than 20
(41%)

20-99
(29%)

100-499
(17%)

500+
(13%)

Top Industries Among Women-Owned Businesses

- The industries with the highest average number of employees per firm are **employment services, depository credit intermediation,** and **school and employee bus transportation.**

- For employer firms, those in **basic chemical manufacturing** have the highest average annual receipts per firm **($21.3 million).**

For nonemployers, **motor vehicle parts and supplies merchant wholesalers** have the highest average annual receipts per firm **($120,000).**

Data source: 2012 Survey of Business Owners, U.S. Census Bureau. Firm growth rate
unavailable due to methodology changes. High-patenting industries are identified by 2012
NAICS codes: 3330, 3341, 3342, 3344, and 3345.

FIGURE 7.1   Government Statistics

Discussion Questions

1. What was Charlotte's business plan for her company? What is the significance of a well-developed business plan for a start-up?

2. Charlotte's idea was revolutionary, had the potential to change the world, and make investors loads of money. Did these three outcomes blind the investors and media from the setbacks that took place over 9 years?

3. Despite mounting evidence that the device was not functional, Charlotte continued to be featured on news programs, talk shows, and other media outlets to promote the company. It appeared that she believed with more money, more time and brainpower, her invention would be a success.

   a. Why did Charlotte continue down the path of pursuing a device that was hopeless for almost a decade?

   b. What could she have done differently to keep the company from "toppling" and protect the investors?

4. Female entrepreneurs are a rarity in the technology start-up arena. Charlotte was a young and charismatic woman who believed deeply in her idea and appeared sincere.

   a. Did her gender influence the media to give more hype to the idea than it deserved?

   b. Were the media and investors blinded by the image of the person they saw versus the reality of the technology in front of them?

   c. Did Charlotte's attractiveness affect how people viewed her and her invention?

   d. If this case had featured a young male researcher instead of Charlotte, do you think the media, medical, science, and investment communities would have continued to support the device development and change the ending of the story? Support your response with your opinion or facts from the case.

5. The author portrays Charlotte as a driven person who wants to help patients. Is she just a fraud who took advantage of the investors for her personal gain?

Assignments

1. There is a cliché to "never put all your eggs in one basket." Suppose you were given $10 million to invest. Would you choose to put your money into a company with one potential "blockbuster" product or a company with five potential products and none labeled as a "blockbuster"? Why?

2. There are numerous ways someone can fund a business. Start-ups are often funded personally or from family and friends. Research the different types of investors, and define the differences between an angel investor, crowdfunding, and venture capitalist.

3. Identify four successful companies started in the past 10 years. Locate two started by male entrepreneurs and two businesses started by women. Compare and contrast the similarities and differences and reasons that each is successful. Also, comment on whether the reason for success is gender-based in any way.

4. Thomas Edison invented the lightbulb, Albert Einstein developed the theory of relativity, and Bill Gates created Microsoft. These are ideas and products that are revolutionary and created by men. Name three ideas or products that were developed by women that you would consider revolutionary. Explain why these are important to you.

References

Arora, R. (2020, March 10). Why male entrepreneurs in the US make double their female counterparts. CNBC. https://www.cnbc.com/2020/03/10/why-male-entrepreneurs-in-the-us-make-double-their-female-counterparts.html

Better Business Bureau. (2021). Welcome. https://www.bbb.org/

Jamil, H. (2014, July). Crowdfunding's potential for minority and women-owned enterprises. Crowdfund Capital Advisors. http://crowdfundcapitaladvisors.com/images/CrowdfundingImpactonMinorityWomenOwnedFirms.pdf

Minnesota Legislature. (2016, August). Why are women-owned businesses overall smaller than men-owned businesses? Office on the Economic Status of Women. https://www.oesw.leg.mn/PDFdocs/Why%20do%20women%20start%20disproportionately%20fewer%20businesses%20than%20menv2.pdf

Mundy, L. (2017, April). Why is Silicon Valley so awful to women? *The Atlantic*. https://www.theatlantic.com/magazine/archive/2017/04/why-is-silicon-valley-so-awful-to-women/517788/

National Association of Women Business Owners. (2021). https://www.nawbo.org/

Score. (2021). Women entrepreneurs. https://core.score.org/topics/women-entrepreneurs

U.S. Census Bureau. (2017, March 31). Women-owned businesses. https://www.census.gov/library/visualizations/2017/comm/women_owned_businesses.html

U.S. Census Bureau. (2020, May 19). Annual business survey release provides data on minority- and women-owned businesses. Release Number CB20-TPS.24. https://www.census.gov/newsroom/press-releases/2020/annual-business-survey-data.html

U.S. Census Bureau. (2021, February 21). Percentage of employer firms by size of firms. https://www.census.gov/library/visualizations/2021/comm/employer-firms.html

U.S. Department of Labor. (2016, April 28). Entrepreneurship and the U.S. economy. https://www.bls.gov/bdm/entrepreneurship/entrepreneurship.htm

U.S. Securities and Exchange Commission. (2021). https://www.sec.gov/

U.S. Small Business Association. (2016, May 1). Survey of business owner facts. Women-owned businesses in the United States. https://cdn.advocacy.sba.gov/wp-content/uploads/2019/06/10112558/Women-Owned-Businesses-in-the-United-States.pdf

Vilorio, D. (2014, June). Self-employment: What to know to be your own boss. U.S. Bureau of Labor Statistics https://www.bls.gov/careeroutlook/2014/article/self-employment-what-to-know-to-be-your-own-boss.htm

Figure Credit

Fig. 7.1: Source: U.S. Small Business Administration.

Second Choices

Overview

They say a person experiences several developmental stages in their adult life. Researchers have different names for these stages, but most identify three key phases. In her book *New Passages*, the well-known author Gale Sheehy (1996) defines them as (a) provisional adulthood (18–30 years), (b) first adulthood (30–45 years), and (c) second adulthood (45–85 years).

Frannie Donchi is in the early stages of her second adulthood. Her children are grown, and she has been successful in her career. But in her heart, she knows it is time for something else. She is tired doing "the same thing at work" and has lost the passion for her job. Some might call this a midlife crisis. Frannie calls it "her time" to do what she wants. And, all she wants is to be her own boss. Wendy Alina is in a similar situation and is also looking for a "second career." In "Second Choices," Frannie and Wendy take similar approaches to starting their own company, but with different results.

Objectives

- Define the stages of adult life.
- Explain the motivations for becoming a business owner in relationship to the stages of adult life.
- Summarize the process for purchasing a franchise business.
- Explain the total financial and personal commitment with franchise ownership.

Key Concepts and Words

brand, business model, business plan, demographics, franchise, franchise agreement, franchisee, franchisor, personal goals, profit, royalty, small business owner, trade name, trademark

FIGURE 7.2   Business Owner Age Demographics

Scenario 1

Frannie's idea for a business (ad)venture came from her parents. Her mother and father were in their early 80s and lived in an independent living facility. This meant they resided in an apartment with support services. To help residents, the facility provided one hot meal a day, housekeeping, and various social activities. Residents such as Frannie's parents could also contract with a company for personal assistance services such as dressing and bathing. Frannie knew the United States had an aging population

(U.S. Census, 2019), and based on the experience with her parents, she began to explore the possibility of operating a personal services and companion care company. For Frannie, the most logical way to approach starting this type of business was to purchase a franchise.

While "doing her homework," Frannie learned that acquiring a franchise was like being hired for a new job (Libava, 2009). The franchise executive team must like you, you must like the company, and you must agree to follow the company's rules. After much research, Frannie seriously explored and considered the company "3C's" for a possible franchise purchase. The company's motto, "Caring, Compassionate and Considerate," appealed to Frannie's empathetic personality. It also had great Internet ratings from customers, and its marketing materials were quite compelling.

Frannie made contact and met with a local franchise owner, Carmen Gray, in her home state of Pennsylvania. She was impressed with the 3C's Montgomery County franchise and how inspiring Carmen was in describing her business, 3C's operational principles, and the reasons why she selected 3C's as a "partner." After the meeting, Frannie was so motivated that she completed the franchise application process and emailed it that day.

After just 2 days, Frannie received a follow-up phone call from the franchise director confirming receipt of her application. During the chat, she was invited to the corporation's headquarters for a "meet and greet" located in Farmington, Iowa. Frannie was told how much 3C's valued its franchise owners and how it treated them as "one big family." She was also strongly encouraged to bring her spouse, Bill, to the event. It seemed a bit strange that the 3C's representative wanted Bill to attend. But as the director explained, "With married couples, it is important that both parties be 'on board,' as the financial and time commitment involved both spouses even if only one person is buying the franchise." Frannie immediately agreed they both would attend. The meeting, interestingly, was to be held at the CEO and owner's home, Danielle Grandy.

Three weeks later Frannie and Bill traveled to Iowa. Twenty prospective franchise owners attended the orientation. Grandy's husband, Sam, was also present at the meeting. He was responsible for the business's accounting functions. His participation reinforced 3C's family values, which once again delighted Frannie.

The meeting took place in the Grandys' dining and living rooms and began promptly at 9 a.m. As everyone poured juice and coffee, Frannie's husband Bill started telling jokes to the group. Danielle was irritated as it made it difficult to focus the group's attention on the agenda and begin the business meeting. After the short delay, introductions were made by the 3C's team, and each prospective owner similarly gave an introduction and indicated the reason for their interest in 3C's. When it was Bill's turn, he stated he wasn't particularly drawn to the franchise. He accompanied his wife only as requested by the 3C's team.

The philosophy of the company and its mission were discussed. Danielle covered the history of the company and why they felt they had a proven business model. Sam explained the financials and balance sheet for 3C's. The Grandys stated that just a single franchise purchase offered the franchisee the potential for a solid return on their money.

At this point in the meeting, Bill had several questions for Danielle and Sam. He questioned their income and expense projections for new franchisees. He challenged an owner's ability to find qualified caregivers for potential clients, and he aggressively requested a copy of the franchise agreement. (It was eventually given to the potential investors at the end of the day.) There was no time allotted to review or ask questions for clarity. This bothered Bill because he thought potential owners should have the opportunity to understand the investment thoroughly. It was evident in Bill's tone that he simply did not like or trust the Grandys.

In contrast to Bill, Frannie took a different approach. She asked a few operational questions about the franchise such as the uniform rules for personal care assistants, the average pay per hour for caregivers, and how most owners located employees. The day ended with a casual and fun barbeque in the Grandys' backyard.

On their drive back home, Frannie and Bill discussed 3C's and the ability to be successful with the business. Frannie was insistent this was the right opportunity for her, while Bill continued to question the monetary return on the investment. She signed and returned the franchise agreement, despite her husband's reservations.

Frannie put the $10,000 down for the franchise fee, and she agreed to pay 3C's, 17.5% of her net income[1] (called a royalty), with a required minimum royalty payment of $25,000 per year. Additionally,

---

1   Net income is the income left during a tax year after the payment of all expenses including taxes.

the agreement was written as a 5-year contract with a 5-year renewable term. Frannie was excited about this opportunity and borrowed the $10,000 franchise fee from her elderly parents. After raising five children who were now adults, Frannie and her husband had little savings and next to nothing put away for retirement. Without her parents' financial assistance, her only option for the down payment was an equity loan on her home.

After 3 months of operating her business, Frannie was very frustrated and stressed. She doubted herself and her decision. First, she had difficulty obtaining clients. Second, the marketing offered by 3C's was ineffective. Third, the franchise payments were due. Frannie had little income from the business, and there were additional start-up expenses that she never anticipated. She did not recall reading about any of these in 3C's franchise materials.

At the beginning of the sixth month, Frannie closed the doors to her franchise location. She still owed the $25,000 annual royalty fee to the 3C's for the next 5 years, and she needed to repay the $10,000 loan to her parents. This totaled $135,000! Frannie blamed the Grandys for failing to provide the support services they had discussed at their home and misrepresenting the income potential for the business. The Grandys insisted they had a winning business model, and it was quite unusual for a franchise owner to have such a negative experience.

Scenario 2

Wendy's idea for a business came from her four sisters. The sisters were close in age, and all five women were quite intelligent and creative. Wendy and her sisters had a favorite uncle who was a widower and lived in a small tourist town in northern Michigan. Their Uncle Chester had no children, and he was their father's only sibling. The house where he lived was very old but inviting, and it had many personal memories. For one, it was Wendy's grandparents' original home, and they lived in it their entire married life. Second, both her father and uncle were born there. Lastly, it was full of old and unique furniture that one would find in a high-end antique store.

When Uncle Chester was in his late 80s, he became ill and passed away. This left the responsibility of cleaning the house to Wendy and her siblings. They approached the task with enthusiasm as the home had personal items belonging to their grandparents and even a few things belonging to their great-grand-mother. The excitement of uncovering the treasures soon turned to extreme stress. After people living almost a century in the home, the house was filled to the brim!

The sisters slowly went through the house, which required six weekend trips over 3 months. One problem was that three of the sisters lived in Virginia, one lived in Illinois, and one in Ohio. This meant the culling and cleaning not only had to be coordinated between the five of them, but each sister had to travel from their home state to Michigan. Also, the process had to be accelerated because the home had been sold. Forced decisions were being made about the belongings and because of the time crunch, most of the valuable items were packed, shipped, and eventually stored in Wendy's garage. It was not a good situation. Her garage was now filled to the brim instead of her uncle's house!

Wendy knew there had to be a better way to accomplish emptying a home, and she was confident with an aging U.S. population (just like Frannie thought in Scenario 1), she and her sisters were not the first to handle this task. Wendy also believed many families with aging relatives were faced with this dilemma. This motivated her to think about starting a home and estate liquidation service.

As she dreamed about a possible business venture, it seemed there were two parts to her business: 1) sorting, cleaning, and removing the contents; and 2) selling the personal property that had value for maximum profit. Wendy believed this could be done with an online auction, an estate sale, or selling the valuable contents to a company on consignment.

Wendy, however, had no business experience. She was an elementary school teacher, who was considering a small side job that could grow into her second career upon her retirement. So, she explored franchise opportunities and came across a downsizing and personal property liquidation franchise that intrigued her. The company, EMK Treasures and Liquidation, had franchises available in her area, so she applied to its headquarters and heard back the next day. The representative provided Wendy with an overview of the company, interviewed her, and asked about her goals for owning and operating a franchise.

They spoke again a week later, and this time the representative identified the available territories. During that meeting, Wendy evaluated the demographics for her proposed territory, which included an affluent zip code close to her hometown in Ohio. It also had a breakdown of the population by age, the average net worth of the homes in the area, and the average income of working adults. Using that information, Wendy compiled a spreadsheet that projected her expenses and potential earnings. At this point, she realized that she would need to contract with three to four estates each weekend for 42 weeks to clear a profit of $50,000. When Wendy broke this down further, she realized that this was more than a part-time business and that the time commitment to be successful was beyond what she was willing to give for the small return on her money.

AVERAGE (ESTIMATED) PROFIT PER ESTATE

(does not include federal and state income taxes to be deducted from "profit")

Average (estimated) profit per estate = $300

Average weekly profit (based on *one* estate per week) = $300 × 1 = $300

42 weeks × $300 = $12,600

Average weekly profit (based on *two* estates per week) = $300 × 2 = $600

42 weeks × $600 = $25,200

Average weekly profit (based on *three* estates per week) = $300 × 3 = $900

42 weeks × $900 = $37,800

Average weekly profit (based on *four* estates per week) = $300 × 4 = $1200

42 weeks × $1200 = $50,400

Wendy had spent over 50 hours investigating and evaluating all aspects of the business, but she was comfortable with her final decision not to invest. The numbers for the franchise did not add up. Even though her heart wanted to make the deal, her head told her otherwise. She walked away without any regrets.

Discussion Questions

1. Frannie said she "did her homework" before she visited the Grandys. Do you agree?

2. Based on the financial numbers discussed in Scenario 1 what questions would you have had for the CEO, Danielle Grandy?

3. The 3C's franchise was not successful for Frannie. Discuss the reasons. In your opinion, what were the top two reasons for its failure?

4. In contrast, Wendy in Scenario 2, made the decision not to pursue EMK Treasures and Liquidation. Do you agree with her decision?

5. What process did Wendy follow to evaluate her potential franchise?

6. Wendy planned to operate the franchise as a part-time business until she retired. Do you think she would have been successful starting this way? Do you believe she and other franchises should be started as full-time careers?

7. How would you compare Frannie and Wendy as potential business owners? If you had to choose, which person would you prefer to be your business partner and why?

Assignments

1. Do you have the personality to be an entrepreneur? Take the entrepreneur quiz at https://www.entrepreneur.com/article/246454. What did you learn about yourself?

2. Research the top five franchises in the United States in the most current year available, and summarize the characteristics of the owners. Are there similarities? What differences did you uncover?

3. Research a failed franchise in your state during the last two years. Summarize why the company failed.

4. Assume you have $75,000 to invest. Research franchises that seem to be a match for you. Select one and explain the reason for your choice. Include a brief history of the franchise, why you feel you would be successful as an owner, and discuss the amount of the initial investment and income needed to sustain the business for a minimum of 3 years (assuming there is no profit until then). With this limited information, explain whether you would purchase the business.

5. Research the site https://www.sba.gov/ for information on franchising. Summarize its content. If you were starting a business, which three topics would be most important to you? Explain.

References

Franchise 500 rating (2021). Entrepreneur. https://www.entrepreneur.com/franchise500/2021

Caminiti, S. (2015, May 5). 5 gutsy career moves at any age. CNBC. http://www.cnbc.com/2015/05/08/5-gutsy-second-career-moves-for-any-age.html

Forbes. (2011, October 11). *How to plan for a second career.* https://www.forbes.com/pictures/el45elilk/dont-make-rash-moves/#5915dcbd2111

International Franchise Association. (n.d.). Franchise opportunities. http://www.franchise.org/

Libava, J. (2009). Is buying a franchise really buying a job? Small Business Trends. https://smallbiztrends.com/2009/08/buying-franchise-buying-job.html

Rampton, J. (2014, July 27). 50 signs you need to start your own business. *Entrepreneur.* https://www.entrepreneur.com/article/235224

Roth, C. (n.d.). Quiz: Do you have what it takes to be an entrepreneur? *Entrepreneur.* https://www.entrepreneur.com/article/246454

Sheehy, G. (1996). *New passages: Mapping your life across time.* Ballantine Books.

Strauss, C. (2019, June 19). Meet the new Burger Kings—and the rest of America's best (and worst) franchises to buy in 2019. *Forbes.* https://www.forbes.com/sites/karstenstrauss/2019/06/19/best-worst-franchises-buy-own/?sh=2db63517d79d

Tavris, C. (1995, June 25). Forward to middlescence. *New York Times.* https://www.nytimes.com/1995/06/25/books/forward-to-middlescence.html

Towner, B. (2011, June 20). 50 jobs for a second career. *AARP Bulletin.* http://www.aarp.org/work/working-after-retirement/info-06-2011/jobs-for-a-second-career.html

U.S. Census Bureau. (2019, October 9). An aging nation: Projected number of children and older adults. https://www.census.gov/library/visualizations/2018/comm/historic-first.html

U.S. Census Bureau. (2020, September 25). Business owners ages: Over half of U.S. business owners were age 55 and older. https://www.census.gov/library/visualizations/2020/comm/business-owners-ages.html

U.S Small Business Administration. (n.d.). 10 steps to start your own business. https://www.sba.gov/business-guide/10-steps-start-your-business

U.S. Small Business Administration. (n.d.). Buy an existing franchise or business. https://www.sba.gov/business-guide/plan-your-business/buy-existing-business-or-franchise

Figure Credit

Fig. 7.2: Source: U.S. Census Bureau.

Rose's Thorns

- Explain the value of self-education in purchasing and operating a successful business.
- Describe the importance of selecting the "right" business partner for a new business venture.
- Summarize the value of hiring external professionals to provide expert operational and financial advice.
- Explain the personal and professional toll of closing a company due to financial distress.

Key Concepts and Words

business ownership, decision-making, due diligence, entrepreneur, investing in your dream, partnership, trust, vocational education

Overview

Rose's Thorns is a story about a creative and talented high school student who dreams about owning a flower shop (florist). She is fascinated by the design of floral arrangements and is confident that her life goal will come true if she opens her own business. Rose purchases her first store believing it will be successful. She discovers that "following your dream" might cause a never-ending "chase" of your dream.

Scenario

Rose was a 16-year-old high school student who was never interested in school. She was a teenager who rebelled against her parents partly due to strong social pressures. Recreational drugs and a free spirit were the social themes within her circle of friends. Rose, like many teenagers, rejected the idea of formalized education (such as attending college after high school). For Rose, it was not the acceptance of her peers or the rebelling against her parents that influenced her decision not to attend college. Instead, it was a passion for doing something that she loved.

During Rose's sophomore year, her school district opened a career and technical education center that allowed students to enroll in vocational classes held on its own campus. The school promoted its courses as part of a program that would lead to a career immediately after graduation. The program that attracted Rose the most was "Floral Arts and Design." She was energized by the beauty of the flowers, the harmonic balance of flowers and leaves in arrangements, and best of all, the calming fragrance of flowers, like "Stargazer" lilies.

On the first day of vocational school, Rose jumped on the bus with other students, feeling inspired. She was motivated by this new method of learning, and it was far more desirable than sitting in a class all day. When she arrived at the campus, she was immediately intrigued. The room was designed like an actual retail florist, complete with wooden workbenches. It had all the materials available to create flower arrangements such as shears, green floral tape, wires, vases, arrangement containers, and flowers. The scent of the flowers was overwhelmingly beautiful to Rose. Her favorite lilies and irises were there, and the orange blossoms, gardenia, baby's breath, carnations, and roses instantly created a sense of peace. Rose immediately knew this was "her place."

In the program, Rose learned about every aspect of floral design. She was educated on the most desired flowers by consumers and how to clean the flower stalks efficiently. She was also taught how to choose the appropriate containers for a floral arrangement based on size, color, and occasion. Finally, the program covered the management of front store responsibilities. The latter included how to greet and interact with customers, the creation of inviting displays, and how to wrap bouquets of fresh cut flowers and tie with ribbon bows. However, the program did not include coursework on running a business or the importance of business planning, accounting, and finance (i.e., how to make a profit).

At the end of her senior year in high school and after 2 years of floral training, Rose was excited with the prospect of being hired as a designer. After graduation, she attended an 8-week course at a competitive, specialized trade school, where students were invited to participate after submitting a flower arrangement. It was judged by instructors as a part of the application process. This institute was considered the "best of best" schools for the "best of the best" floral designers in the industry. When Rose received her acceptance letter, she couldn't contain her excitement. The specialized training was an invaluable education, and Rose maximized the experience by networking and collecting business cards from the other designers.

Soon after finishing the institute program, Rose was hired by a local florist, Daisy Petal. She continued to learn and excel with her unique ideas. After 1 year on the job, Rose left Daisy Petal to achieve her lifelong dream and operate her own florist, but first, she needed a business partner.

Rose worked with a woman at Daisy Petal named Debbie. Debbie also had a desire to purchase a business and to "be her own boss." The women were good work friends and seemed like a great match. Rose wanted to focus on floral design, and Debbie was more interested in the operational side of the business. Unlike Rose's formal training, Debbie's education in the floral business came solely from her 3 years of work experience at Daisy Petal.

Rose and Debbie purchased their floral shop, Elita's Flower & Design, from a gentleman who owned the store for about 20 years. It was located in an excellent area for foot traffic. The store was on the corner of a shopping center with large, expansive windows ideal for attracting customers. Business neighbors included a popular Middle Eastern cuisine restaurant and a nationally known printing and mailing company. The mall was busy with potential customers throughout the entire day. Not far away was another flower shop, but it was small and connected to a high-end grocery store.

As a part of the purchase negotiations, the previous owner agreed to work in the shop for 2 weeks to assist in transitioning the business to Rose and Debbie. Both of them felt confident to operate the business when he left the store. They shared good wishes, and the previous owner turned over the keys. The partners also purchased the customer lists from the seller, which included 5,100 names and addresses of previous clientele. Rose felt they were set up for success.

Owning a business was exciting to Rose. She was happy and making people happy because she was doing what she loved. The business thrived, and the partners took a monthly salary. At the end of the first year, they "broke even." They weren't losing money or making a profit, but they were pleased to have a monthly income.

Reasons for the flat financials may have resulted from making small bad decisions that didn't even register with Rose. For example, she occasionally paid cash for flowers at the wholesaler when she forgot the card with the business tax identification number. This meant she received no price discount from the vendor, and she had to pay sales taxes on her merchandise. It occurred because she could not document she was a reseller and exempt from sales tax. And, at least once a week, the co-owners would treat themselves to lunch by taking cash directly from the register, not thinking about documenting the spending. These were not the best practices of business ownership, as Rose would later learn.

Quick Facts: Floral Designers	
2020 median pay	$29,140 per year $14.01 per hour
Typical entry-level education	High school diploma or equivalent
Work experience in a related occupation	None
On-the-job training	Moderate-term on-the-job training
Number of jobs, 2019	51,800
Job outlook, 2019–29	-20% (Decline)
Employment change, 2019–29	-10,400

What Floral Designers Do

Floral designers arrange live, dried, and silk flowers and greenery to make decorative displays.

Work Environment

Most floral designers work in retail businesses, usually flower shops and grocery stores.

How to Become a Floral Designer

Most floral designers have a high school diploma or the equivalent and learn their skills on the job in a few months.

Pay

The median annual wage for floral designers was $29,140 in May 2020.

Job Outlook

Employment of floral designers is projected to decline 20% from 2019 to 2029. Many floral designers work in the florist industry, in which overall employment is projected to decline.

(US Bureau of Labor Statistics, 2021)

Rose was thrilled that her dream was coming true, and she was a proud owner of Elita's Flower & Design. She secretly celebrated that she did this without a formal college education, like many successful business owners she read about on the Internet. She was a bit jealous that her sisters had all earned college degrees and were very successful. But her business was growing quickly, regardless of her lack of formal education which made her proud. With the company doing so well, Rose and her husband decided to have a baby. Instead of hiring childcare, Rose brought her son to the store. It worked out well because the baby slept most of the day. When awake, she put the baby in his carrier on the workbench next to her. This way Rose could play and talk to him like all mothers did, and she could still work.

The business continued to grow and made a small profit of just $5,000 the second year. Shortly after the beginning of the new year (its third in business), the owner of the building complex where Elita's was located, approached the women. He offered to move them to another location in the shopping center. The new space was not on the corner of the mall, but the landlord offered 3 months' free rent and included all expenses for the move. The square footage for the new location would be smaller, but this change would decrease expenses and improve the profit margin of the business. Packing up and relocating was a short-term inconvenience for a long-term gain. Rose and Debbie agreed with little discussion and looked forward to their new store.

However, after the move, the partners noticed their foot traffic decreased. They no longer attracted customers with their creative window displays. In the past, Elita's had appeared in a local magazine for weddings and events, and it had featured (for free) their unique and beautiful designs. Because there was only one small window for displays at the new location, the magazine no longer came monthly to take pictures. This was a significant disappointment to Rose. It was the only marketing they had needed for the business and an advertisement in a magazine or online would be expensive.

In the fourth year of operation, Debbie decided that she no longer wanted to be an owner and offered to sell her share of the business to Rose. This came as a big surprise to Rose, but she liked the idea of being a sole business owner. Their certified public accountant (CPA) prepared the sales documents, attached the current financials, and the two women agreed on a number. According to the CPA, the financial books were in order. Rose paid her partner in full, and she celebrated her new sole ownership with a family and friends' party!

Now all the responsibility fell on Rose. Her first week passed without incident, and the shop opened and closed as it always did. Orders from customers came in, deliveries were made, and the transition was seamless. In the second week, though, Rose had to complete some new tasks. She had to pay her employees, pay the wholesaler for last month's flowers and materials, and learn how to balance the cash register and reconcile the books. This meant she had to enter in the transactions and payments from customers, deposit checks, review expenses, and pay all the bills.

Unfortunately, the mail piled up because Rose was designing the floral arrangements, handling the customers, and managing the financial side of the business. When she found a moment, she was horrified to open a letter from the Internal Revenue Service (IRS) for unpaid back taxes. Not only was there $23,000 in unpaid taxes, but it also included a penalty of $2,200. The business had not paid taxes for its first 3 years!

Rose panicked. She called her older sister, who also owned a business, and sought her advice. Her sister told her to call the CPA immediately and demand an explanation. The accountant said she would investigate the situation. Rose called again after 2 days because she had spoken with the IRS, and it stated it would freeze her bank accounts if the taxes were not paid within 10 days.

That evening, Rose sat on the floor in the store and just cried and cried and cried. "How could this be happening to me?" she asked. "Everything was fine with Debbie, and now this!" Rose tried calling Debbie, but her former partner never returned her calls. In reality, the business had been struggling all along.

When Rose arrived at the CPA's office 2 weeks later, she was greeted by a different accountant. This person told her that she had bought the previous CPA's business. The new CPA said the books were "not in order" as represented.

It was true. The taxes had not been paid. The business file showed that Rose's former partner had signed for several certified letters from the IRS, but Rose never knew these communications existed. The landlord had also changed the terms and conditions of the rental contract when they moved. She learned that Elita's Flower & Design was now paying rent plus partial fees for the mall upkeep, including snow removal and landscaping. Debbie never told Rose about this either. There was a letter in the files dated 14 months ago, signed by Debbie, acknowledging those new leasing terms. Finally, there were bills for flowers and materials that had not been paid for months, and the business was buying items on credit with steep interest rates.

Because Debbie was running the business financials, Rose never asked questions. Both were taking their salary monthly, and this meant that the financials were solid to her. In fact, there were 2 months where Debbie said they both could take an extra $200 in pay. She never thought to review anything with Debbie. They were equal owners, and she trusted her.

Rose brought in an auditor to evaluate the financials for the company. The auditor discovered that Debbie had been forging financial documents and even the tax returns for the business. It also showed that several bank deposits had never been made. Rose felt everything that Debbie had done for the business was a lie! Debbie was a thief!

Even worse was that Debbie had disappeared along with the original CPA, so Rose had no option of holding either one responsible. The new CPA took no accountability because she not been their accountant when the inaccuracies took place. To add to the sadness of the situation, Rose discovered that Debbie, her former business partner, and their original CPA were best friends. It seemed they had been conspiring together and secretly.

The extensive debts forced Rose to make the painful decision to close the shop. Rose considered filing for bankruptcy, but she and her husband thought that financial decision would haunt them for the rest of their lives.

Rose was forced to pay the Internal Revenue Service the back taxes and late fines. She also had to pay off the remaining loan on the business. This nearly destroyed her and her husband financially. The business cost Rose and her husband their family home, and eventually, she went back to working at Daisy Petal. There, she excelled once again but had the energy only to work part-time. Rose was embarrassed by her failure, but her sister had been encouraging. "You went after something you wanted in life and loved. No shame with that!"

Discussion Questions

1. Rose did not have a college degree. Explain why it may or may not have made a difference in the success of her florist.

2. Rose thought she was "set up" for success. What do you think she meant by that?

3. Were there any early signs that Debbie was not a good partner? Support your position with examples.

4. When Rose described Debbie as a good partner for her business, explain why she thought the two would succeed. What traits or skills did each partner bring to the business? Was her logic sound at the time?

5. What is the importance of trust in a business relationship?

6. Discuss the advantages and disadvantages of owning a business by yourself or with a partner.

7. Identify at least three mistakes Rose made in her business. Which one or two were most responsible for the failure of the florist? Explain why.

8. If someone close to you recommended their accountant or attorney, would you take their word for the individual's professional competency and credibility?

Assignments

1. Research and define the term "due diligence." Did Rose and Debbie perform due diligence before purchasing the business? For example, Rose and Debbie purchased a customer list of 5,100 clients from the prior owner. How did they know the list was legitimate and contained the contact information for active customers, such as those who purchased from Elita's in the past year?

2. Do you have a creative idea or dream you think could be made into a successful business? What type of research would you need to do to turn your vision into a reality?

3. Research how to choose the correct partner for a business. Identify the evaluation process and traits of a strong partner.

4. Every business needs professional support as well. How does one research and select a professional, such as an attorney, accountant, or marketer, who can be trusted? What national and local organizations where you live could help you in finding a professional? When is the appropriate time in the business cycle for you to hire the support?

Additional Learning

- The U.S. Small Business Administration provides excellent educational materials on starting and operating a business. Topics include (a) plan your business; (b) launch your business; (c) manage your business; and (d) grow your business. Visit the SBA at https://www.sba.gov/business-guide. How could Rose have used the SBA resources to her advantage?

- Certain professionals such as an attorney or a CPA must have a special license granted by the state where their business is located. Locate the licensing requirements in your state for these specialists.

- Research how to file a formal disciplinary complaint against either attorneys or certified public accountants. How important would this information be when deciding whether to hire an accountant or attorney?

- Filing bankruptcy has many personal and professional implications. There are three different bankruptcy proceedings: Chapter 7, Chapter 11, and Chapter 13. Visit the website for the U.S. Bankruptcy Courts located at http://www.uscourts.gov/services-forms/bankruptcy/bankruptcy-basics. Define each type of bankruptcy. How are they the same or different?

References

Business Dictionary. (2017). http://www.businessdictionary.com/

Entrepreneur. (2017). How to buy a business. https://www.entrepreneur.com/article/79638

Robert Half International (2017, May 12). Accounting professionals: The most important small business hires? https://www.roberthalf.com/accountemps/employers/hiring-tips/how-to-hire-an-employee/why-the-right-accountant-could-be-the-most-important-hire-for-your-small-business

Society of American Florists. (2021). Trends and statistics. https://safnow.org/trends-statistics/

U.S. Courts. (2011, November). *Bankruptcy basics,* (3rd ed.). http://www.uscourts.gov/services-forms/bankruptcy/bankruptcy-basics

U.S. Department of Labor. (2021, April 9). Floral designer. Bureau of Labor Statistics. https://www.bls.gov/ooh/arts-and-design/floral-designers.htm

U.S. Small Business Administration. (n.d.) Come in we're open [Photograph]. https://www.sba.gov/assets/images/homepage/open-for-business-blogs-photo.jpg

U.S. Small Business Administration. (2021). Browse business topics. https://www.sba.gov/

U.S. Small Business Administration. (2021). Write your business plan. https://www.sba.gov/business-guide/plan-your-business/write-your-business-plan?interiorpage2015

U.S. Small Business Administration. (2021). Buying an existing business or franchise. https://www.sba.gov/starting-business/how-start-business/business-types/buying-existing-businesses

U.S. Small Business Administration. (2021). Women-owned businesses. https://www.sba.gov/starting-business/how-start-business/business-types/women-owned-businesses

Wasley, P. (2016, May 20). 8 critical considerations for choosing the right business partner. Entrepreneur. https://www.entrepreneur.com/article/273813

Ethics and Personal Values

8

Should Truth Prevail (or Not?)

Overview

Charlotte Laurus is a laboratory chemist working for the cannabis medicinal company, Marimed Ltd., based in Groves, Massachusetts. She has been employed by Marimed for 4 years and creates formulas for new cannabis products. The company has recently expanded to sell its brands in Canada, forcing the reorganization of its corporate structure. Charlotte has a new supervisor whose management style is dramatically different than previous leadership. The new supervisor is directing Charlotte to "cut corners" and "stretch the truth," making Charlotte very uncomfortable both personally and professionally.

Scenario

Charlotte graduated from Dartmouth College with a major in chemistry and a minor in philosophy. During college, she had worked in the chemistry lab at Marimed Ltd. Marimed offered part-time employment in the summer, intending to recruit recent graduates. Marimed hired only the best students with the highest grades in biology and chemistry.

Objectives

- Explain how to professionally disagree with your boss or superior.
- Describe the consequences of disagreeing with management.
- Compare and contrast the differences between personal values and professional values.
- Define the term "whistleblower."

Key Concepts and Words

chain of command, ethics, integrity, internal promotion, personal values, professional values, whistleblower, workplace disagreements

During the summer months of her junior year, Charlotte worked on a project to create a cannabidiol (CBD) anti-inflammatory lotion that was successfully tested on rabbits for skin sensitivity. The ingredients of the Mint Leaf Calming Lotion were altered several times until its clinical effect was stable and the rabbits did not experience any rash or irritation. The formula for the lotion was difficult to stabilize because some ingredients could break down quickly. This meant that the final lotion could turn out to be too thick and sticky or have too much liquid, if it was not mixed in the correct proportions. In addition, the effectiveness could be impacted.

Once Charlotte understood how to adjust the active ingredients with the mint and cannabidiol content, she successfully created the lotion. During that time, she learned the importance of precise measurements and experiment documentation. Charlotte became more excited about the project as the company ultimately planned to seek approval of the product for human topical use.

Charlotte personally loved creating the lotion because her family grew mint plants at their house when she was a child. They used to make mint sun tea, which calmed her upset stomach, so she was thrilled about this new use. When you rubbed the leaves between your hands, the fragrance seemed calming to the spirit as well. Hence, the name Calming Lotion.

After graduation, Charlotte joined Marimed as a permanent employee. She enjoyed her job as a chemist and was passionate about her work. She was particularly interested because she would work on the launch of the Calming Lotion in the retail market. For 4 years, she worked with a manager (during summers and as a permanent employee), who frequently recognized her for her ingenuity and attention to detail. Regardless of the project, Charlotte was meticulous in her notes and was known for her dependability and integrity. She worked with five other chemists and they regularly collaborated with one another. Her manager, Tammie, was proud of the team, and they were often featured in the CEO's "State of Address" and during meetings with its company's investors. Charlotte was considered the informal lead among her peers since she had the most experience and tenure.

After the recent business update, Charlotte's manager received a promotion, and a new supervisor, Phoebe Clems, was named to Charlotte's team. Phoebe had been a manager at Marimed for 2 years in the warehouse and distribution area of the company and had no lab knowledge. Charlotte was disappointed that Phoebe was chosen because she had hoped to learn more about laboratory management from a new boss. She also felt the company could have selected a person with specific chemistry experience within the cannabis medicinal industry externally who would have been a better fit.

Nevertheless, Charlotte embraced Phoebe and sent her a text congratulating her and offering to help with her transition. Phoebe responded 3 days later and told Charlotte that she was meeting everyone the following week. She also included in the body of the text, in capital letters, that Phoebe was late completing company laboratory documents and sent a photo listing the items due. Charlotte was stunned by the tone and content of the reply. She hadn't met Phoebe, and the first communication was requiring her to finish some lab documents. Charlotte replied that the documents were "optional" and had not been needed to be completed for any of their past projects. This was supported by her previous manager, Tammie. She assumed that Phoebe was not likely aware of this because she had never worked in a lab.

Pressure Point #1

Monday morning, Phoebe announced her arrival at the laboratory with a strong and deliberate look on her face. She gave her new employees a history of her work achievements at Marimed and quickly changed the content from her introduction to asking Charlotte about the tardy documents. Phoebe demanded that Charlotte complete them within a week. She reminded Charlotte that SHE was the manager now, and her previous supervisor's direction was obsolete. The other five chemists were shocked by Phoebe's tone, knew she was wrong but continued their work in silence. Charlotte felt disrespected and was embarrassed by Phoebe's scolding of her in public in front of her colleagues.

Pressure Point #2

The following day when Charlotte and her colleagues arrived at work, they found their laboratory was completely rearranged. The document files were placed in new binders and labeled differently. In addition, their assigned workstations changed location, meaning Charlotte was now working at the station closest to the door and Phoebe's office.

Charlotte and the others were frustrated. They didn't understand why the changes had occurred, and the new procedures and lab design delayed their work because they were unfamiliar with Phoebe's placement of their data and reports. The shelves, supplies, ingredients, and chemicals were also rearranged.

Throughout the first few days, the chemists frequently grabbed the wrong items for their experiments and analyses. Sometimes, Charlotte and the others didn't realize they had grabbed the wrong item until it was too late. This forced them to start their project all over.

After the fourth day, one chemist, Michael, brought this to Phoebe's attention. She scoffed and said to "use the failed or inaccurate tests and just bury them in the paperwork." She instructed everyone to include those failures in the total number needed for production approvals. "Final summary reports will be submitted on time. We will not miss any deadline under any circumstances because we had to do something over," she said. The reports were critical to launch dates, and they needed to be certified with the Federal Drug Administration (FDA) on time. Michael was worried. He defined this behavior as fraudulent but complied with Phoebe's direction.

Pressure Point #3

During Phoebe's second week as the new manager, she posted checklists on the walls providing direction on how to complete tasks. The chemists were irritated because there was no need for the checklists. Their group had functioned well and exceeded timelines and objectives consistently day after day and month over month. Tammie, the previous manager, trusted the team, and they were tenured and competent.

Charlotte asked Phoebe about the lists and why they were posted. Phoebe replied that things had not been getting completed on time in the past, so this would ensure compliance. She also required that the chemists initial the notes she placed on their workbenches to ensure they had read them. She demanded the notes be placed in a chronological binder used by all employees at their lab station. Phoebe told the team that she would be reviewing the binder daily to be certain they followed her protocols, and she would "spot-check" their knowledge. At any given time, she warned that "she could ask them a question and they had better know the answer."

Pressure Point #4

Despite her changes, Phoebe was still not happy with the department's operation and felt there was more room for improvement. Starting the third week, Phoebe changed the chemists' work schedules without any warning. When asked about the change in work shifts, Phoebe told the chemists she did not need a reason nor was she required to check with them for their approval. The six chemists had been working the same hours Monday to Friday, 8 a.m. to 5 p.m. for as long as the company had been in business. With a consistent Monday through Friday schedule, the team could depend upon each other to solve problems that they could not resolve independently. It also meant they could assist each other if they fell behind in meeting deadlines.

Everyone was surprised with a new Sunday to Saturday schedule. This meant the six chemists would not be present in the lab working together each day, and they would be alternating workdays and splitting shifts. Because their projects were multifaceted, chemists were responsible for different steps. Only the person who had the knowledge and expertise could complete certain phases. When a chemist completed their step, the project moved to the next chemist to complete their specific job. Unfortunately, if that second chemist was not working the same day, the project was stalled. Charlotte shook her head, and the others rolled their eyes. The consequence of not having all the chemists working together on the same days would cause missed deadlines.

Specific to balancing work with home life, the change was a disaster for some of them. One chemist didn't drive and had depended upon her neighbor for transportation to and from work. When the employee communicated this, Phoebe told the chemist she would have to take an Uber or determine other ways to get to work. Another person had three children involved in sports, and weekends were booked with activities. In frustration, that person complained to Charlotte and not Phoebe. Both of them felt they shouldn't say anything because they might get fired. The change was also inconvenient for Charlotte, who taught a lab course on Saturdays at the local community college and couldn't imagine how she would manage this schedule. Charlotte was frustrated due to her manager's lack of transparency and unwillingness to discuss this significant alteration in the work schedule.

Pressure Point #5

Charlotte and her colleagues had hoped this was the end of the changes. However, by month's end, Phoebe announced that the team needed to hasten the post-marketing analysis on the Mint Leaf Calming Lotion. This meant they needed to quickly produce additional quantities of the product. However, this was impossible as the mint and cannabidiol oils would break down if heated faster than the formula required. The end result would be a foul odor and a lotion that would irritate the consumer's skin. When Charlotte brought this problem to Phoebe, she demanded the team follow her instructions and document that the lotion was heated for the original time necessary. Phoebe argued that 15 minutes of higher temperature would not destroy product integrity.

Charlotte refused to change the process and lie in the documentation, but the other five chemists listened to Phoebe and did what was required by their new manager. Charlotte also knew that the law required submitting a new application when any of the processes changed in production of their lotion. When that was suggested, Phoebe replied that it was not necessary. This created angst between Phoebe, Charlotte, and the five other chemists. Phoebe's request angered Charlotte. Changing the process of the Mint Leaf Calming Lotion would create an inferior product. She knew the goal of the lotion was to be "calming" for customers, and the time alterations could interfere with its anti-inflammatory action and cause skin irritations.

What to Do?

Charlotte became worried, as did Michael, about the actions of Phoebe and her lack of regard in following lab protocols. She considered speaking with Phoebe's boss, Sulieman, yet Charlotte didn't know him well, and she respected the "chain of command." She thought about a second option which was speaking with Human Resources. A third idea was to phone the confidential ethics and compliance phone line of Marimed.

The "ethics and compliance hot line" was an established 1-800 phone number for any employee to call and disclose ethical issues at Marimed. Since it was "confidential," there would be no information documenting the person who made the call and alerted the company. Marimed also used a third-party vendor to ensure confidentiality.

Charlotte was conflicted. She was confident she was correct that the processing time should not be accelerated, and she knew this was the ethical thing to do. Yet she believed, whether true or not, it was inevitable she would be recognized as the "informant." Because of Charlotte's public challenge of Phoebe's directive, it would be easy to deduce who likely made the complaint as the "whistleblower." Charlotte knew what she had to do. She dialed the number and did not tell any of the other chemists about her call.

A Potential Consequence?

After Charlotte reached out to the ethics and compliance line, there was no immediate change. While in the laboratory, Charlotte and her colleagues discussed their frustration daily. Sometimes their conversation continued over lunch in the employee breakroom. The six of them felt they had no choice but to agree to the requests of their new boss. Unbeknownst to them, their frustration was overheard by an employee of another department. That person mentioned it to their boss. A day after one of these lunches, Phoebe announced that the team was required to attend a mandatory meeting outside of work hours on a Sunday morning at 10 a.m.!

Charlotte and the other chemists were upset again. They already gave up family time when they were assigned to work a Sunday in the lab. Now, all of them had to immediately prioritize this meeting. They were also nervous about this last-minute request. They knew they had to participate and started worrying about the security of their jobs. When Charlotte asked why the meeting was occurring, Phoebe responded, "You'll find out when you all get there." This scared Charlotte because she remembered the phone call she had made to the "ethics and compliance hot line." The agenda for the Sunday meeting seemed secret. But Charlotte decided to be an optimist and influence the team. She suggested that it might be a meeting for recognition since one of their latest cannabis calming perfumes was launched at a large department store the previous week.

On Sunday, the group walked into the lab to find Phoebe and Suleiman, her boss, waiting for them. The chemists were surprised and felt more insecure again. Phoebe had a list of items she wanted to discuss, which she passed out on an agenda. They were all negatives: performance, gossip, attitude, product completion, and documentation, among other things. When a question was asked, the team responded and tried to explain, yet they were cut off by Phoebe or Phoebe's boss. In fact, questions and commentary were phrased in the negative and often contained a reference to Charlotte. For example, "Since Charlotte can't solve issues with some of the projects, you all need to contact me (i.e., Phoebe) with issues." Or, "I (Phoebe) arranged the shelves with the formula ingredients so it is easier to find supplies. It was so difficult before with the way Charlotte had it organized. Wouldn't you agree?"

Then Phoebe's boss separated the other chemists from Charlotte and asked them questions about Phoebe's and Charlotte's interactions. Next, Suleiman cornered Charlotte by herself and lectured her about not being supportive of Phoebe. Charlotte ended the discussion by confirming that she had always been supportive, yet it was challenging to maintain the team's previous record of top performance when Phoebe was constantly changing the "rules." There seemed to be no reason to "fix what doesn't need fixing." A couple of months ago, everybody seemed happy, and the team was lauded for their creations. Now, the environment in the lab was different. Everyone was stressed.

Charlotte and her colleagues returned to work on Monday, even more disillusioned. They felt broadsided by the meeting. They agreed, though, they would try to keep a positive mindset. Charlotte, the eternal optimist, made statements to support Phoebe and tried to keep the team dynamic spirited.

During the coming weeks, Phoebe asked the chemists to take on additional tasks in the lab that were completed by their previous manager. They barely had enough time to finish their current projects yet take on responsibilities that their new boss should be doing. One chemist decided that she couldn't work under Phoebe and planned to look for a new job. Charlotte decided the same. Charlotte and her chemist colleagues continued to create lotions, potions, and perfumes, but did so with less enthusiasm. In fact, their performance declined.

A month later, Charlotte was contacted by Phoebe to attend a meeting regarding Mint Leaf Calming Lotion. Sales had plummeted, and several lawsuits were pending. Phoebe said she wanted to get her feedback since she was the original person who discovered and perfected the lotion. But it was too late. That morning Charlotte had accepted a new job with a competitor with an increase in pay and regular shift hours. When she met with Phoebe, she handed Phoebe her resignation letter and simply left. It was time to move on.

CANNABIS

- *Cannabis sativa L.* is a plant that contains over 80 different naturally occurring compounds called "cannabinoids"
- Two well-known cannabinoids:
    - **Cannabidiol (CBD)**
    - **Tetrahydrocannabinol (THC)**
- Plants are grown to produce varying concentrations of cannabinoids – **THC** or **CBD**
- These plant variations are called cultivars

Cannabis-derived compounds

- Compounds occurring naturally in the plant – like **CBD** and **THC**
- These compounds are extracted directly from the plant
- Can be used to manufacture drug products
- Example: highly-purified CBD extracted from the plant

Cannabis-related compounds

- These synthetic compounds are created in a laboratory
- Can be used to manufacture drug products
- Some synthetic compounds may also occur naturally in the plant and some may not
- Examples: synthetically-derived dronabinol (also naturally occurring) and nabilone (not naturally occurring)

FIGURE 8.1   Cannabis (FDA, n.d.)

Discussion Questions

1. Explain the environment in the laboratory before the new manager Phoebe arrived and then after she started managing the team.

2. List the conflicts that existed between Phoebe and the six chemists.

    a. Why did the conflicts exist?

    b. Which of these would you consider a conflict of personal or professional values?

3. Phoebe tells Charlotte she has missed deadlines on her first communication, which was by "text." How did this impact Charlotte? Do you believe Phoebe's treatment of Charlotte impacted her decision to call the ethics and compliance line? Explain.

4. Charlotte decides to contact the hotline rather than speak with Phoebe's boss, Suleiman. Why do you think she made that decision? Would it have been appropriate to bypass the chain of command and go directly to Suleiman. Why or why not?

5. Assume you found an egregious situation in your workplace that differed from your values.

    a. Would you come forth and report it? Yes or no, and why?

    b. If the situation would *harm* a person or animal, would you come forth and report it? If the situation would *not harm* a person or animal, would it change your decision? Discuss.

    c. If you knew there was a possibility that you would lose your job, does your answer differ to the questions above? Why or why not?

6. Why did Charlotte decide to look for new employment?

7. Do you think Phoebe really wanted to ask for Charlotte's expertise at the end of the scenario or for another reason? Explain.

8. There are several ways this workplace scenario could have ended. Describe at least two differing outcomes.

Assignments

1. Research how to disagree with your boss and summarize the most effective way of dialoguing with them.

2. Summarize the meaning of "chain of command." Identify two organizations or industries that have a well-defined chain of command. List the benefits and limitations of this structure and control. (Hint: Military)

3. Research and define the difference between personal and professional values. Explain the impact on an employee when their values are opposite their employers.

4. Define a "whistleblower." Find a workplace whistleblower example within the last 10 years. Summarize the scenario and the outcome. Then, include an explanation of when it is appropriate to operate outside of the "chain of command" to report unethical behavior.

References

Campbell, S. (2018, September 27). 6 effective tactics for handling a toxic boss. *Entrepreneur*. https://www.entrepreneur.com/article/320696

Dunham, A., & Stout-Jough, S. (2020, February 26). Are ethics hotlines effective? SHRM. https://www.shrm.org/hr-today/news/hr-magazine/spring2020/pages/are-ethics-hotlines-effective.aspx

Grenny, J. (2014, November 25). How to disagree with your boss. *Harvard Business Review*. https://hbr.org/2014/11/how-to-disagree-with-your-boss

Muse Editor. (2021). 10 brilliant tips for dealing with a difficult boss. The Muse. https://www.themuse.com/advice/10-brilliant-tips-for-dealing-with-a-difficult-boss

National Whistleblower Center. (2021). Know your rights. https://www.whistleblowers.org/know-your-rights/

U.S. Department of Agriculture. (n.d.). OIG hotline. Office of Inspector General. https://www.usda.gov/oig/hotline.htm

U.S. Department of Labor. (2021). The whistleblower protection program. Occupational Safety and Health Administration. https://www.whistleblowers.gov/

U.S. Food and Drug Administration. (n.d.). FDA and cannabis: Research and drug approval process. https://www.fda.gov/news-events/public-health-focus/fda-and-cannabis-research-and-drug-approval-process

Vlachoutsicos, C. (2013, January 31). When your values clash with your company's. *Harvard Business Review*. https://hbr.org/2013/01/when-your-values-clash-with-yo

Watkins, M. (2002, June 3). How to succeed with your new boss. Harvard Business School. https://hbswk.hbs.edu/item/how-to-succeed-with-your-new-boss

The Unsophisticated Counselor

Objectives

- Explain how youth and lack of sophistication can hinder a person's professional career.
- Describe the importance of confidentiality between an attorney and a client.
- Evaluate the career and reputation implications of being "blacklisted" in an industry.

Key Concepts and Words

attorney-client privilege, client confidentiality, code of professional responsibility, ethics, naivete, professional skills, pyramid scheme, trust account

Overview

Susan McAllister is a newly licensed attorney. When she was a law student, Susan began her career with the law offices of attorney Jayson Reid as a paralegal. Upon graduation from law school, J.R. (as his clients called him) offered Susan a permanent position as an associate attorney, making it a two-attorney law office. Susan was hired to perform all the legal work for the firm's clients, leaving Mr. Reid the time to handle his client's business investments and legal negotiations, both of which were his specialty. However, the job was short-lived due to a combination of Susan's naivete and Reid's opportunistic personality.

Scenario

Susan McAllister grew up in Skyway City, Nevada, as the oldest of three children. As a teenager, she was very achievement-oriented, and she was very anxious to earn her diploma and quickly graduate from high school.

School had never challenged her. Although her parents spoke to the teachers about Susan "skipping" a grade in elementary school, her teachers discouraged it. They said that academically gifted students learned more, but it could hurt their social development. However, during her senior year of high school, Susan took advantage of her school district's dual-enrollment program, and she completed her last year of high school at a state university. Susan jumped at the chance to leave what she considered basic education and unsophisticated teachers.

Because she had forgone her last year of high school and blended it with her first year of college, Susan was a young freshman at 17 when she started at West Valley State University. Like most college students, she did not understand what direction she should take with her major. She remembered when she was young that her Uncle Ray told her to "pick something you like" and "just finish it!" Susan reflected on that advice often during her freshman year and chose sociology as her major. She knew that choice would force her to earn a master's degree to be marketable in the workforce, but she was comfortable with that plan.

When Susan was in her final semester at West Valley State, she needed that "one last class" to graduate. While looking for an elective, she decided to enroll in a business law class. She had never taken a business course let alone a law class in college, but, to her surprise, she became passionate about the topic. She quickly developed a love for the law. Immediately, her initial plan for graduate school changed to law school. She submitted three applications for that fall semester and was accepted for enrollment at a Nevada law school.

The first year (often referred to as 1L) was challenging. At 20, Susan was the youngest in her class. The other students were older and had more life experiences than she. This often made it more difficult to understand the business concepts in her law courses. Susan would take detailed notes, create study outlines, work in study groups, and try any learning strategy she could to ensure success. But, after the first year, Susan's grades were ordinary; she was discouraged and seriously contemplated quitting. Then, she remembered what Uncle Ray said. She heard a voice in her head that kept saying, "FINISH!" "Why waste a year of education, time, and money?"

Summer break arrived. Like most law students, Susan needed a job to pay for tuition in the fall. She was interested in law-related summer employment, but she had no family members who were lawyers and no immediate leads for work. Until law school, she had never met an attorney in her life. So, Susan looked at her options and decided her best chance for employment was to contact her old employer,

Mr. Keelin Brown. Keelin owned a local automotive repair shop called K.B. & Sons Auto. During high school, Susan had been a cashier at K.B., and Mr. Brown had always complimented her on her work ethic. After Susan's initial phone call to him, she was working at her old job the next day!

The job was not in the legal field, which Susan had wanted, but as many would say, "It paid the bills!" After a month at K.B., a very interesting customer came into the garage. He was picking up his car, a classic Chevrolet Corvette, that had needed service. Susan struck up a conversation with him and found out he was a local attorney with a business practice who advised and assisted start-up companies. This customer, Jayson Reid, had an engaging personality, was flamboyant, and appeared very smart. But, most of all, he was passionate about his clients.

As the summer progressed, Reid frequently stopped by the store, and he and Susan discussed the stresses of law school. During one of those conversations, J.R. caught Susan off guard. He suggested Susan come work for him during her second year of law school (2L) as a paralegal. She was delighted at the offer and excitedly accepted.

The stress of the second year of law school was worse for Susan than the first. But, the excitement of working with J.R. and his clients motivated her to continue with this educational path. She worked for him throughout her third (3L) and last year of law school. It was a challenging job, and Susan enjoyed the clients and the work. There was another attorney who worked in the building as well. His name was Marck Cahster, and he was a sole practitioner attorney with about 15 years of family law experience.

During her last semester of law school, Marck stopped by one afternoon to chat with Susan. He asked her how things were going with the job and what her career plans were after graduation. It was a very collegial conversation. Strangely, Marck ended it by telling Susan that she shouldn't consider J.R.'s firm as an employment option. He didn't provide her with a reason but told her to "be careful." Susan did not understand why he would give her this advice, but she politely thanked him as he returned to his office.

When graduation was within reach, Susan began her job hunting for a permanent full-time position as an attorney. Her search efforts were happily cut short because J.R. surprised her again with a job offer as an associate attorney. He told Susan he wanted to spend more time with the financial and business management side of his client's businesses, leaving the law practice to her to manage. This decision meant she would work with new clients setting up their companies and creating all the appropriate business documents. To Susan, this was a win-win as she would do something she enjoyed, while J.R. would finally have the time to focus on building the client base and manage their investments. J.R. also included in the financial package a leased car that would replace her old, rickety car she bought at an auction while in college!

Things continued to go well in Susan's life, and she easily passed the bar exam the November after she graduated. She was 23 years old and had received her law license. Life was good! She was even able to move into her own apartment not far from her parent's home. However, dark clouds were coming her way.

The first indication was a break-in at the office right before the winter holidays. The firm was located in the first floor of a historic centennial farmhouse. One Monday morning, Susan opened the door to the law office and found a window broken in their law library, with a large rock lying on the floor. As she explored further, doors had been opened to all the offices in the firm, including J.R.'s. Nothing appeared stolen, and the client files appeared intact, so J.R. told Susan there was no need to file a police report. He attributed the break-in to local teenagers. Susan thought it odd not to file a police report, but it made sense since nothing was amiss.

A few weeks later, something else unusual happened. Susan had finalized an employment case, and the firm had received a settlement check for the client. According to protocol, settlement checks were deposited in a separate bank account reserved for client funds called a client trust account. This way, client funds were protected from the firm funds and expenses. After the check was deposited and cleared, Susan asked their secretary Becky to process a check for payment to the client and have J.R. sign it. That afternoon, Becky handed Susan a client letter for her to sign with the check attached.

As Susan reviewed the documents, she looked closer and saw an unfamiliar signature on the check. The signature was Becky's! Immediately, Susan realized that their secretary had access to the firm's client trust account. The Nevada Rules of Professional Conduct governed use of the trust account.[1] Susan thought it was strange that a nonlawyer managed and had the primary signature access to the account.

---

1   See https://www.leg.state.nv.us/courtrules/rpc.html.

J.R. assured her it was common in the legal community, but Susan knew this practice was bordering on professional ethics violations.

Two months later, the dark clouds turned into a storm. It was a Tuesday afternoon on a frigid day in February. J.R. was out of the office and on vacation in the Caribbean. Susan was working on an employment contract for a client when her secretary Becky came rushing into the office with a ghostly look on her face. Becky was so shaken she could almost not talk. When her secretary gained her composure, she finally told Susan that seven people with badges and guns, were standing at the front door with a search warrant!

Susan was surprised as well and confused. She quickly met the law enforcement officers in their small lobby area and confirmed they had a warrant from a county judge to search the office. Susan closely read the warrant and saw it authorized the police to look specifically for Skyway City Hospital bonds. She did not understand what these were and why the police would want to locate them. However, Susan's first reaction was to isolate the client files, as the information in these files was protected by ethics rules. Any information inside them was confidential. She courageously told the officers that the files were off-limits and protected by the attorney-client privilege. The detective in charge threatened Susan with arrest, but she stood firm on restricting their access.

After the search was over, Susan sat down in her chair in deep thought. The group of seven men had comprised local police, state police, and special investigators from the state attorney general's office. "What could this possibly be about? What am I missing?"

Susan had had her law license for only 4 months. She didn't want to confide in her colleagues and let them know about the search warrant. To her dismay, the search was all over the evening news! One local television station even had a clip showing a photo of J.R.'s office with Susan's name on it. She was horrified and embarrassed. The truth had come out. J.R. was being accused of committing investment fraud.

During the remainder of the week, Susan stood firmly by J.R.'s side. To her astonishment, he continued his Caribbean vacation. He told Susan there was nothing to worry about, and he would return home that weekend as originally planned. While he was gone, she fielded client calls, avoided the news media, and ensured that client interests were put first. Then, reality set in. Susan knew nothing about J.R.'s investing efforts on behalf of his clients. Did J.R. really cheat clients out of their money? She started to think. Maybe the police were correct.

Three days later, Susan was contacted by a detective in the local police department to be interviewed. Because she had nothing to hide, she agreed to meet with him. But her youth and naivete did her an injustice. While at the Skyway City Police Department, she was asked a few general questions, told she was a suspect in the investigation, and then given her required Miranda[2] rights. When she heard those fateful words, "You have the right to remain silent," Susan became physically sick. She had no clue that the police thought she was a co-conspirator in this case! Susan refused to answer further questions, walked out the door, and collapsed inside her car. She arrived at home, closed the door to her bedroom, and slept all weekend long.

When Monday arrived, Susan faced the reality of the situation. She tried to regroup her thoughts and contacted one of her colleagues for the name of a "good" criminal law attorney. Susan met with him and was speechless when he told her he required a retainer of $25,000 to represent her! "How could this happen?" she thought. "All I wanted to do was be a good lawyer and represent my clients the best I could!" Susan had no money and several thousands of dollars of school debt. Her only option was to ask her Aunt May for a loan to secure the services of an attorney for herself.

Susan thought it was strange, again, that J.R. stayed in the Caribbean after his law office was searched and he had not immediately returned to the states. He seemed relatively unfazed by the search warrant for the office. She struggled with the possible truth in front of her and what might be an explanation for the situation. Then Susan recalled Marck Cahster's conversation with her to "be careful." Susan immediately quit her job with the firm and borrowed money from Aunt May to secure the legal advice and representation. She hired one of the best criminal law attorneys in the county, Sam Sanders.

When Sam spoke with the investigators, he learned that the prime reason Susan was considered an "unindicted" co-conspirator was that she had unwittingly signed for the delivery of a package at J.R.'s law office. That package contained 50 fraudulent Skyway City Hospital bonds that J.R. presented to his

---

2   Miranda rights are required by the 1966 U.S. Supreme Court case, *Miranda v. Arizona*.

clients as valid investments. While Susan was practicing law, J.R. was selling the forged bonds to clients as legitimate investments. He would take the client's funds and place them in the general law firm checking account (instead of the client trust account), all the while living off the proceeds. When an interest payment was due to a client, J.R. would find another client to purchase more bonds and use those new funds to pay interest to the "earlier and established" clients. The clients had no reason to suspect anything was fraudulent because their investment was being paid to them on time and in full. Susan had no knowledge of this and was shocked. J.R. operated an investment pyramid scheme.

How does the story end?

The local district attorney never brought charges against Susan, but she was forced to take a lie detector test to persuade law enforcement officers she was not involved in the scheme. Her first goal was to find another job to repay Aunt May for her generous loan.

To this day, Susan has never set foot in a courtroom or practiced law again.

Discussion Questions

1. There were subtle hints at the law office that suggested problems in the firm. Identify these and talk through the implications.

2. The author describes Susan as naive.

   a. Do you agree? If so, discuss her actions that prove this to be true.

   b. Does naivete support her ignorance of J.R.'s actions, or does she have other personality traits that explain her dedication to her boss?

3. Attorneys have an obligation to protect the confidentiality of client information, referred to as an attorney-client privilege. Do you think Susan did the right thing when the law enforcement officers arrived with the search warrant? Why or why not?

4. Why didn't Susan quit her job the day the police came to the office with the search warrant? Did Susan create her own problem with the police by appearing to support J.R.? Or, was her situation just caused by a set of unfortunate circumstances?

5. Explain why you believe that J.R. did not return from his vacation immediately.

6. Susan did not return to practicing law. What lessons do you think she learned? Based on your response, discuss how the story could be rewritten.

Assignments

1. Was it a problem that Becky had access to the client trust account that held client funds? Why or why not? (See Rule 1.15 of the Nevada Rules of Professional Conduct on Safekeeping Property located at https://www. leg.state.nv.us/courtrules/rpc.html.)

2. Research your state's rules of confidentiality that attorneys must follow. They are typically described as ethical rules or rules of professional conduct. What did you learn?

3. Choose another profession, such as a physician or a cleric, that requires its members to comply with confidentiality rules. Summarize the confidentiality requirements.

4. After this experience, Susan never returned to work in the law. One reason may have been that she was "blacklisted." Define this term in the workforce. Debate whether this was the reason for not returning to a job she found exciting and rewarding.

5. Since Susan chose her career in law based on a single class, do you think it was a good fit for her? Why or why not? Discuss if you or someone you know decided their career path based on a single event or experience. Share the story and describe if the person is successful or not and if that decision has/had any bearing on their success and professional and personal happiness.

References

Buckner, C. J. (2011). IOLTAs and client trust accounts. *American Bar Association GP Solo, (28)*5. https://www.americanbar.org/groups/gpsolo/publications/gp_solo/2011/july_august/ioltas_client_trust_accounts/

Findlaw Attorney Writers. (2018, November 28). Malpractice and the attorney client trust account. FindLaw. https://practice.findlaw.com/how-to-start-a-law-firm/malpractice-and-the-attorney-client-trust-account0.html

Nevada Rules of Professional Conduct. (2021). https://www.leg.state.nv.us/courtrules/rpc.html

Nevada Rules of Professional Conduct (2021). Rule 1.15, Safekeeping property. https://www.leg.state.nv.us/courtrules/rpc.html

Pinkasovitch, A. (2021, January 29). Ponzi vs: pyramid scheme: What's the difference? Investopedia. https://www.investopedia.com/

    ask/answers/09/ponzi-vs-pyramid.asp

Trustbooks. (2015). A client's guide—Understanding a lawyer's trust account. https://nmcdn.io/e186d21f8c7946a19faed23c3da

    2f0da/556712d9bf0f4cb2a916cc810687d52b/files/risk-management-resources/articles/clients-guide-to-understanding-a-lawyers-

    trust-account/Clients_Guide_-Understanding_a_Lawyers_Trust_Account.pdf

I Wish I Would Have Known

The reader is advised that this case contains sensitive or disturbing content. For those that may be experiencing sexual assault, you are encouraged to seek assistance at the National Sexual Assault Hotline: 1-800-656-4673 or https://rainn.org/get-help/national-sexual-assault-online-hotline.

Overview

Sadie Wray is the middle child of seven siblings who live in Shaleville, Tennessee. She is only 14 years old. In this case, her father helps her get hired at the local hardware store as a part-time cashier. While there, she learns about "do-it-yourself" (DIY) home improvement, as well as farming and ranch needs. There are many types of field crop fertilizers, for example, and there is modified "feed" for thoroughbred horses being groomed for racing. Every day she acquires knowledge and experiences something new.

Now, 10 years later, Sadie and her family have gathered for a family reunion and a party to celebrate their great-grandfather's 101st

Objectives

- Explore appropriate work environments for teenagers.
- Explain the process to develop personal values and ethics from childhood to adulthood.
- Describe the problem-solving process used to make moral and ethical choices.
- Define how early work experiences influence one's future personal and professional life.

Key Concepts and Words

ethical dilemmas, ethics, Fair Labor Standards Act, naive, personal values, sexual innuendo, work environment birthday. While enjoying the festivities, she reminisces about her teenage years with her two older sisters and reveals that she grew up way too soon. She just didn't know it ... at the time.

FAIR LABOR STANDARDS ACT

"The Fair Labor Standards Act (FLSA) sets wage, hours worked, and safety requirements for minors (individuals under age 18) working in jobs covered by the statute. The rules vary depending upon the particular age of the minor and the particular job involved. As a general rule, the FLSA sets 14 years old as the minimum age for employment, and limits the number of hours worked by minors under the age of 16.

Also, the FLSA generally prohibits the employment of a minor in work declared hazardous by the Secretary of Labor (for example, work involving excavation, driving, and the operation of many types of power-driven equipment). The FLSA contains a number of requirements that apply only to particular types of jobs (for example, agricultural work or the operation of motor vehicles) and many exceptions to the general rules (for example, work by a minor for his or her parents). Each state also has its own laws relating to employment, including the employment of minors. If state law and the FLSA overlap, the law which is more protective of the minor will apply." (U.S. Department of Labor, 2021, para. 1–2)

Scenario

Sadie Wray was an awkward teenager of 14 years old. She grew up in a family of eight children with two older sisters, four younger brothers, and a younger sister. Her family lived on a 40-acre working chicken farm, and they had a contract with a large organic egg company to sell their eggs. They were very popular with local customers because their chickens were fed with vegetarian feed, and the eggs had a very light taste. The Wray farm was surrounded by acres and acres of fields owned by their neighbors who were horse owners and also boarded and trained thoroughbred racing horses. Some of these farms specialized in breeding and training horses for the famous Triple Crown[1] races.

---

1   The Triple Crown refers to a series of three horse races (Kentucky Derby, Preakness Stakes, and Belmont Stakes) that take place each spring. A Triple Crown "winner" is a horse who wins all three races in the same year.

Because they lived in a small community, Sadie and her family knew just about everyone in town. Her father was an ironsmith and known for his creation of horseshoes that fit the hoof perfectly. This was critical for keeping a horse healthy and sound. He was well respected in the industry, and he was always gifted four tickets annually by one of the owners of the neighboring ranches to attend the Preakness, Belmont Stakes, or the Kentucky Derby races.

Since she had grown up understanding horses and the racing industry, Sadie wanted to earn money for college and thought she might get a job at a stable. Her parents were able to afford college for her older sisters, Sarah May and Ada. However, she wasn't sure her parents would have the money to help her with college when she graduated from high school. She had a stepbrother with physical disabilities, and any extra family money was spent to take care of his needs. Sadie decided to plan ahead because she had all intention of going to a big university. She knew getting a scholarship might not be possible, but she was a whiz at mathematics.

When her sisters Sarah May and Ada had turned 16 years old, their dad, Warner, had helped them find a cashier position at Colts Feed and Hardware. Colts was a local store that carried all the usual stuff one might need for "do-it-yourself" (DIY) home projects, from screws and tools to building supplies, as well as feed and fertilizer. If a person had a house problem, Colts was the place to go. Everyone in town came to Colts when they needed a part to make a repair. The staff was very neighborly, and it was rare that the store didn't carry what someone needed.

Sadie had been to the Colts store many times with her dad. With the exceptions of the cashiers, it was "just guys" who worked at Colts. When she would visit, she would be greeted by one of the Hester brothers, John and Jeremy. They were always smiling and joking around with customers. There were also two older men, Gene and Greg, who knew the answer to any and all questions. For example, eliminating pests from the garden was a common inquiry as well as questions about what size nut or bolt was needed to fix an old hinge on a gate. Occasionally, a younger teenage boy, Jeff, followed one of the older men around. He helped load heavy boxes and bags of feed into the customer's car or truck.

Annabelle, the owner's sister, rounded off the group of employees. The owner, Alvin, would usually be there during the 9 to 5 shift.

When Sadie's dad told her that he had gotten her a job at Colts Feed and Hardware, she was somewhat happy. She had hoped to work at the local grocery store or a ranch, but her sisters worked at Colts before, so she thought she knew what to expect. April 1 was her first day, and she came dressed in jeans, a t-shirt, and boots. The guys who worked there dressed the same. After all, it was a feed and hardware store, and everyone left with dusty, dirty, and sometimes smelly clothes at the end of their shift.

Annabelle acted as the head cashier and the accountant for the business. She taught Sadie the "ropes." The ropes included how to wait on customers, charge them for their purchases, and give them change. Colts Feed and Hardware did everything by paper, and Sadie couldn't believe that in the year 2010, the store still used an old-fashioned cash register. It was like a toy one that her 4-year-old sister used for playing "bank." It had manual push buttons for numbers and opened to a drawer with slots for the bills and different compartments for the coins.

The cash register didn't compute the sales tax, but Sadie was good with math, and she was able to calculate the 7% tax in her head. Annabelle and Sadie would use a small notepad to write up the items that were purchased. Between two pieces of paper was a sheet of carbon that produced an exact copy of the top page. Sadie had to press firmly with the pen to be sure the writing transferred and came through clearly on the second page. The copy was given to the customer as their receipt.

At the end of the night, Sadie was taught how to add up all the charges and balance the money in the cash register. If the store had a computer, this would have been done electronically, but not in this small town at Colts. Alvin thought about buying one, but the paper system worked fine for years. "No need for it, nothing to fix" he said when Sadie suggested the idea to Alvin and Annabelle. Charges were also processed on paper. Colts was a rural town, and high-speed, wireless Internet service wasn't available. They could connect to the internet only via a voice line and modem.

Some nights, the closing process took 30 minutes to complete because it was done manually and with a calculator. There could be upwards of 200 paper receipts to review and total. Many of the purchases were small. For example, someone might buy 10 screws for $1 or a single lightbulb for $1.75. However, receipts could be hundreds of dollars if someone purchased aluminum siding, lumber, or salt by the truckload. At the end of the day, the money from the cash register was placed in a fabric drawstring bag and hidden about

12 inches below the surface of a big barrel filled with birdseed. Every other day, it was deposited in the bank by "one of the guys." Again, Sadie thought, how antiquated; Colts didn't even have a safe for the money!

Those first few weeks, Sadie waited for her dad to pick her up because she couldn't drive yet. She told him that the job was simple, especially since math was easy for her. The customers were friendly, and Sadie had learned quite a bit about the business. She couldn't wait to get her first paycheck, open a savings account, and apply for a debit card at the bank. The agreement with her parents was, she could keep her entire paycheck if at least half of it was put into savings for her college.

Over the next several months, Sadie continued to learn about the business from the guys. One morning, a male customer asked a specific question about plumbing. John, one of "the guys," was eager to teach Sadie about plumbing basics and asked her and the customer to follow him back to aisle 9 to the plumbing area.

Sadie did not realize it at the time, but gender is used to describe the connections and pipe fittings in plumbing. John started explaining the differences between male and female fittings, and the customer laughed uncontrollably. He said that it's essential that the male and female parts fit well together to make sure the connection is tight. John further went on to talk about bolts and nuts. They follow the same male and female premise, he said with a grin. Bolts have threads that screw into a nut, and those two parts are commonly purchased together. At that point, one of the older sales guys, Gene, told Sadie she was needed upfront to cash out customers.

Sadie liked working with the guys and she told her sisters that they were always nice. They often put their arm over her shoulder to let her know she was doing a "great job" and she was just "one of them." Being young, she didn't comprehend that they were actually flirting with her. They complimented her on how pretty she looked day after day. In particular, they said she looked best in her blue t-shirts that just happened to be the ones that fit tightly around her chest. Although she was only 14 years old, she developed physically much younger than most girls her age. Another day a customer remarked that her belly button was "winking at him." He had said this when she reached above her head for twine to tie a box. Unknown to her, her shirt lifted high above her navel. She thought his comment was funny, and they both laughed, not recognizing what he might have been suggesting.

Much of the same occurred over the next year. The suggestive comments continued, and because Sadie was naive, she continued to appreciate the attention the guys and the customers gave her. Sadie was very impressionable and started to be influenced and perhaps be manipulated by the guys as well.

For example, Jeremy, the younger Hester brother, suggested that they take their breaks at the same time during their shifts. They would hang out at the back door of Colts and talk about general stuff. This was how Sadie was introduced to smoking cigarettes. Jeremy offered her a "smoke." Sadie, wanted to be liked and decided to do what he was doing. She didn't like the taste, but she did it anyway, thinking it might make Jeremy like her more than just a cashier at Colts.

Later that day at the end of her shift, her dad picked her up. When she got in the car, he asked if she had been smoking because she clearly smelled of cigarettes. Sadie denied it and said that Alvin had been smoking a cigar during the past hour at the store.

After taking breaks together for a couple weeks, there was an occasion when they were nearing the end of their 15 minutes and Sadie was getting ready to go back into the store. However, Jeremy wasn't following her. He kept smoking and asked her to punch him back in. This way he could finish his cigarette and the employee time clock would show he has returned from his break. He said he would come back in 10 minutes and make up the time during his lunch the next day. Sadie went back inside and took both timecards and punched them at the same time. She liked having a secret with Jeremy, and the smoking and punching of his timecard became a ritual whenever they worked together.

Another time, Annabelle opened the store, took the money from the seed bin, and filled the cash register with the money for the day. She put $300 in the register as a starting amount. The remainder, $1,244, was the amount to be deposited into the bank. However, when the money was counted, it was $60 less than marked on the deposit slip. Annabelle asked Sadie if she had double-counted the money the evening before, which was part of the nightly process. She confirmed that she had and then placed it in the cloth bag in the seed bin. What she didn't share is that she thought she saw John standing around the seed bin after she went to get her backpack to leave Colts. She did not see John take any money, but she thought it was possible he might have stolen it.

More money continued to disappear, and Sadie kept quiet. Annabelle finally thought she had it solved. There was a cashier, Elle, who worked part-time. Only on those days was the cash balance wrong. It was suspected that Elle was stealing from the till. Annabelle decided to "set up" a situation to confirm what she surmised. Annabelle counted the money from the cash register. It totaled $240.50. When Elle started her morning shift, Annabelle asked her to count the register money. This was part of the daily process before they opened the store, so the request was not unusual. When she finished the count, Elle told Annabelle there was $200.50. Forty dollars has disappeared, and there was absolutely no other explanation for the money to be missing than for Elle to have taken it. When confronted, Elle said she needed something from her locker in the breakroom. Sadie arrived a minute later, and Annabelle asked her to watch if Elle was putting money in her wallet. The answer was yes. Elle was fired on the spot. Sadie felt like a "spy" and that she was responsible for getting Elle fired.

Sadie enjoyed her job, but she longed for a break. A couple of months later, three girlfriends from school asked Sadie to go rafting with them on the upper Pigeon River. Sadie had been working the entire summer and really wanted to go. In fact, she was working more than 50 hours a week and was tired. Forty hours was the most the law allowed in the summer for a teen, but her dad said to "grin and bear it" and that she was lucky to have a job.

Sadie thought about what her dad had said, but she had always wanted to learn how to raft and needed a break from Colts. She decided to go to work at 8 a.m. and then, after an hour, pretend she didn't feel well. She dressed in her normal clothes and told her mom that her friend, Piper, and her sister, who was the driver, were picking her up at the end of her shift. They were going to watch another friend, Riley, train for the Junior National Finals Rodeo (Jr. NFR) and would be home about 7 p.m.

It worked! She had the entire day free! Piper picked her up, and then they drove to the river. Sadie had so much fun that she wished she could do this every weekend. She never knew how exciting whitewater rafting could be. However, there was a bit of a problem. Sadie's dad needed something from Colts that day. He didn't see Sadie at the cashier's counter and thought she was probably helping a customer in the back of the store. As he left, Annabelle said that she hoped Sadie felt better and that she would be well enough to work tomorrow. You can imagine what her dad had to say when Sadie arrived home!

The last experience that Sadie shared with her sisters was this. One night, when she was almost 15 and a half years old, she needed a ride home from Colts. For some reason, none of her family members could pick her up. The Hester brothers offered to drive her, but they had an old Corvette. John was the one who said she would have to sit on her brother's lap because the car was only a two-seater. Sadie had a crush on Jeremy, the younger brother, and any opportunity to spend time with him made her happy. She agreed.

The minute Sadie's mother learned of this, she taught Sadie how to drive an old 1989 Ford pickup truck they owned. It was a stick shift, and that week, Sadie applied for her driver's learner permit. Her mother told her not to accept a ride home from anyone, "under any circumstances." After that, one of her sisters or her parents drove her to work and picked her up. On the day she turned 16, her mother drove her down to the department of transportation to get her "intermediate license." This allowed Sadie to drive unsupervised to and from work with written permission from a parent.

But there was more. On one occasion, the gate on the back of the truck fell open when she drove to work. She used all her force to lift it to close, but it wouldn't budge. She saw John when she walked into Colts and asked if he wouldn't mind helping her. He said he was more than happy to jump in the bed of the truck with her and stay there as long as she needed.

At this point of hearing the experiences from Sadie, her sister Sarah May started to cry and asked her to stop telling her any more. Her other sister, Ada, agreed and was disturbed by what she learned. Neither sister had been exposed to anything like Sadie.

Sarah May's experience was the opposite. She said the guys rarely spoke to her and she felt slighted that she was not invited to their parties. They met their ranch friends on Friday nights in the fields and drank and danced to music. She knew one of the guys at Colts smoked marijuana because a joint fell out of his pocket in front of her. She wanted to try it and even hinted how fun it would be to join them. But they never took her up on her offer. Ada shared that she didn't recall the guys or the customers making innuendos or saying anything suggestive or sexual.

The three sisters sat quietly for a while, and then Sadie started to talk again with anger:

"Looking back, there are so many things I wish I would have known. I was stupid. I did think some of what I heard was wrong. But we were taught to respect our elders, our teachers, and those who had authority. Never did I once realize that things told to me by those in authority were not absolute. I wish I would have known I had a voice. There was no reason for me to stay quiet at all. If something was wrong, I should have had the courage to tell someone that it wasn't right or that I was offended by something someone said. Never did I realize that attention from boys or men could be given with ill intent or lack of respect. In hindsight, I am glad the one older guy, Gene, looked out for me, and so did our mother. I wonder if I had spoken up if someone would have listened to a young girl anyway."

After a long pause, Sadie reflected on what she just had said. "I wish I would have known I had a voice." She realized that she does have her voice now. Her resolution was to find a way to use it.

She and her sisters felt they could influence young girls and women by inspiring them with confidence and self-worth. They started a grassroots effort with female teenage horse wranglers who competed in rodeo events like roping and barrel racing. These young girls spoke at various community and school events to demonstrate the impact of bravery and courage not only in the rodeo arena or horse-riding ring but also in daily life. Sadie decided to continue her higher education and earn a professional ethics degree to continue to be a model and mentor to girls and young women.

Discussion Questions

1. Warner Wray, the daughters' father, was able to secure a job for his children at Colts Feed and Hardware. Why do you think he chose the hardware store as a job for them as young teen girls, an environment frequented by mostly men?

2. Do you think Mr. Wray shared an ignorance of the sarcasm and the sexualized environment he was exposing his daughters to at Colts? What about Mrs. Wray's knowledge?

3. Sadie knew that Jeremy and perhaps John were falsifying their timecards from breaks, yet she said nothing to Alvin or Annabelle. Why do you think she helped Jeremy with the falsification?

4. Sadie's older sisters said they had no recollection of being exposed to sexual innuendos.

   a. Do you think they were being truthful? If not, why would they not share their stories?

   b. Do you think they did have a similar work experience and were as naive as Sadie? Explain.

5. Sadie articulates, as an adult, "I wish I would have known …." What determines when a person develops their values and ethics? Can they change over time? Explain and provide examples.

6. Should teenagers work during their high school years? Why or why not?

7. Are there specific work environments that are not optimal or recommended for a teenager? How can a parent or guardian engage with an employer to make certain their teen has secured a "good job"?

8. Sadie's awareness of her early experience created a path to give back to the community and influence young girls. For children and teenagers exposed to similar situations, what might be the negative impact on their adult life?

Assignments

1. Jeffery Epstein (deceased) and his girlfriend, Ghislaine Maxwell (incarcerated awaiting trial in 2021), are accused of recruiting and manipulating young girls under the guise of making money and helping teenagers to "make it" in the music industry (Bryant, 2020). During interviews of these girls, they reveal they never suspected they would be exposed to sexual situations. Research the case and federal charges against Maxwell. Using the Epstein-Maxwell scenario, explain how a stranger, especially an adult, can exert power over a teenager.

2. Both the U.S. Department of Labor (DOL) and state labor departments have rules about the number of hours a teen can work. Research both the DOL and your state labor department and provide an overview of the restrictions for 14-year-olds.

References

Bryant, L. (Director). (2020). *Jeffrey Epstein: Filthy Rich* (Episode 1), [Netflix 4-part series]. RadicalMedia; JP Entertainment; Third Eye Motion Picture Company.

Eveleth, R. (2015, November 27). A modest proposal for re-naming connectors and fasteners. The Last Word on Nothing. https://www.lastwordonnothing.com/2015/11/27/a-modest-proposal-for-re-naming-connectors-and-fasteners/

Kakatos, M. (2021, May 14). Dozens of women who "recruited girls for pedophile Jeffrey Epstein" say THEY are victims, with at least one claiming compensation from his victim's fund. *DailyMail.com.* https://www.dailymail.co.uk/news/article-9580407/Dozens-women-recruited-teenage-girls-Jeffrey-Epstein-abuse-claim-victims.html

Knox, A. (2016, July 27). I'm a woman working at a hardware store, and literally no one trusts me. SheKnows. https://www.sheknows.com/living/articles/1126707/woman-hardware-store-sexism/

Lytle, T. (2018, April 16). HR tips for managing teen workers. Society for Human Resources Management. https://www.shrm.org/hr-today/news/hr-magazine/0518/pages/hr-tips-for-managing-teen-workers.aspx

Mortimer J. T. (2010). The benefits and risks of adolescent employment. *The Prevention Researcher, 17*(2), 8–11.

National Young Worker Safety Resource Center. (2021). Teen workers—Rights and responsibilities. https://youngworkers.org/rights/teenworkers/#what-if-i-am-being-sexually-harassed-at-work

Norfolk Plumbing. (2021). A plumber's dictionary. https://norfolkplumbinginc.com/a-plumbers-dictionary/

Simpson, K. (2020, June 9). Gender terminology for electrical connectors and fasteners. https://forum.digikey.com/t/gender-terminology-for-electrical-connectors-and-fasteners/7180

Time, F. (n.d.). Tips on employers who employ teenagers. Chron. https://smallbusiness.chron.com/child-labor-laws-many-hours-can-17yearold-work-60420.html

Triple Crown Races. (2021). Your guide to the races of the triple crown of horse racing. https://triplecrownraces.com/

U.S. Department of Labor. (2021). Youth and labor. Age requirements. https://www.dol.gov/general/topic/youthlabor/agerequirements

U.S. Department of Labor (2021). Young workers. Wage and Hour Division. https://www.dol.gov/agencies/whd/youthrules/young-workers

U.S. Department of Labor (2021). Young workers—You have rights! Occupational Safety and Health Administration. https://www.osha.gov/youngworkers/

Valley, N. (2014, September 12). Fix-It Friday: Adult plumbing glossary … 10 rude sounding terms that are proper plumbing lingo. Women You Should Know. https://womenyoushouldknow.net/about/

Whyte, A. (2021). The pros and cons of allowing a teenager to work. Evolve. https://evolvetreatment.com/blog/pros-cons-teenage-jobs/

Why Now?

Objectives

- Define and describe what is considered sexual misconduct in the workplace.
- Explain the relevance of the term "quid pro quo" in the business environment.
- Define, compare, and contrast the terms ethical, moral, and legal workplace behavior.
- Describe the historical basis of the #MeToo movement.

Key Concepts and Words

business ethics, career mobility, empowerment, legality, moral, personal values, quid pro quo, sexual misconduct, toxic work environment, work culture

Overview

Sexual misconduct in the workplace has been headlined in the news for the past several years. What is now known as the "#MeToo[1] movement" began with allegations of sexual assault against several prominent men.

For example, well-known actor Bill Cosby, Roger Ailes, former CEO of Fox News, Harvey Weinstein, a Hollywood movie producer, and Matt Lauer, cohost of the popular *Today* show, have been accused in some of the most documented cases. In addition, former staff members of the Ellen DeGeneres show have also come forth to accuse her and her staff of a toxic work environment, suggesting that this issue is not unique to a single gender, sexual orientation, age group, or to a single industry.

Not only is this issue one of power, but it lends itself to discussions on how sexual misconduct in the workplace crosses the lines between

---

1   Tarana Burke is credited in 2006 with the coining the phrase "Me Too," as a way to promote awareness of sexual abuse to women of color (Gill & Rahman-Jones, 2020). In 2017, after allegations against Harvey Weinstein were publicized, actress Alyssa Milano used the phrase on Twitter, which now is used to represent sexual harassment and abuse in the workplace.

ethics, morality, and the law. Ask yourself: Why and how have the victims now become courageous and feel empowered to speak up? What has changed? And how are society and the workplace improved because of this knowledge and awareness?

Scenario

Sadie Wray is an adjunct professor at Shaleville Community College in Tennessee. She is teaching a synchronous, virtual course on "ethics, morality and the law." This week's lecture topic uses sexual misconduct in the workplace as the foundation for the discussion. She experienced it first-hand as a teenager while employed as a cashier at a feed and hardware store. She starts by asking the students:

> *"What are words?"* Most would agree, a single word or words are used to communicate and express one's thoughts. Words can have different meanings to different people. The reasons for this are many. Someone's use or interpretation of a word could be based on a person's life experiences. Perhaps, their use of a word is based on context from the language they grew up speaking.

Professor Wray then writes the word **hot** on her computer screen. She tells the students to "think about it for a moment, and then type in *your* definition of the word in the chatbox." The students respond, and the following pop up: sunshine, unberable (yes, spelled incorrectly), attractive, sexy, burning, Mama-mia, belle, sweating, and need a shower. She tells students,

> *"As you can see, you have defined this commonly used word in diverse ways. Hot defines a room or outside temperature, perhaps a sexually suggestive term, someone's appearance, or the spiciness of food."*

Image 8.1

She then asks, *"Have I got your attention? Please respond with an "emoji" in the chat or unmute yourself."* Sadie gets an affirmative and continues.

  "Just as words have different meanings, there can be a different interpretation of acceptable behavior at work. This can be explained, in part, by the workplace culture. Personal experiences and values can also influence it."

Image 8.2

"Now, consider the meaning of ethical conduct." She scribbles **ethical** on her screen. *"How would you define the concept?"* She pauses again to give the students time to reply. *"Like the word 'hot,' what if there were a disconnect between an employer's definition of ethical behavior and that of the employee? A common occurrence, for example, is for people to recognize when someone gets their hair cut and remark that it looks nice. If that were said to you, would you find the comment acceptable?"* Once again, respond with either a thumbs up or down.

Sadie reveals that 94% of students agree. This leaves 6% disagreeing.

She continues, "Even if it were one person who disagrees, it makes my point."

The professor flips her screen so the students can fully see her in her office and writes on a flip chart the word **Moral** in bold cursive.

"Ponder, how would morality be characterized? And, is there a relationship between ethical conduct and moral behavior? Are they the same? What do you think? We will look at academic definitions in a minute if some of you find yourself confused. We'll discuss how and why these ideas differ but also intersect."

Image 8.3

"Let's finally add in the law. What is considered legal? Can ethical or moral behavior be legal, or is it always a violation of the law?

Image 8.4

Think through this. A person might feel it is ethical to perform a particular action that under the law could subject that person to criminal prosecution. Ethical, moral, and legal—many experts, including scholars, are befuddled, interchange these words, and can debate the definitions for hours at a time. My job today is to help you understand the differences. Let's review the three words and their closely related definitions."

The table below takes up Professor Wray's entire screen.

TABLE 8.1   **DEFINITIONS**

Ethical	Moral	Legal
"conforming to accepted standards of conduct"	"conforming to a standard of right behavior"	"conforming to or permitted by law or established rules"

(Merriam–Webster, 2021, para. 1)

Sadie walks the students through the Merriam-Webster meanings. She emphasizes that the lack of absolute clarity between these terms is evident in three "real-life" situations of accused sexual misconduct in the workplace. The accuser and the accused have their own perspective. Professor Wray asks the students to read through the situations that she has summarized by themselves. She tells them that their homework is to discuss their personal reactions before next week's class with two or three peers. They should keep referring to the table as they read through the following stories.

Situation 1

Roger Ailes, founder and former CEO of Fox News, resigned from his company in 2016 after Gretchen Carlson, a former network anchor at the company, sued Ailes, alleging he sexually harassed her (Koblin, 2016). The lawsuit, filed in July 2016 in the Superior Court of New Jersey, alleged that Ailes "unlawfully retaliated against Carlson [terminated her] and sabotaged her career because she refused his sexual advances and complained against severe and persuasive sexual harassment" (*Carlson v. Ailes,* para. 4).

After the lawsuit was filed, several others made similar allegations against Ailes including former Fox star Megyn Kelly. Kelly, "in her memoir *Settle for More,* … described how women at the network secretly banded together to share their stories with investigators, ultimately ousting Ailes in July 2016" (Yu, 2016, para. 1)

Only 2 months after the lawsuit filing, the Fox Network settled the case against Ailes for $20 million and made a public apology to Carlson (Yu, 2016). Soon after the settlement, Carlson, in a news interview, said she was "grateful that the parent company of Fox News took 'decisive action' to quickly settling her sexual harassment claim" (Brackett, 2016, para. 1) Roger Ailes died in May 2017 at 77, denying all allegations up to his death.

"When he spoke directly with Carlson, Ailes injected sexual and/or sexist comments and innuendo into their conversation, by:

    a. Claiming that Carlson saw everything as if it 'only rains on women' and admonishing her to stop worrying about being treated equally and getting 'offended so God damn easy about everything.'

    b. Describing Carlson as a 'man hater' and a 'killer' who tried to 'show up the boys' on Fox & Friends.

    c. Ogling Carlson in his office and asking her to turn around so he could view her posterior.

    d. Commenting that certain outfits enhanced Carlson's figure and urging her to wear them every day.

    e. Commenting repeatedly about Carlson's legs.

    f. Lamenting that marriage was 'boring,' 'hard,' and 'not much fun.'

g. Wondering aloud how anyone could be married to Carlson, while making sexual advances by various means, including, stating that if he could choose one person to be stranded with on a desert island, she would be that person.

h. Stating 'I'm sure you [Carlson] can do sweet nothings when you want to.'

i. Asking Carlson how she felt about him, followed by: 'Do you understand what I'm saying to you?'

j. Boasting to other attendees (at an event where Carson walked over to greet him) that he always stays seated when a woman walks over to him so she has to 'bend over' to say hello.

k. Embarrassing Ms. Carlson by stating to others in her presence he had 'slept' with three former Miss Americas but not with her.

l. Telling Carlson, she was 'sexy, but too much hard work.'"

(Carlson v. Ailes, paragraph 20)

Situation 2

In October 2017, news services were flooded with accusations of sexual misconduct, including rape allegations against the movie producer Harvey Weinstein. These charges came from women who were: (a) young with dreams of Hollywood success and (b) established actresses such as Angelina Jolie, Gwyneth Paltrow, Ashley Judd, and Rosanna Arquette (Fortin, 2017). Their stories, however, were all very similar and alleged that Weinstein sexually harassed and/or forced the women to perform sexual acts with him (Kantor & Twohey, 2017). Weinstein, who cofounded the Weinstein Company, was quickly fired by the board of directors as the news spread (Kantor & Twohey, 2017).

An investigation by the *New York Times* reported that allegations against Weinstein went as far back as 30 years (Kantor & Twohey, 2017). Media reports stated that Weinstein's sexual reputation was well known in the movie industry (Farrow, 2017). What is unique in the Weinstein case is the number of men in Hollywood who have been asked and have failed to comment on the Weinstein charges (Levin & Wong, 2017).

Also interesting is the length of time Weinstein continued to harass and demand sexual favors from women without any of these allegations being uncovered by the media sooner. One reason was simple: It was money. Weinstein, one of the most successful producers in Hollywood, was an extremely wealthy man who was able to "pay off" his accusers and who was so influential in the movie industry.

After Weinstein's firing from his company, his wife left him, and he reportedly sought residential treatment for sex addiction (Holmes, 2017). He departed after only 1 week of therapy (Italiano, 2017, para.1). In May 2018, Weinstein was charged with the rape of two women and other charges of sexual abuse. Multiple charges were added, with Weinstein finally going to trial in January 2020. He was found guilty in February 2020 of a first-degree criminal sexual act and a third-degree rape. In March 2020, Weinstein was sentenced to prison for 23 years (Dwyer, 2020).

Situation 3

In spring 2020, the well-known television host and comedian Ellen DeGeneres made headlines as current and former employees alleged that the work environment on her set was "toxic" (Yang, 2020). Further investigation expanded these allegations beyond Ms. DeGeneres to include "sexual harassment and misconduct against three of the daily talk show's executive producers" (Tsioulcas & Del Barco, 2020, para, 1). One wonders the extent of Ms. DeGeneres's knowledge and complacency with these new allegations (Yandoli, 2020).

Professor Wray resumed class the following week. She started the hour with the following on her screen and asked,

> *"Define this word."*

Image 8.5

She waited until everyone had provided a response and programmed the words to pop up on the screen one at a time. She said,

> *"You are empowered to live your life ethically, morally, and legally. I hope last week's lecture and conversation with your peers provided you with this awareness. Although you cannot control the behavior of others, you should realize that you can influence others. Know that you can be the change you want to see in the world."*
>
> *"Take the step or a giant leap to make that happen and do it now. If you commit to this, you are all getting an 'A' for your final exam."* Please respond on the screen with a thumbs up or down emoticon.

It was the fastest response Professor Wray had ever gotten from one of her online questions. Class dismissed!

Discussion Questions

Use the definitions provided in Table 8.1 to assist with these questions.

1. Many of the women in the situations described above accepted the sexual overtures because they felt they had no option, and they would lose their job if they resisted. Are their actions moral? Are they ethical?

2. Quid pro quo means "something for something." Some individuals may accept sexual overtures from a person in power to advance their career. Is that moral? Is that ethical?

3. Two aggressors described, Ailes and Weinstein, were men pursuing women. What if the roles were reversed and it were a female in power demanding sexual favors from an employee (of any gender or sexual orientation), or a male in power demanding sexual favors from another male (Garcia-Roberts, 2017)? Would there be the same reaction from the media about these behaviors? Why or why not?

4. How should companies handle employees charged with sexual misconduct? For example, upon receipt of an accusation and prior to a review of the facts, should the employee be suspended? And, at what point in the investigation should an employee be terminated?

5. What is your personal definition of empowerment? How does a person become empowered at work?

6. Discuss your knowledge of the #MeToo movement.

   a. How did it start?

   b. Why did it start?

   c. Has the meaning and the purpose of the campaign changed over time?

7. Many major news outlets (e.g., CNN, *New York Times, Washington Post*) have reported that former Fox News anchor Bill O'Reilly made a $32 million payment to a network analyst who worked with O'Reilly at the network (Steele & Schmidt, 2017, para. 1). After the payout, the Fox News network extended his contract for 100 million dollars for 4 additional years. The *New York Times* also reported this was the sixth known harassment claim that O'Reilly had settled out of court (Steele & Schmidt, 2017, para. 3). At the time of the contract extension was made, O'Reilly was the most popular anchor at Fox (Steele & Schmidt, 2017). Was it moral, ethical, or legal for the parent company of Fox News, 21st Century Fox, to extend O'Reilly's contract with knowledge of the sexual misconduct claims?

8. *The Weekly Standard* is a well-known magazine published every other week. Soon after the Harvey Weinstein's sexual misconduct claims were made public, the magazine published an article titled "There's an Awakening Against Sexual Assault, So Why Is No One Talking About Bill Clinton" (Hemingway, 2017). Why does no one talk about the former president and the public affair with his former intern, Monica Lewinsky?

Assignments

1. Research the first two situations (Ailes, Weinstein), and locate the lawsuits filed against the men. Are there any common "threads" in their stories? What motivated and empowered these women to take their complaints to the legal system and not simply "live with" or "take" the abuse anymore?

2. Ellen DeGeneres announced in May 2021 that she was ending her television show (Yandoli, 2021).

   a. She stated that the reason had nothing to do with the allegations brought against her and her staff. Explain if you believe this to be true.

   b. Ellen made a statement that she takes responsibility for her staff. Three accused individuals were fired, but her namesake show continued to air and was not cancelled by the network. Research and explain how she demonstrated she personally took responsibility for her staff behaviors.

3. Professor Wray asked the students to evaluate the real-life situations as they were reading. Complete the following table, noting if you believe the accused behavior falls into each of the three categories of conduct. Select one of the cases and summarize why you responded in the way you did.

Case	Ethical	Moral	Legal
	"conforming to accepted standards of conduct"	"conforming to a standard of right behavior"	"conforming to or permitted by law or established rules"
Roger Ailes			
Harvey Weinstein			
Ellen DeGeneres			
Ellen DeGeneres Staff			

(Merriam-Webster, 2021, para. 1)

4. Provide your definition of ethical behavior. Secondly, summarize how you demonstrate ethical behavior in your personal and professional life with two specific examples.

Additional Learning

- Locate and watch the 1994 movie *Disclosure* starring Demi Moore and Michael Douglas, an adaptation of the Michael Crichton (1993) book by the same name. In the movie, Ms. Moore is the sexual aggressor, and Mr. Douglas is the employee being harassed. While viewing, compare the sexual misconduct portrayed in the movie with the three situations discussed in this case.

References

Authur, K., & Setoodeh, R. (2019, October 8). Ronan Farrow book alleges Matt Lauer raped NBC News colleague. *Variety.* https://variety.com/2019/tv/news/matt-lauer-rape-nbc-ronan-farrow-book-catch-kill-1203364485/

BBC News. (2020, April 7). Harvey Weinstein timeline: How the scandal unfolded. https://www.bbc.com/news/entertainment-arts-41594672

Bowley, G. (2020, December 1). Bill Cosby case: Judges review decision to allow multiple accusers. *New York Times*. https://www.nytimes.com/2020/12/01/arts/television/bill-cosby-appeal.html

Bowley, G., & Hurdle, J. (2018, April 26). Bill Cosby is found guilty of sexual assault. *New York Times*. https://www.nytimes.com/2018/04/26/arts/television/bill-cosby-guilty-retrial.html

Brackett, E. (2016, September 6). Gretchen Carlson vs. Ailes a cultural/media/workplace flashpoint. *USA Today*. https://www.usatoday.com/story/money/business/2016/09/06/gretchen-carlson-case-against-ailes-culturalmediaworkplace-flashpoint/89908084/

Carslon v. Ailes. Docket Number _____, Superior Court of New Jersey Law Division. (2016) https://www.documentcloud.org/documents/2941030-Carlson-Complaint-Filed.html

Carmon, I. (2017, November 12). Why are so many men confused about what sexual consent means? *New York Times*. https://www.washingtonpost.com/outlook/what-counts-as-improper-sexual-contact-its-becoming-harder-to-tell/2017/10/13/b15506c6-af8e-11e7-9e58-e6288544af98_story.html?hpid=hp_no-name_opinion-card-c%3Ahomepage%2Fstory&utm_term=.1b77cb247dc3

Crichton, M. & Levinson, B (Producers), & Levinson, B (Director). (1994). *Disclosure* (Motion Picture). United States: Warner Bros.

Dwyer, C. (2020, March 11). Harvey Weinstein sentenced to 23 years in prison for rape and sexual abuse. NPR. https://www.npr.org/2020/03/11/814051801/harvey-weinstein-sentenced-to-23-years-in-prison

Farrow, R. (2017, October 23). From aggressive overtures to sexual assault: Harvey Weinstein's accusers tell their stories. *The New Yorker*. https://www.newyorker.com/news/news-desk/from-aggressive-overtures-to-sexual-assault-harvey-weinsteins-accusers-tell-their-stories

Fortin, J. (2017, October 10). The women who have accused Harvey Weinstein. *New York Times*. https://www.nytimes.com/2017/10/10/us/harvey-weinstein-accusations.html

Garcia-Roberts, G. (2017, October 20). "Stranger Things" star Finn Wolfhard leaves APA as his agent is fired amid claims of sexual assault and harassment. *Los Angeles Times*. http://www.latimes.com/topic/crime-law-justice/crime/sexual-assault/02001005-topic.html

Gill, G., & Rahman-Jones, I. (2020, July 9). Me-Too founder Tarana Burke: Movement is not over. BBC News. https://www.bbc.com/news/newsbeat-53269751

Hemingway, M. (2017, October 20). There's an awakening against sexual assault, so why is no on talking about Bill Clinton? *The Weekly Standard*. http://www.weeklystandard.com/theres-an-awakening-against-sexual-assault-so-why-is-no-one-talking-about-bill-clinton/article/2010150

Holmes, L. (2017, October 12). Harvey Weinstein can't blame "sex addiction" for his alleged assaults. *Huffington Post*. https://www.huffingtonpost.com/entry/harvey-weinstein-sex-addiction_us_59de3b6be4b04fc4e1ea8dd9

Italiano, L. (2017, October 21). Weinstein leaving sex rehab but still "working with doctors." *The New York Post*. https://pagesix.com/2017/10/21/weinstein-leaving-sex-rehab-but-still-working-with-doctors/

Ivey, I. (2018, June 19). 42 universities on the status of Bill Cosby's honorary degrees. *New Yorker*. https://www.vulture.com/2015/10/bill-cosby-honorary-degrees.html

Kantor, J., & Twohey, M. (2017, October 5). Harvey Weinstein paid off sexual harassment accusers for decades. *New York Times*. https://www.nytimes.com/2017/10/05/us/harvey-weinstein-harassment-allegations.html?_r=0

Kim, K., Littlefield, C., & Etehad, M. (2017, June 17). Timeline: Bill Cosby: A 50-year chronicle of accusations and accomplishments. *Los Angeles Times*. http://www.latimes.com/entertainment/la-et-bill-cosby-timeline-htmlstory.html

Koblin, J. (2016, July 16). Gretchen Carlson, former Fox anchor, speaks publicly about sexual harassment lawsuit. *New York Times*. https://www.nytimes.com/2016/07/13/business/media/gretchen-carlson-fox-news-interview.html

LegalNews.com (2015, July 8). Bill Cosby: A decade in the making. http://www.legalnews.com/detroit/1408878

Levin, S., & Wong, J. C. (2017, October 10). Hollywood men silent over Weinstein allegations as women speak out. *The Guardian*. https://www.theguardian.com/film/2017/oct/09/harvey-weinstein-hollywood-men-actors-directors

Merriam Webster. (2021). Definition of ethical. https://www.merriam-webster.com/dictionary/ethical

Merriam Webster. (2021). Definition of moral. https://www.merriam-webster.com/dictionary/moral

Merriam Webster. (2021). Definition of legal. https://www.merriam-webster.com/dictionary/legal

Morris, W. (2017, June 18). How to think about Bill Cosby and "The Cosby Show." *New York Times*. https://www.nytimes.com/2017/06/18/arts/television/how-to-think-about-bill-cosby-and-the-cosby-show.html?auth=login-email

Setoodeh, R., & Wagmeister, E. (2017, November 29). Matt Lauer accused of sexual harassment by multiple women. *Variety*. https://variety.com/2017/biz/news/matt-lauer-accused-sexual-harassment-multiple-women-1202625959/

Steele, E., & Schmidt, M. (2017, October 21). O'Reilly settled new harassment claim, then Fox renewed his contract. *New York Times*. https://www.nytimes.com/2017/10/21/business/media/bill-oreilly-sexual-harassment.html

Strauss, V. (2014, November 14). Bill Cosby's doctoral thesis was about using "Fat Albert" as a teaching tool. *Washington Post*. https://www.washingtonpost.com/news/answer-sheet/wp/2014/11/24/bill-cosbys-doctoral-thesis-was-about-using-fat-albert-as-a-teaching-tool/?utm_term=.fdc9140a1ef6

TMJ-4. (2021). 30 celebrities accused of sexual assault since Harvey Weinstein. https://www.tmj4.com/news/30-celebrities-accused-of-sexual-assault-since-harvey-weinstein#

Tsioulcas, A., & Del Barco, M. (2020, July 20). "Ellen" producers face another round of allegations, including sexual misconduct. NPR. https://www.npr.org/2020/07/31/897646026/ellen-producers-face-another-round-of-allegations-including-sexual-misconduct

Yandoli, K. (2020, July 31). Dozens of former "Ellen Show" employees say executive producers engaged in rampant sexual misconduct and harassment. BuzzFeed News. https://www.buzzfeednews.com/article/krystieyandoli/ex-ellen-show-employees-sexual-misconduct-allegations

Yang, R. (2020, August 28). A timeline of the allegations against Ellen DeGeneres and her producers. Entertainment. https://ew.com/tv/timeline-allegations-ellen-degeneres-producers/

Yu, R. (2016, July 16). Report: Megyn Kelly told Fox investigators Ailes sexually harassed her too. *USA Today*. https://www.usatoday.com/story/money/2016/07/19/report-megyn-kelly-told-fox-investigators-ailes-sexually-harassed-her-too/87292092/

Yu, R. (2016, September 16). Fox settles Carlson's sexual harassment lawsuit against Ailes for $20 M. *USA Today*. https://www.usatoday.com/story/money/2016/09/06/fox-settles-carlsons-sexual-harassment-lawsuit-against-ailes-20m/89904346/

Figure Credits

Index